To Mac as ever

U.S. POLICY TOWARD JAPAN AND KOREA

A CHANGING INFLUENCE RELATIONSHIP

CHAE-JIN LEE
AND HIDEO SATO

STUDIES OF INFLUENCE IN
INTERNATIONAL RELATIONS

Alvin Z. Rubinstein, General Editor

D1287875

PRAEGER

PRAEGER SPECIAL STUDIES • PRAEGER SCIENTIFIC

Library of Congress Cataloging in Publication Data

Lee, Chae-Jin, 1936-
    U.S. policy toward Japan and Korea.

    (Studies of influence in international relations)
    Bibliography: p.
    Includes index.
    1. United States—Foreign relations—Japan.
2. Japan—Foreign relations—United States. 3. United
States—Foreign relations—Korea (South) 4. Korea
(South)—Foreign relations—United States. I. Sato,
Hideo, 1942-   II. Title. III. Series.
E183.8.J3L43   327.730519′5   81-22656
ISBN 0-03-053471-2   AACR2
ISBN 0-03-053466-6 (pbk.)

To Marshall E. Dimock

and

H. Arthur Steiner

Published in 1982 by Praeger Publishers
CBS Educational and Professional Publishing
a Division of CBS Inc.
521 Fifth Avenue, New York, New York 10175, U.S.A.

© 1982 by Praeger Publishers

23456789   145   987654321

Printed in the United States of America

EDITOR'S PREFACE

The cornerstone of U.S. policy in East Asia is the preservation of Japan and South Korea as independent states firmly linked to the Western world. Although this policy rests on a relatively solid foundation, since the early 1970s the edifice of interlocking diplomatic, military, and economic interests has increasingly experienced periodic shocks that threaten permanent damage to United States-Japanese and United States-South Korean relationships. These bilateral ties have grown more complex and difficult to cement, even as they become more inter-dependent and institutionalized. This study explores the key issues and developments that have shaped those relationships and the ways in which each party has tried to influence the outcome on matters of special concern to it.

The dynamics of United States-Japanese and United States-South Korean relations reflect the extraordinary international and regional changes of the past two decades: the emergence of the Soviet Union as a superpower and the global-ization of the United States-Soviet rivalry; the end of the Sino-Soviet alliance; the U.S. defeat in Vietnam and the subsequent erosion of its credibility as an ally and patron; the development of Japan and South Korea as strong economic powers; the energy crisis and growing salience of economic considerations in the policies of all these countries; and the United States-Chinese rapprochement, started by President Nixon in 1972, which tends to reinforce rather than diminish the importance of United States-Japanese and United States-South Korean relations.

Japan and South Korea have come a long way from the years immediately after World War II when they were subordinate to Washington. They have each developed strong, cohesive, highly nationalistic societies; built productive, impressive economies, and sought greater latitude in foreign policy. They perceive the United States as weaker in the 1980s than it was in the 1960s, but they are highly vulnerable to attack from outside and remain heavily dependent for security on U.S. military protection. Both are apprehensive over U.S. leader-ship but find their options limited. Though the United States is no longer preeminent globally or regionally and its word is no longer fiat, nonetheless, what it does, or does not do is still crucial to the security, stability, and well-being of Japan and South Korea.

Problems aside (and these are developed in extensive and sophisticated fashion by the authors), the United States-Japanese relationship has been an unrivalled success story. From being bitter enemies in war, the two progressed beyond a period of U.S. military occupation that was as statesmanlike as any in modern history to one of military alliance and productive partnership. They are major trading partners and economically interdependent, but this has given rise to serious differences that could, if allowed to fester, undermine their political cooperation in the future. A close military relationship was established in 1960 by the United States-Japan Treaty of Mutual Cooperation and Security, but frictions have arisen over pressure from U.S. officials to have Japan devote more for defense than its current level of less than 1 percent of gross national product (GNP) compared to almost 6 percent for the United States. The inherent tensions must not be ignored.

Japan's wariness of U.S. policy dates back to Nixon's failure to warn it of the imminent reversal toward China. Washington has on a number of occasions acted without consulting Japanese leaders, even though their interests were very much affected as a consequence; for example, President Reagan recently urged Japan to cut down on loans and sales of industrial equipment to the Soviet Union in order to punish Moscow for its invasion of Afghanistan, but then suddenly the United States lifted the grain embargo.

Japan is an economic force in search of a political role in the world. It is particularly vulnerable to crippling attack because of: (1) its highly concentrated population, which is constrained from developing a military capability commensurate with its industrial and technological power because of its constitution and its deep-rooted aversion to nuclear weapons; and (2) its dependence on overseas investments and imports for 80 percent of its essential raw materials. Japan is extremely cautious in world affairs, content to shelter under the protection of the U.S. nuclear umbrella, and reluctant to accede to U.S. requests that it increase defense expenditures. Many of the difficulties besetting the United States-Japanese relationship also stem from Japan's insular society and outlook, epitomized perhaps by the frequently repeated observation that to the Japanese there are two kinds of people in the world — Japanese and foreigners.

A distinctive set of problems characterizes the United States-South Korean relationship. The division of Korea roughly along the 38th parallel, regarded as a temporary expedient in August 1945, was confirmed in the 1950 to 1953 period by war and since then by an intransigent ideological hostility between South and North Korea. In the absence of any progress on unification — and the prospect is extremely remote — South Korea must continue to maintain vigilance and a large military establishment that depends on U.S. arms and, ultimately, the U.S. shield.

South Korea is important for strategic and political reasons. In hostile hands, it would be a dagger pointed at Japan. Any diminution of U.S. credibility as an ally would send shock waves through seismically sensitive Japan. Washington respects the fighting prowess of the Koreans and wants the nation to be strong, but the United States is a grudging giver of modern weapons, fearing a runaway arms race between South Korea and Soviet-supplied North Korea and wishing to keep the South Korean military on a tight leash. Moreover, to the extent that human rights is a priority for any administration, the United States tries to maintain a certain distance between itself and the succession of authoritarian military rulers; its aim is to support Seoul without encouraging its repressive domestic policies. But Washington has often had to alter its principles to accommodate geopolitical reality. The situation in Korea is volatile, and the South Koreans have not been averse to lobbying in Washington for retention of a sizable U.S. military presence in the country.

The Koreans pride themselves on being "the Irish of the Orient." Inheritors of a tragic past, ruled by outsiders for much of their history, faced with a troubled future, they are clannish, pugnacious, and tough. Like Japan, Korea is a cohesive society with a highly literate, politically conscious, disciplined people. It knows that its national security is a vital U.S. interest and, accordingly, drives a hard bargain.

Professors Chae-Jin Lee and Hideo Sato analyze the key diplomatic, military, and economic issues that have dominated the United States-Japanese and United States-South Korean relationships since the early 1970s. Carefully setting the historical framework, they explore the misunderstandings, divergences, and difficulties, and expose the domestic and external considerations guiding the behavior of the three actors. At the heart of their analysis is the attempt to clarify the nature and limits of these important influence relationships.

In Japan and South Korea, form and substance are integrally related and, as the authors make clear, imperious behavior and erratic communication hamper the shaping of partnership, which is the stated U.S. objective. Partnership is difficult because it is rarely tried. Any bargaining situation between a superpower and its ally is inherently asymmetrical, but it can be conducted effectively if both sides are open and sensitive.

This study assesses the problems and prospects facing the United States-Japanese and United States-South Korean relationships and is a welcome addition to *Studies of Influence in International Relations*.

Alvin Z. Rubinstein
University of Pennsylvania

PREFACE

This study examines the development of the United States' complex, asymmetric, trilateral influence relationship with Japan and the Republic of Korea (South Korea) during the 1970s and early 1980s. After a broad historical review of U.S. relations with Japan and South Korea from 1945 through the end of the 1960s, we will analyze at length the most salient policy issues in the areas of diplomatic relations, military affairs, and economic interactions. Specifically, we will focus on: the rapprochement between the United States and the People's Republic of China (PRC) and its impact on Japan; the Koreagate affair and human rights; President Carter's plan to withdraw U.S. ground troops from South Korea; Tokyo's defense budget in light of the larger issue of United States-Japan security relations; the structure of trilateral commercial relations; and specific trade disputes over textiles and color television sets. Some readers may find our detailed, substantive issue analysis very useful; for others the generalizations drawn from our study may hold greater interest. In any case, our central concern is with the way in which the United States has managed (or mismanaged) its diplomatic, military, and economic policies toward these two Northeast Asian allies in a changing systemic environment, and the extent to which the United States has succeeded (or failed) in maintaining a viable influence relationship with them.

The decision to focus our inquiry on the last two decades is based on the fact that just prior to and during the early part of this period, important systemic changes had taken place, thereby forcing the United States to readjust its relations with its postwar allies. The passing of the cold war, bipolar international system substantially reduced U.S. as well as Soviet superpower influence in the attempted management of global and regional affairs. This trend is particularly evident in the postwar development of U.S. influence relationships with Japan and South Korea.

After the Pacific War (1941-45), the United States virtually dictated the domestic and foreign policies of occupied Japan and the southern part of a divided Korea. Even after South Korea formally established a new government in 1948 and Japan regained its political independence in 1952, the United States, as leader of the Western coalition against the communist bloc, successfully maintained a preponderant patron-client relationship during the 1950s and early 1960s. In return for the deference given to U.S. leadership, the two Northeast Asian client-states benefited from U.S. military protection, diplomatic patronage, and generous economic policies. U.S. relations with these countries were thus generally smooth, intimate, and cooperative. This situation gradually changed over time, but most markedly from the late 1960s with the emergence of detente and the decline of the U.S. economic position in the noncommunist world. Today the United States is no longer the unchallenged patron of Japan and South Korea, but increasingly finds itself engaged in economic disputes or facing diplomatic tensions within an often strained alliance. The emerging pattern of U.S. influence relationship with Japan and South Korea seems characterized by a complex mixture of cooperative and conflictual triangular interactions and by the growing manifestation of asymmetric interests and perceptual dissonance.

As used in our study, "influence is manifested when A affects through non-military means, directly or indirectly, the behavior of B so that it rebounds to the policy advantage of A."[1] Insofar as influence is a relational concept, (that is, relates A's original policy preference to B's behavior), it is both a process and a product. In order to facilitate our examination of the United States' influence relationship with Japan and South Korea, we will be guided by the following set of questions. These questions will serve as conceptual reference points, if not as the basis of a rigorous research design.

1. To what extent is the concept of unequal power useful for understanding influence relationships among members of the Western alliance system? If U.S. superiority vis-à-vis Japan or South Korea is evident in the descending order of military power, diplomatic ability, and economic performance, will the efficacy of the U.S. influence relationship with either ally likely decrease in the same order?

2. Does greater accommodation in interalliance relations (that is, relations between the United States on the one hand and China or the Soviet Union on the other) increase or decrease policy flexibility for U.S. allies? Does it have different effects on different allies, specifically, Japan and South Korea?

3. Under what circumstances can a junior or weaker member of an alliance system afford to be more intransigent and defiant in its tactical moves, or increase its leverage vis-à-vis stronger members?

4. Does the fact that a given political system is open or closed in any way affect the degree of external influence or penetration it experiences? If so, how does the character of an influence relationship between the United States and an authoritarian polity like South Korea differ from that resulting between the United States and a plural democracy like Japan?

5. Is the influence relationship between the United States and Japan in relation to South Korea a zero-sum game? In other words, can we say that as Japan exerts more influence on South Korea, U.S. influence over that country will correspondingly decrease or vice versa? Or, is the game played differently over military, diplomatic, and economic issues?

6. Can different types of issues be linked, explicitly or implicitly, to maximize influence for these allies in dealing with one another? If so, under what circumstances?

7. How essential is an intergovernmental alliance of two countries for maximizing their influence over a specific policy of a third country within the Western alliance system?

8. How salient is the concept of transnational alliance in influence relationships among three countries within the same bloc?

9. How important is *style*, as opposed to *substantive issues*, in conditioning the effectiveness of U.S. influence relationship with Japan or South Korea, or the effectiveness of Japanese influence relationship with South Korea?

Our study may not answer all the questions in a satisfactory or balanced way, but we will attempt to discuss the substantive issues in the overall context of these questions.

NOTES

1. Alvin Z. Rubinstein, ed., *Soviet and Chinese Influence in the Third World* (New York: Praeger, 1975), p. 10.

ACKNOWLEDGMENTS

In the process of preparing this book we have been indebted to a large number of diplomats, scholars, businessmen, military specialists, and friends in the United States, Japan, and Korea. They have generously helped us in various ways — obtaining research materials, agreeing to be interviewed, or offering comments and suggestions. We deeply appreciate their cooperation, but it is simply impossible to list all of their names in this limited space, and we understand that many of them prefer to remain anonymous.

However, we feel compelled to specifically acknowledge a few individuals who have been particularly helpful to our research. They are Mike Mansfield, William P. Bundy, William Clark, Jr., Hugh Patrick, and David Blakemore in the United States; Sunobe Ryozo, Ogawa Heishiro, Ishikawa Tadao, Kubo Takuya, and Okazaki Hisahiko in Japan; and Kim Yong-shik, Yu Chong-ha, Kim Jae-ik, and Sakong Il in South Korea. (The positions held by them are omitted. Please note that the surnames are written first for Japanese, Chinese, and Korean individuals mentioned in the text of our book, except for Syngman Rhee.)

We are grateful to Professor Alvin Z. Rubinstein, who, as our series editor, has given us wise counsel and critical insights. We also thank Randall Oestreicher, Tae-dong Kim, Anne Wallace, Anne M. Shaw, and Nancy Kaul for their able and dedicated assistance. Our wives — Kyung Shin Lee and Akiko Sato — deserve special recognition for their intellectual stimulation and sustained support. One of us wishes to acknowledge the research grants provided by the Joint Committee on Japanese Studies of the Social Science Research Council and the American Council of Learned Societies, and by the University of Kansas General Research Fund.

This book is dedicated to Professors Marshall E. Dimock and H. Arthur Steiner, to whom we owe much of our scholarly and professional growth. Of course, we alone are responsible for the contents of this book.

Chae-Jin Lee
Hideo Sato
January 1982

CONTENTS

LIST OF TABLES

LIST OF ABBREVIATIONS

AAPSG	Asian-African Problems Study Group
ADB	Asian Development Bank
ADC	Advanced Developing Country
AID	Agency for International Development
ASEAN	Association of Southeast Asian Nations
ASPAC	Asian and Pacific Council
CCP	Chinese Communist Party
CFC	Combined Forces Command
CHINCOM	China Committee (of the COCOM)
COCOM	Coordinating Committee
COMPACT	Committee to Preserve American Color Television
CPV	Chinese People's Volunteers
DMZ	Demilitarized Zone
DPRK	Democratic People's Republic of Korea
DRP	Democratic Republican Party
EC (EEC)	European Community (European Economic Community)
ECA	Economic Cooperation Administration
FMS	Foreign Military Sales
GARIOA	Government and Relief in Occupied Areas
GATT	General Agreement on Tariffs and Trade
GHQ	General Headquarters
GSP	Generalized System of Preferences
ITC	International Trade Commission
JCP	Japan Communist Party
JCS	Joint Chiefs of Staff
JSP	Japan Socialist Party
KCIA	Korean Central Intelligence Agency
KMAG	Military Advisory Group in Korea
KMT	Kuomintang
LDC	Less-Developed Country
LDP	Liberal Democratic Party
MFA	Multi-Fiber Agreement
MITI	Ministry of International Trade and Industry
NATO	North Atlantic Treaty Organization
NDP	New Democratic Party
NSC	National Security Council
NTB	Non-Tariff Barriers
ODA	Official Development Assistance
OMA	Orderly Marketing Agreement
OPEC	Organization of Petroleum Exporting Countries
PL 480	Public Law 480
PLA	People's Liberation Army

PRC	People's Republic of China
ROC	Republic of China
ROK	Republic of Korea
SALT	Strategic Arms Limitations Talks
SCAP	Supreme Commander for the Allied Powers
SDF	Self-Defense Forces
UAW	United Auto Workers
UNC	United Nations Command
UNCK	United Nations Commission on Korea
UNCURK	United Nations Commission for the Unification and Rehabilitation of Korea
UNTCOK	United Nations Temporary Commission on Korea
USAFIK	United States Army Forces in Korea
USOM	United States Operations Mission

1

HISTORICAL PATTERNS

AFTER THE PACIFIC WAR

During and immediately after the Pacific War (1941-45), the United States established itself for the first time as the preeminent power in the Asian and Pacific region. In the 1930s, despite an idealized self-image and public rhetoric, the United States failed to act like an Asian-Pacific power. Militarily, economically, and diplomatically, it remained passive in the face of Japanese imperialist penetration into Manchuria and China proper.[1] However, Japan's surprise attack on Pearl Harbor and the ensuing Pacific War altered the United States' traditional attitude that Europe was the first priority. These events led to the emergence of the United States as a legitimate, credible, and dominant influence in the Pacific.[2]

Although the new U.S. involvement in Asia developed more as a reaction to external circumstances than as a consciously adopted policy initiative, by the winter of 1944-45 U.S. policy makers had developed a "fairly clear notion" of postwar policy in Asia.[3] Through a series of interagency planning sessions and international conferences, they decided that the United States should take an active role in shaping and leading Asia's new regional order. For example, at the Yalta Conference (February 1945), President Franklin D. Roosevelt affirmed the desirability of preponderant U.S. influence in the Pacific Ocean, while allowing for the reestablishment of Great Britain's prewar position in Southeast Asia and the extension of the Soviet Union's territorial and economic interests in Northeast Asia.[4] Even though Roosevelt did not regard China as

1

a great power, which was equal with the Big Three, he expected that with the cooperation of the Big Three, an independent and unified China, led by a coalition government of the Kuomintang (KMT) and the Chinese Communist Party (CCP), would fill the regional power vacuum created by Japan's certain defeat. U.S. hopes of effecting a lasting compromise between the rival KMT and CCP and of United States-Soviet Union cooperation in China proved naive.

U.S. Policy toward Japan

By contrast, the United States never intended to apply the notion of a Big Three concert in Japan. Unlike in Germany where the United States acquiesced to the establishment of separate occupation zones, Washington opposed all Soviet maneuvers to institute the zonal occupation of Japan. A semblance of formal, allied cooperation was maintained in such ceremonial and organizational areas as acceptance of the Japanese surrender instrument, the eleven-nation Far Eastern Commission (in Washington), the four-nation Allied Council (in Tokyo), and the International Military Tribunal for the Far East. For all practical purposes, the Allied occupation of Japan was exclusively a U.S. operation. U.S. government agencies planned and executed all important occupation policies in Japan. Washington appointed the Supreme Commander for the Allied Powers (SCAP), who possessed "all powers" necessary to effectuate the surrender terms and other occupation policies for Japan.

As stated in the government document entitled "United States Initial Post-Surrender Policy for Japan," the fundamental objectives of U.S. policy in Japan were:

(a) To insure that Japan will not again become a menace to the United States or to the peace and security of the world.
(b) To bring about the eventual establishment of a peaceful and responsible government which will respect the rights of other states and will support the objectives of the United States as reflected in the ideals and principles of the Charter of the United Nations.[5]

The document identified four instrumental goals for achieving these objectives: (1) clarification and limitation of Japan's territorial sovereignty; (2) the complete disarmament and demilitarization of Japan; (3) encouragement of the respect of fundamental human rights by the Japanese people and formation of democratic and representative organizations; and (4) economic development adequate for the peacetime requirements of the Japanese people. Unlike U.S. officials in Germany where the indigenous government ceased to exist, General Douglas MacArthur as SCAP was instructed to "exercise his authority through Japanese governmental machinery and agencies, including the Emperor, to the extent that this satisfactorily furthers United States objectives."

This document and other government directives, which Professor Robert Ward has characterized as remarkably prescient, reasonably clear, and operationally feasible,[6] shaped the substantive evolution of occupation policy. With full understanding of the psychology of the Japanese people, General MacArthur dominated Japan's early postwar development as a "benevolent but absolute master."[7] He effectively disarmed and demobilized 2.6 million troops repatriated from abroad. He supervised the dismantling of all existing and potential war-making and war-servicing facilities. MacArthur ordered the removal from public office of about 200,000 elite members of military, bureaucratic, political, ultranationalistic, business, and communications organizations.[8]

The most important legal prescription for Japan's permanent demilitarization was incorporated in Article 9 of the revised Japanese Constitution. This article proclaimed:

> Aspiring sincerely to an international peace based on justice and order, the Japanese people forever renounce war as a sovereign right of the nation and the threat or use of force as means of settling international disputes.
> In order to accomplish the aim of the preceding paragraph, land, sea, and air forces, as well as other war potential, will never be maintained. The right of belligerency of the state will not be recognized.[9]

This provision was reminiscent of the Kellogg-Briand pact as well as the Spanish (1931) and Filipino (1935) constitutions. While Prime Minister Shidehara Kijuro may have initiated Article 9, the ideal for an unarmed, neutral, and pacifist Japan coincided with MacArthur's design to make Japan "the Switzerland of the Pacific." It also expressed the strong antiwar sentiment that existed among the Japanese people.[10] With the end of the occupation during which the U.S. military guaranteed both Japan's internal and external security, the article became a source of constitutional controversies over Japan's self-defense forces and military alliance commitments.

In promoting Japan's democratization and socioeconomic reform, the occupation approach was a mix of dominance and tutelage, which sometimes adopted and sometimes only suggested various measures. In the political area, democratization strategies embraced universal suffrage and free elections, constitutional revision, bureaucratic reorganization, and local self-government. Socioeconomic measures included the breakup of monopolistic industries, land reform, progressive taxation, unionization, textbook and curriculum revision, and religious freedom. The occupation also undertook a costly relief and economic rehabilitation program that was addressed to wartime economic devastation, the loss of foreign trade and raw materials, and the influx of several million repatriates. Between September 1945 and December 1951, U.S. economic aid to Japan amounted to $2.1 billion.

Professor Edwin O. Reischauer has characterized U.S. occupation policy in Japan as "basically healthy and mutually beneficial."[11] Critics in Japan and abroad argue that U.S. occupation authorities reigned as arrogant, insensitive overlords, summarily dispensing "victor's justice" to Japanese war criminals, conducting "vindictive" and "indiscriminate" wholesale purges, and imposing a "guided democracy" upon Japan, especially through "alien" constitutional revisions. Yet, even these commentators agree that the occupation was a reasonably successful experiment in planned political change.[12]

This U.S. policy success was due in large part to a combination of careful wartime planning, sound judgment, genuine goodwill, and a commitment to reform, which was especially powerful during the first two years of the occupation. In addition, MacArthur's strong personality and charismatic leadership sustained the occupation's authority and vitality.[13] A unified occupation situation and the system of indirect administration were no less important. Finally, much credit must be given to Japan's leaders and people. Although the Japanese were physically exhausted and psychologically demoralized by their first experience with alien domination, they were willing to cooperate with the occupation authorities in rebuilding their war-torn nation. Highly educated and disciplined elements among the surviving population played a key role in the diffusion and assimilation of the changes flowing from occupation policy directives. Emperor Hirohito and Prime Ministers Shidehara Kijuro and Yoshida Shigeru cooperated personally with General MacArthur to attain maximum policy coordination.[14]

Occupation policies reflected the changing realities of the United States' global and regional position. In 1947 and 1948, responding to the cold war conflicts with the Soviet Union and the CCP's rapid ascendancy in the Chinese civil war, Washington downplayed the punitive aspects of its occupation policy and moved to transforming Japan rapidly from a vanquished enemy to a viable ally in the U.S. anticommunist containment system. Consequently, U.S. policy makers assigned priority to the rehabilitation of Japan's economy and its integration with U.S. security interests in East Asia. George F. Kennan (director of the Policy Planning Staff, State Department in 1947-49) recalls that by 1947 the United States realized that Japan was more important than China as a potential factor in international political developments, despite the United States' strange fascination with China and traditional exaggeration of China's real importance.[15]

Thus, the United States initiated the "reverse course" in many important areas of its political, diplomatic, economic, and military policies toward Japan. The occupation placed restrictions on the freedom of radical political movements and labor strikes led by the Japan Communist Party (JCP). It rehabilitated a large number of purged Japanese leaders, who returned quickly to positions of political influence.[16] These new policies neutralized the effects of the JCP's aggressive campaign of subversion and bolstered the conservative, pro-United States power structure in Japan. As early as March 1947, General MacArthur spoke of the urgency of ending the occupation and of negotiating a peace treaty restoring Japan's sovereignty.

With the onset of the cold war in 1947, the United States began to convert Japan from a liability to an economic asset for the free world through various economic stabilization policies (including the so-called "Dodge Line") and through financial aid and loans, which allowed Japan to import needed food-stuffs and raw materials from the United States. As seen in Table 1.1, U.S. aid covered a major part of Japan's import financing before 1950.

An important part of the U.S. loan program was directed to the rebuilding of Japan's textile industry. In 1947 the SCAP created a $500 million industrial loan fund and a separate $100 million revolving cotton credit fund to facilitate cotton purchases. Japanese sources financed the reequipping of the factories.[17] By 1948 the United States had abandoned its efforts to strengthen China at Japan's expense, to deliver Japanese industrial facilities to China as reparations, and to slow the postwar reconstruction of Japan's heavy industry. Professor Martin Bronfenbrenner contends that in 1948 U.S. policy was altered in favor of "the restoration of Japan's prewar position as the 'workshop of Asia' and the preservation of her economy as far as possible from Socialist encroachments."[18]

In November 1948, based on George F. Kennan's recommendation, the National Security Council decided to reinforce and reequip Japan's paramilitary capability for anticommunist internal security.[19] In spite of Article 9 of the

TABLE 1.1
Japan's Foreign Income from U.S. Aid and Special Procurement: 1945-56

(in million dollars)

Year	Aid	Procurement*	Value of Imports
Sept. 1945-Dec. 1946	193	—	306
1947	404	—	526
1948	461	—	684
1949	535	—	905
1950	361	149	974
1951	164	592	1,995
1952	—	824	2,028
1953	—	809	2,410
1954	—	596	2,399
1955	—	557	2,471
1956	—	595	3,230

*Procurement includes Allied military expenditure in dollars and pounds, yen purchases for Joint Defense Account, expenditure of Allied soldiers and civilians in Japan, and payments in respect of certain offshore procurement contracts.

Source: Ministry of Finance and Economic Planning Board. Taken from G. C. Allen, *Japan's Economic Recovery* (London, New York, and Toronto: Oxford University Press, 1958), p. 203.

Japanese Constitution, preliminary plans for Japan's gradual remilitarization were drawn up under the auspices of General MacArthur. Even though the "reverse course" signaled the beginning of processes that were expected to restore Japan's independence, Japan remained under the United States' dominant influence throughout the seven-year occupation. Deliberate U.S. efforts to assure continuous influence over an independent Japan were well underway.

U.S. Policy toward Korea

In contrast to the carefully prepared, well-staffed, and relatively successful, if not always consistent, occupation policies in Japan, U.S. postwar policy with regard to the Korean peninsula was largely improvised, deflected by misconceptions, and filled with frustrations. Prior to the Pacific War, U.S. involvement in Korea had been peripheral and inconsequential. As epitomized by President Theodore Roosevelt's benign acceptance of Japan's paramount influence over Korea in 1905, Washington had largely ignored or even condoned Japan's subsequent colonial subjugation of Korea.[20] During the Pacific War, the United States viewed the Korean question primarily in the context of the military struggle against Japan. At the Cairo Conference (December 1943), President Franklin D. Roosevelt joined Prime Minister Winston Churchill and Generalissimo Chiang Kai-shek in expressing their joint resolve to "restrain and punish the aggression of Japan." They declared: "The aforesaid three great powers, mindful of the enslavement of the people of Korea, are determined that in due course Korea shall become free and independent."[21] The conferees did not specify the length of time implied by the phrase "in due course." Apparently, the participants of the Cairo, Teheran, and Yalta Conferences tacitly agreed that Korea would not be ready for independence immediately following Japan's defeat and that a period of multipower trusteeship over Korea would be required.[22] Roosevelt believed that, as in the case of the Philippines, the Korean people needed an apprenticeship of up to 40 years to compensate for a limited experience in self-government and representative democracy.[23] In addition, a series of planning documents prepared by the U.S. government in the spring of 1944 envisioned no unilateral U.S. operation in Korea (unlike Japan) and proposed the creation of centralized administrative structure in Korea.[24]

In the last days of the Pacific War, the United States hastily proposed and the Soviet Union agreed to the use of the 38th parallel as a temporary line for dividing the responsibilities of processing the Japanese surrender in the Korean peninsula. With Soviet troops well-positioned to sweep the entire peninsula in a few days, Washington decided upon the 38th parallel as a way of checking the probable southward Soviet advance and thus protecting U.S. occupation interests in Japan. This line was also chosen to block Soviet access to the capital city of Seoul and to Kaesong (an ancient capital), both of which were south of the 38th parallel.[25] Soviet acceptance of the 38th parallel may have stemmed from Moscow's expectation that the United States could be persuaded to accept a similar compromise in Japan. Soviet and U.S. military occupation of Korea was thus assured. With the de facto division of Korea into two zones of foreign occupation, the issues of Korean unification and independence became intertwined inevitably with the postwar evolution of United States-Soviet Union relations.

Almost a month after the Soviet troops' entrance into North Korea, the 24th Army Corps, commanded by Lieutenant-General John R. Hodge, was redeployed from Okinawa to Inchon. On the basis of intelligence reports and a widely read pocket guide, corps members correctly perceived Korea as a liberated nation and not as an enemy territory. However, unlike the occupation forces in Japan, General Hodge and his men lacked any real appreciation of the history, culture, and aspirations of the country to which they were assigned. This was symptomatic of the inability of U.S. policy makers to formulate and articulate a clear, comprehensive statement of U.S. objectives regarding Korea.

In contrast to the "United States Initial Post-Surrender Policy for Japan" by which Washington guided General MacArthur, the comparable "Basic Initial Directive," which General Hodge received in piecemeal fashion, was ambiguous and contradictory. While upholding the "rights of assembly and public discussion," this directive ordered Hodge to "immediately place under control all existing political parties, organizations, and societies" and to abolish those whose activities were inconsistent with the requirements of the military occupation.[26] Unlike MacArthur in Japan, Hodge received no clear instructions for political democratization or sweeping socioeconomic reforms. Undoubtedly, Washington concentrated much of its early postwar attention and resources on Japan and China, and concern over the future internal evolution of Korea received lower priority. While controversy persists as to whether the U.S. command simply committed policy "blunders" or whether it implemented "conscious planning for counter-revolution,"[27] there is little disagreement that Hodge was convinced he had a mandate to suppress any political group or activity associated with the communists and to strengthen the rightist forces.

Viewing the Korean People's Republic and the local People's Committees as procommunist, formed by left and center political forces at the end of the Pacific War, Hodge denied the legitimacy of these indigenous institutions. Similarly, he distrusted the self-styled Korean provisional government, which had returned from exile in Chungking. While disarming and repatriating Japanese soldiers expeditiously, Hodge, in a move that ignored the bitter Korean experience with Japanese police state tactics, used Japanese police and officials temporarily to maintain law and order.[28] As John M. Allison observed, Hodge did not possess the "political sensitivity of General MacArthur" and took a harsh attitude toward the Korean people.[29] Unlike the system of indirect occupation administration used in Japan, the United States established its own military government in Korea (similar to the one in Germany) and appointed Major General Archibald V. Arnold as its first military governor. Arnold reported to

General Hodge, commanding general, United States Army Forces in Korea (USAFIK). Washington's gradualist approach to Korean independence "in due course" greatly upset many Korean political leaders who impatiently anticipated immediate independence. Much of the initial goodwill generated by U.S. liberation of Korea was lost. While MacArthur, as a conqueror, was guided by a clear sense of national purpose and used authority confidently and wisely to influence the internal political development of Japan, Hodge and Arnold, as liberators, felt constrained from providing Korea's highly fragmented political forces with effective tutelage. Uncertain about U.S. Korean policy objectives, both internally and externally, they were bewildered by the seemingly endemic cycle of violent demonstrations, strikes, plots, and assassinations. They found themselves drawn into bitter bickering with Syngman Rhee and other strong-willed politicians. It was easier for MacArthur to reconstruct a thoroughly defeated and demoralized nation than for Hodge and Arnold to build a viable political order in a liberated but divided nation. Yet, U.S. economic programs were indispensable to South Korea's postwar survival. Between 1946 and 1948, the United States provided $181 million economic aid to South Korea (versus $980 million to Japan during the same period). In late 1945, the U.S. military government organized and trained a modest defense constabulary to ensure South Korea's internal order and border security. The constabulary attracted many persons who had served in the Imperial Japanese Army.

As an extension of the wartime agreements, the Big Three foreign ministers met in Moscow in December 1945 and agreed to set up a provisional Korean democratic government, a Soviet-United States joint commission, and a four-power trusteeship over Korea for a period of up to five years.[30] The repeated failure of the joint commission to implement the Moscow agreement throughout 1946 and 1947 reflected the increasing competition between the two global powers in Korea and elsewhere. Washington's appreciation of Korea's regional importance grew from a new awareness that either Japanese or Soviet domination of Korea "lessens the prospect of a strong and stable China, without which there can be no permanent stability in the Far East."[31] Moreover, the U.S. military government encountered overwhelming opposition within South Korea to the notion of trusteeship and feared that if a unified provisional government were established, the well-organized and disciplined communist forces might prevail. Hence, the United States did not support the indigenous Korean movements for negotiated unification.

In 1947, as the cold war spread both globally and regionally, the United States apparently decided to scrap the Moscow accord and to embrace a two-Korea solution, whereby the historically volatile peninsula would become a buffer area in Northeast Asia. In the fall of 1947, the Soviet Union rejected a U.S. proposal to hold separate, parliamentary elections in the two zones and to constitute a provisional national legislature whose membership would reflect the 2-to-1 proportion between the populations in South and North Korea. In response, the United States removed the Korean question from the context of bilateral United States-Soviet Union relations and referred it to the United Nations General Assembly where Washington could count on a predictable voting majority.[32] The U.N. resolution called for free elections throughout the Korean peninsula under the supervision of the new nine-nation United Nations Temporary Commission on Korea (UNTCOK), but the Soviet Union blocked UNTCOK's access to North Korea. Consequently, the UNTCOK-supervised elections were held in the United States-occupied zone only. On the basis of these elections, the independent Republic of Korea (ROK) under President Syngman Rhee was formally proclaimed on August 15, 1948. A few weeks later, the Democratic People's Republic of Korea (DPRK) under Premier Kim Il-song was established in the Soviet-controlled zone. Although the United States and the Soviet Union legally terminated their three-year Korean occupation, the coexistence of their respective client-states across the 38th parallel compelled the persistence of the Soviet Union-United States rivalry in the Korean peninsula.

Policy Assessment

The U.S. decisions to undertake "reverse course" in their Japanese occupation policy and to freeze Korea's territorial division during the late 1940s were logical extensions of the Truman Doctrine. In March 1947, President Truman declared:

> It must be the policy of the United States to support free peoples who are resisting attempted subjugation by armed minorities or by outside pressures. . . . The free peoples of the world look to us for support in maintaining their freedoms. . . . Totalitarian regimes imposed on free peoples, by direct or indirect aggression, undermine the foundations of international peace and hence the security of the United States.[33]

The Truman Doctrine signaled the concentration of U.S. economic resources and military strength in Europe, which was confronting the most serious and direct Soviet challenge to "free peoples." However, in Asia the CCP's victory was accepted as the "product of internal Chinese forces," which the United States tried to influence but could not.[34] The doctrine, when applied to Asia, led to a selective policy of solidifying U.S. political and military presence in Japan, while undertaking gradual military disengagement from the East Asian continent.

As early as April 1948, President Truman endorsed the National Security Council's assessment that the United States had "little strategic interest in maintaining its present troops and bases in Korea."[35] The Joint Chiefs of Staff (JCS) considered South Korea indefensible and thus a strategic liability for the United States. General MacArthur, who did not regard Korea as vital to the defense of Japan, shared this view.[36] Accordingly, by June 1949, all U.S. troops had completed their withdrawal from South Korea, except for the 500-man Military Advisory Group in Korea (KMAG). Washington sought to minimize the risk of a communist takeover of South Korea after the U.S. withdrawal by using KMAG to train the greatly expanded South Korean Army (which grew from 65,000 in March 1949 to 98,000 in June 1950) and by supplying it with about $200 million in military equipment, with more military aid promised. By early 1949, U.S. policy makers had ruled out guarantees of South Korea's political independence and territorial integrity by force of arms if necessary. Strategists in Washington had concluded that this option carried an unacceptable risk of U.S. involvement in a major war in an area in which "all of the natural advantages would accrue to the Soviets."[37] Although U.S. intelligence monitored a substantial military buildup in North Korea, the U.S. government denied President Rhee's repeated requests for immediate military aid. At least three factors shaped the U.S. response: the low priority of Korea in U.S. strategic planning; the fear that Rhee might try to follow through on his public pledge to invade North Korea;[38] and the depletion of U.S. military stockpiles.[39] This latter fact appears to account for delay in the delivery of $11 million in military aid promised under the Military Assistance Program for fiscal year 1950. Prior to the outbreak of the Korean War (June 1950), less than $1,000 worth of the military equipment pledged under this program had reached South Korea.[40]

U.S. economic assistance to South Korea was modest too. At the beginning of 1949, the Economic Cooperation Administration (ECA) took responsibility for implementing the Department of the Army aid programs and administered the GARIOA (Government and Relief in Occupied Areas) funds, which the military government had not yet spent in South Korea. ECA requested $410 million in aid for South Korea for the years 1950-53, but Congress was reluctant to allocate the funds. When urging Congress in June 1949 to appropriate $150 million in aid to supplement the $60 million already earmarked for South Korea in fiscal year 1950, President Truman argued: "If we do not do it, we are absolutely certain that the whole situation in Korea will collapse and Korea will fall into the Communist area."[41] Congress appropriated the requested amount, but through the end of fiscal year 1950 only $110 million had been spent for South Korea.[42] In contrast to the constrained policies in the military and economic fields, U.S. diplomacy labored actively on behalf of South Korea's international status. Notwithstanding vigorous Soviet protest, Washington succeeded in getting the United Nations to accord a degree of international recognition to the Republic of Korea. The U.N. resolution, adopted in December 1948, stated that:

> there has been established a lawful government [the government of the Republic of Korea] having effective control and jurisdiction over that part of Korea where the Temporary Commission was able to observe and consult and in which the great majority of the people of all Korea resided; that this Government is based on elections which were a valid expression of the free will of the electorate of that part of Korea which were observed by the Temporary Commission; and that this is the only such government in Korea.[43]

The resolution also reorganized UNTCOK into a seven-nation United Nations Commission on Korea (UNCK), whose primary function was to work for the unification of Korea. The continuing presence of UNCK in South Korea intensified the diplomatic rivalry between North and South Korea. The United States and other pro-U.S. governments promptly recognized the ROK government as the only lawful government on the Korean peninsula.

Seeking to encourage South Korea's renewed relations with Japan, General MacArthur invited President Rhee to meet with Japanese officials in Tokyo during October 1948, and in January 1949 received a South Korean diplomatic mission accredited to the SCAP General Headquarters (GHQ). Mindful of the historical conflict between Japan and Korea, U.S. officials nevertheless ventured a cautiously optimistic prognosis about the prospect of bilateral relations. A top secret State Department memorandum, dated January 31, 1949, observed:

> While Koreans harbor deep resentment against Japan and find it difficult to sympathize with certain U.S. policies which they regard as inconsistent with Japan's status as a defeated aggressor, there is recognition, at least by more realistic Koreans, of the advantages to Korea of maintaining commercial ties with Japan. Geographical propinquity and an increasing realization of one another's requirements may be expected to lead to the development of a new pattern of increasing contact.[44]

However, this sanguine expectation was effectively disappointed by President Rhee's anti-Japanese policy.

CONTAINMENT AND PATRONAGE: 1950s

In summary, U.S. policy toward East Asia underwent substantial revision and adjustment in the immediate postwar era. The Soviet Union-United States honeymoon ended, and the differences between the wartime allies appeared irreconcilable. The U.S. search for a preeminent regional leader had to be reconsidered as the fall of China grew imminent.[45] In spite of the mounting Congressional outcry against the "loss" of China, President Truman adopted a wait-and-see approach as the People's Republic of China (PRC) was established in October 1949. In January 1950, he stated that the United States would neither use its armed forces to defend Chiang Kai-shek's Taiwan nor provide military aid or advice to it.[46] Reiterating this point in a broader context, Secretary of State Dean Acheson excluded both Taiwan and South Korea from the U.S. Pacific area "defensive perimeter," which ran from the Aleutians to Japan and the Ryukyus and then enclosed the Philippine Islands. Acheson made it very clear "that there is no intention of any sort of abandoning or weakening the defenses of Japan and that whatever arrangements are to be made either through permanent settlement or otherwise, that defense must and shall be maintained."[47]

Meanwhile, the PRC, along with the Soviet Union, espoused a doctrinaire, "two-camp" international outlook, and took an ideologically inspired, revolutionary hardline against the United States and Japan. Chinese spokesmen assailed the alleged plan of the United States to protect Taiwan and to remilitarize Japan. In the 30-year Treaty of Friendship, Alliance and Mutual Assistance signed in Moscow in February 1950, the PRC and the Soviet Union agreed to adopt "all necessary measures" for their common objective of preventing the revival of Japanese imperialism and the resumption of aggression on the part of Japan or "any other state [meaning the U.S.] that may collaborate with Japan directly or indirectly in acts of aggression."[48] While the PRC saw in the treaty a needed vehicle for safeguarding its new government against external threats and interference, the Soviets took the occasion to express their continuing disappointment with the U.S. exclusive occupation of Japan.

The Sino-Soviet military alliance aroused considerable apprehension among U.S. and Japanese leaders, who wished to restructure the occupation system along lines consistent with the new bipolar regional alignment. Guided by his hope for bipartisan foreign policy, President Truman appointed John Foster Dulles, a Republican Party foreign policy spokesman, to negotiate a peace treaty with Japan. Although outwardly ambivalent toward U.S. long-range interests in Korea, Truman preferred to preserve the status quo in Korea during the first half of 1950. While Washington acknowledged South Korea's regional significance and declared the strengthening of South Korea's defense capabilities as an important policy objective, it was unable to provide military and economic assistance comparable to that received by the Soviet-supported North Korea. Yet the secretary of state refused to guarantee the security of those Pacific areas — such as South Korea and Taiwan — beyond the U.S. "defense perimeter" because such a guarantee was "hardly sensible or necessary within the realm of practical relationship." Acheson expressed his hope that in the event of a military attack those areas would rely initially upon their own defensive efforts and then upon "the commitments of the entire civilized world under the Charter of the United Nations."[49] The Truman-Acheson disengagement policy on Taiwan remained operational for a while, though it was vehemently opposed by General MacArthur, the Joint Chiefs of Staff, and some conservative Republicans in Congress.

Korean War

The outbreak of the Korean War on June 25, 1950 not only prompted Secretary Acheson to reverse his position on the defense of South Korea and Taiwan; it led Washington to revamp the U.S. East Asian policy.[50] For President Truman, this crisis was not a civil war precipitated by North Korea's quest for national unification. Rather, the president instinctively believed that this invasion by the well-armed forces of a Soviet satellite was a harbinger of Moscow's global military design against the United States. From the very beginning, he was determined to draw the line and to use U.S. forces in Korea if necessary. Secretary Acheson, too, felt that the war was "an open, undisguised challenge to our internationally-accepted position as the protector of South Korea, an area of great importance to the security of American-captured Japan."[51] Gone was his earlier reference of U.S. "defensive perimeter" in the Pacific. As President Truman recalls in his memoirs, there emerged a complete consensus among all major U.S. policy makers, both civilian and military, that "whatever had to be done to meet this aggression had to be done."[52]

On June 25, the United States took the initiative diplomatically by convening an emergency session of the United Nations Security Council, which passed a resolution calling on North Korea to cease hostilities and to withdraw its forces to the 38th parallel. UNCK was to monitor compliance and to keep the Security Council informed on developments in Korea.[53] This maneuver was aided by the conspicuous absence of the veto-wielding Soviet delegation, which had walked out of the Council in January 1950 to protest Nationalist China's representation. On the same day, President Truman held a top-level policy session at Blair House, which was the temporary White House.[54] He authorized General MacArthur to provide air cover for the evacuation of U.S. citizens from Seoul and to supply South Korea with arms and other equipment. In fact, MacArthur was told that in order to assist the evacuation, he could use, if necessary, the Air Force and the Navy to prevent the Inchon-Kimpo-Seoul area from falling into North Korean hands. The chairman of the Joint Chiefs of Staff, General Omar N. Bradley, suggested that the United States act in Korea "under the guise of aid to the United Nations." Truman instructed the Departments of State and Defense to identify the next probable Soviet target and asked the Air Force to prepare plans for destroying all Soviet bases in the Far East. The president ordered the Seventh Fleet to the Taiwan Straits to prevent either China or Taiwan from attacking the other. The U.S. decision to defend Taiwan was made in the context of the perceived global Soviet threat. Relatedly, the Philippines and Indochina were to be strengthened by U.S. military aid.

At another Blair House meeting on June 26, Air Force Chief of Staff General Hoyt S. Vandenberg read the text of a just-issued order authorizing the Air Force to take "aggressive action" against any planes interfering with its Korean mission or operating in a manner unfriendly to the South Korean forces.[55] President Truman responded to the reported downing of the first North Korean "Yak" fighter by expressing his hope that it would not be the last. The president approved Secretary Acheson's proposal to provide the United States' all-out naval and air support to South Korea. Such evidence establishes indisputably that the United States unilaterally had decided to commit U.S. forces to Korea at least a full day prior to the June 27 passage of the U.N. Security Council's collective security resolution. This resolution recommended that "members of the United Nations furnish such assistance to the Republic of Korea as may be necessary to repel the armed attack and to restore international peace and security in the area."[56] Undoubtedly, the U.N. decision helped legitimize U.S. direct military involvement in the Korean War, but it was not a decisive factor in the ensuing U.S. war effort. On June 30 President Truman ordered that a regimental combat team and then two army divisions be redeployed from Japan to South Korea, in response to General MacArthur's urgent request issued after his daring inspection trip to the South Korean frontline.[57] On July 8, General MacArthur was designated as United Nations commander in Korea and put in charge of the forces contributed by U.N. member-states, following the Security Council resolution of June 27. A week later, President Rhee, upon Washington's request, agreed to place his armed forces under General MacArthur's command authority for the duration of the hostilities.[58] In fact, the confused and demoralized South Korean government was under the effective control of U.S. Ambassador John J. Muccio.[59]

The full-scale commitment of U.S. combat troops during July and August 1950 failed to stop the North Korean armed forces. By early August, the North Koreans had swept the entire peninsula, except for a small southeastern coastal strip stretching from Taegu to Pusan. Only MacArthur's dramatic Inchon landing and counteroffensive in September turned the tide of the war.[60] MacArthur's U.N. forces pursued the retreating North Korean troops across the 38th parallel and advanced rapidly into North Korea. In this new situation, the United States changed the ultimate objective of its war efforts from the repulsion of North Korean aggression to total military victory and Korean unification.[61] On October 15, General MacArthur confidently told President Truman at their Wake Island meeting that victory would be achieved in a very short time. MacArthur suggested that there was little chance for Chinese intervention in Korea, but, should it occur, he felt that the Chinese would encounter the "greatest slaughter."[62] As events soon demonstrated, General MacArthur erred in his assessment of Chinese motives and capabilities.

Peking, perceiving a threat to its own security and spurred by a sense of solidarity with its beleaguered communist neighbor, sent large numbers of Chinese People's Volunteers (CPV) across the Yalu River in late October and November.[63] The PRC's massive armed intervention against the United States dramatically reversed the tide of battle and saved the North Korean communists. With the U.N. forces in desperate retreat, the CPV captured Seoul in early January 1951 and then moved further southward. By July 1951, after a series of pitched battles, the war became stalemated along a line adjacent to the 38th parallel. Meanwhile, Truman had dismissed General MacArthur both as SCAP in Japan and as U.N. commander in Korea and had acted to initiate negotiations on a ceasefire in Korea.[64] Preliminary negotiations were begun at Kaesong on July 10, 1951, but it required two tortuous years for both sides to hammer out the terms of a ceasefire.[65] The negotiated settlement averted a possible U.S. air and naval attack against China and the use of tactical nuclear weapons against North Korea.[66]

The three-year Korean War reestablished South Korea as a U.S. client-state *par excellence* in the areas of military, economic, and diplomatic relations. Having already sponsored South Korea's formal independence in 1948, the United States returned to defend it from armed conquest by North Korea. From the beginning, the United States assumed all major responsibilities vital to South Korea's defense: strategic decisions, operational control, actual fighting, military training, and the supply of war material. The South Korean armed forces, whose numbers fluctuated sharply from 98,000 at the outbreak of the war to half that number in August 1950 and then to 250,000 by 1952, depended completely upon U.S. leadership and support. With the marginal U.N. involvement, the Korean War was, for all practical purposes, the United States' war. Having suffered more than 142,000 casualties, including 33,629 dead, the United States developed a strong vested interest in South Korea's viability.

Seoul's complete military dependency upon Washington was reinforced by an economic dependency that was primarily induced by the war. The enormous physical damage sustained by, but not confined to, urban centers was a central factor. By September 1951, physical losses amounted to almost $2 billion, which was a figure far greater than South Korea's gross national product for 1949. Reeve observes that "industrial plant, public transport, power facilities, and coal and other mining installations, dozens of towns, and hundreds of villages had been partly or completely destroyed. In Seoul over 80 percent of industry, public utilities, and transport, three-quarters of the offices, and more than half of the dwellings were in ruins."[67] Beyond the immense economic dislocations of the war, there was the horrendous human cost. According to the U.N. report of October 1953, South Korean casualties totaled 1,313,836, including a million civilians. Military casualties included 47,000 killed, 183,000 wounded, and 70,000 missing and prisoners of war.[68] A large number of prominent South Korean leaders and other citizens were liquidated for political reasons. Estimates range from 17,000 (cited by U.S. ambassador to the U.N. Henry C. Lodge in a November 1953 speech) to 363,599 (cited by a recent South Korean government report).[69] At least 200,000 South Korean youths joined the Volunteer Force of North Korea. Over five million people were left homeless, and an even greater number suffered from family tragedies, refugee life, and other wartime hardships. The sudden influx of two million North Korean refugees further burdened South Korea's already overtaxed economy. For its economic survival and reconstruction efforts, South Korea had no choice but to rely on the massive assistance programs of the United States.

The war transformed South Korea into a thoroughly penetrated, internationalized polity — one whose domestic affairs were intertwined with its external environments. Through field representatives, especially, Ambassador Muccio and the military commanders, the United States profoundly influenced South Korea's internal policies and virtually dictated its external affairs. The United Nations was the most important international forum through which the

United States protected and promoted South Korea's diplomatic interests. Almost singlehandedly and by sacrificing President Rhee's policy preferences, the United States conducted truce negotiations with the communists at Kaesong and Panmunjom.

The Korean War had far-reaching consequences for U.S. occupation policy in Japan. As soon as the war broke out in Korea, the United States reversed its assumption that Korea was not vital to Japan's defense and affirmed the interdependence of Japanese and South Korean security interests. In response to the transfer of U.S. troops from Japan to Korea in 1950, General MacArthur and Prime Minister Yoshida authorized formation of a United States-equipped 75,000-man National Police Reserve Force, which became the prototype of Japan's Self-Defense Forces (SDF).[70] The war demonstrated the indispensability of U.S. troops and bases in Japan and Okinawa to U.S. regional security objectives. It also dispelled any doubts Yoshida may have had about the desirability of the United States' continuous military presence in Japan after the peace treaty. In addition to the placement of the United Nations Command Headquarters for Korea in Tokyo and designation of SCAP as U.N. commander in Korea, Japan proved its vital strategic importance to the U.S. war efforts. Japanese territory and facilities were used for the training, staging, logistic and material support, medical care, and rest of U.S. forces. Moreover, Japanese personnel were mobilized to man 37 landing ship tanks during the Inchon landing, to conduct minesweeping and dredging operations near Korean harbors, and to serve in various technical and labor functions in Korea (for example, communications, repair, cargo handling, etc.).[71]

The war in Korea spurred the United States to extend the application of its "reverse course" in Japan. Occupation authorities imposed tighter restrictions on communist activities and labor agitation. Six months after the CPV's intervention, the GHQ rescinded permission (granted on March 15, 1950) for Japanese trade with the PRC and ordered a total embargo on Japan's exports to China. This order was a stunning blow to those Japanese who hoped the Sino-Japanese trade would regain the high volume of the early 1940s. Responding to a petition for lifting the embargo, General MacArthur stated that it was wrong for Japan to seek a market in China since it denied human rights.[72] By forcing Japan to import many materials from the United States that had been imported traditionally from China, the embargo deepened Japan's existing postwar trade dependence on U.S. exports of food and raw materials. Thus, while China had supplied 34.0 percent of Japan's iron ore imports, 68.4 percent of its coal, 17.3 percent of its soybeans, and 38.6 percent of its salt between 1934 and 1936, by 1951 the percentage of these items imported from China had dropped to 1.3, 1.1, 2.6, and 0.2 percent respectively. By contrast, in 1951 the United States, which had not sold these items on Japanese markets between 1934 and 1936, was supplying, often at higher prices, 66.6 percent of Japan's iron ore imports, 70.9 percent of its coal, 97.3 percent of its soybeans, and 10.6 percent of Japan's salt.[73]

Yet, despite the China trade embargo, Japan emerged as a principal economic beneficiary of the Korean War because of special procurement arrangements and service contracts concluded with the United States. In fact, the value of U.S. procurement contracts during the three-year war was well above the value of total U.S. aid from 1945 to 1951. This created the so-called "Korean War boom" in Japan, which raised industrial production above its prewar level and set the country on the road to economic recovery. As a price for the restoration of Japan's independence in 1952, Tokyo agreed to the continued deployment of U.S. troops on its territory. As one consequence, Japan continued to receive substantial amounts of money from U.S. military procurement contracts even after the Korean armistice of 1953. Although the Korean conflict greatly assisted Japan's successful economic recovery, the most important effect of the Korean War for Japan was the acceleration of Dulles's negotiations for the termination of the occupation.

The San Francisco System

Washington's new awareness of the interdependency of Japanese and South Korean security gave added importance to the issue of Japan's postwar status. Meaningful progress on this topic hinged on Dulles's skill in securing both bipartisan Congressional support for his diplomatic efforts and a compromise between the positions of the Department of State and the Department of Defense regarding security arrangements with the peace settlement in Japan.[74] As a leading foreign policy spokesman in the Republican Party, he could neutralize any opposition from his party. However, the State Defense cleavage was deep and fundamental. The State Department sought an immediate, nonpunitive peace treaty with Japan, despite Moscow's and Peking's obstructionism. For the Defense Department, any treaty without assurances that U.S. troops would remain in Japan and without the Soviet Union and the PRC as signatories was unsatisfactory. In an effort to reconcile these divergent positions, Dulles proposed to make the peace settlement conditional on a bilateral security treaty with Japan and to urge Japan's substantial rearmament at a level of 350,000 troops.

In resolving the thorny question of which of the two rival Chinese governments should be invited to the forthcoming peace conference, Dulles needed to find an answer that would not jeopardize the alliance between Great Britain and the United States. The United States continued to regard the Republic of China (Taiwan) as the sole lawful government of China, but Great Britain had recognized the PRC in January 1950. Japanese Prime Minister Yoshida, who was basically pro-British in general foreign policy outlook and who had made a realistic assessment of Chinese affairs due to his prewar diplomatic service in Tientsin and Mukden (Shenyang), remained noncommittal. In June 1951, Dulles and British Foreign Secretary Herbert Morrison found a compromise formula whereby both agreed that the United States, as the host country, would invite neither Taipei nor Peking to the San Francisco peace conference. Further, they maintained that "Japan's future attitude toward China must necessarily be for determination by Japan itself in the exercise of the sovereignty and independent status contemplated by the treaty."[75]

At the San Francisco peace conference in September 1951, Secretary of State Acheson rejected Soviet Deputy Foreign Minister Andrei Gromyko's move to invite a delegation from the PRC. On the morning of September 8, Prime Minister Yoshida signed the peace treaty with the United States and 47 other countries, but not with the Soviet Union, Poland, and Czechoslovakia. That same afternoon, he signed a bilateral, mutual security treaty secretly negotiated with the United States.[76] The security treaty was designed to protect an independent but weak Japan and to present a countervailing force to the Sino-Soviet alliance. Thus, the structure of the two rival military coalitions in East Asia was formalized.

Even though Yoshida rejected Dulles's original proposal that Japan undertake full-scale rearmament, the Japanese prime minister not only accepted a U.S. military guarantee of Japan's external security, but also intended to reorganize and expand the 75,000-man National Police Reserve Force for improved internal security. While the United States-Japanese security treaty was frequently justified by reference to the Communist Chinese intervention in Korea, Yoshida discounted the likelihood of a direct military threat from China because it lacked sophisticated naval and air capabilities and the industrial bases for their development. He viewed the security treaty as a deterrent against a potential Soviet attack.

As a "provisional arrangement" for Japan's defense, the treaty granted the United States the right to retain its armed forces and military bases in and about Japan, with Washington assuming a de facto responsibility to protect Japan against external armed attack as well as internal riots and disturbances. Of particular regional importance was Article 1, which stated:

Japan grants, and the United States of America accepts, the right . . . to dispose United States land, air and sea forces in and about Japan. Such forces may be utilized to contribute to the maintenance of international peace and security in the Far East and to the security of Japan against armed attack from without, including assistance given at the express request of the Japanese government to put down large-scale internal riots and disturbances in Japan, caused through instigation or intervention by an outside power or powers.[77]

In an exchange of notes with Acheson at San Francisco, Yoshida agreed to provide Japanese facilities and services in support of any U.N. military action in the Far East. Specifically, this commitment rendered Japan continuously available as a vital support area for the U.S. military activities in Korea. For the same regional security purpose, the United States retained its control over the Ryukyus Islands "as long as conditions of threat and tension exist in the Far East," but Japan's "residual sovereignty" over them was acknowledged.[78]

During the Japanese Diet debates over both treaties, Yoshida indicated his preference for a "two-China" approach in Japan's diplomatic and economic policies. Yet, he was under intense pressure from Washington to announce his pro-Taipei commitment as a *quid pro quo* for obtaining Senate ratification of the two treaties. In a letter to Dulles, Yoshida felt compelled to pledge that his government would conclude a treaty with the Republic of China as soon as it was legally possible.[79] The prime minister disclaimed any intention of concluding a bilateral treaty with the PRC. As justification for this policy, he cited the U.N. condemnation of the PRC as an aggressor, Peking's support of the JCP's violent revolutionary line, and the Sino-Soviet military alliance directed against Japan. This important foreign policy commitment of an independent Japan was formally enunciated while Japan was still under U.S. occupation. On the same day that the San Francisco treaties came into force in 1952, Japan and the Republic of China signed a bilateral peace treaty and agreed to establish diplomatic relations.

The San Francisco system and its adjunct, the Tokyo-Taipei peace treaty, constrained the development of security arrangements and diplomatic relations involving Japan and China over the next two decades. On April 18, 1952, Japan regained its formal independence from the occupation authorities, but Japan remained tied in with the U.S. quest to contain and isolate the international communist movement. Unlike the NATO accords whose signatories were bound by the principle of reciprocal obligations, the United States-Japanese security treaty stipulated Japan's unilateral and unconditional dependency upon U.S. military protection.

However, Japan constituted only one element in the U.S. anticommunist containment structure in the Asian-Pacific region. This structure was quickly extended to embrace the Philippines, Australia, New Zealand, South Korea, South Vietnam, Thailand, Pakistan, and Taiwan. The 1953 mutual defense treaty between the United States and South Korea was negotiated not only as another integral link in the U.S. regional security chain but also as a prerequisite for President Rhee's acceptance of the Korean ceasefire agreements. In June 1953, in an attempt to overcome Rhee's intransigent opposition to a negotiated settlement of the Korean War, the United States submitted a draft treaty to him, which was patterned after the United States-Philippine Mutual Defense Treaty. But Rhee insisted that the Japanese security treaty serve as the model, especially its provision for a continuous U.S. military presence "in and about Japan" (Article 1) and for the indefinite duration of the treaty's effectiveness (Article 4).[80] He also wanted to obtain assurances that the United States would take an automatic, direct military action for South Korea's defense in the event of external attack.[81] Frustrated by the recalcitrant Rhee, the United States devised a contingency plan (code-named "Operation Ever-ready") that would remove him from authority, disarm loyal South Korean army units, and set up a United Nations Command (UNC) military government in South Korea.[82] The plan was not implemented because a combination of persuasion and hard pressure secured Rhee's agreement to the armistice arrangements in July 1953. In turn, the Eisenhower Administration committed itself to the security treaty, substantial economic and military aid, support for Korea's ultimate unification, and cooperation at a postceasefire international political conference on Korea.[83]

After intensive negotiations between Secretary of State Dulles and Rhee at Seoul in August 1953, the United States and South Korea initialed the Mutual Defense Treaty, which would take effect in November 1953.[84] Article 3 declared:

> Each Party recognizes that an armed attack in the Pacific area on either of the Parties in territories now under their respective administrative control, or hereafter recognized by one of the Parties as lawfully brought under the administrative control of the other, would be dangerous to its own peace and safety and declares that it would act to meet the common danger in accordance with its constitutional processes.

Except for a clarification of territorial boundaries and a reference to the U.N. Charter, this article was an exact replica of Article 4 of the United States-Philippine treaty. While the United States denied Rhee's request for the treaty's indefinite effectiveness provision and included a one-year advance notice for termination requirement, Dulles acceded to Rhee's proposal that the United States exercise the right of deploying military forces "in and about" South Korea (Article 4).[85] The U.S. commander in Korea, in his capacity as U.N. commander, was to retain operational command authority over South Korea's armed forces even after the armistice. Although Rhee preferred to nullify this wartime arrangement, Dulles regarded it as essential for preventing South Korea's violation of the armistice agreement.

Policy Assessment

U.S. East Asian policy faced a series of major challenges and adjustments during the first three years of the 1950s. At the cost of considerable human and material sacrifices, especially after Chinese intervention, the United States rescued South Korea from North Korean conquest. This bloody confrontation, coupled with new U.S. commitment to Taiwan's defense, inflicted almost irreparable damage on relations between Washington and Peking. During and after the Korean War, intense anti-Peking feeling was widespread among top policy makers in the United States. Assistant Secretary of State for Far Eastern Affairs Dean Rusk's 1951 characterization of the PRC as a "colonial Russian government — a Slavic Manchukuo on a larger scale" was typical. Rusk rejected the PRC's authority to speak for China's interests.[86] On the other hand, the United States concluded a relatively successful seven-year occupation experiment in Japan, effectively transforming Japan from a defeated enemy to a close military and political ally in East Asia. In addition, while engineering a negotiated truce in Korea, the United States spread its regional security umbrella over South Korea.

The resulting pattern of U.S. Asian policy was marked by assumptions of rigid bipolarity, a tone of moralistic crusade, and the primacy of ideological and security considerations. Insisting on a sharp ideological distinction between the two blocs, Washington divided countries into "friends" and "enemies" and vigorously solidified its anticommunist containment structure. U.S. contempt toward the evil of communism in the Soviet Union, China, and North Korea was intense and pervasive. The United States jealously opposed any initiative directed at interbloc cooperation and labored to sustain its hierarchical, protective influence over its East Asian allies: Japan, South Korea, and Taiwan.

Even though Japan regained its formal sovereign independence in 1952 and joined the United Nations in 1956, the United States still retained the vestiges of its patron-client relationship with Japan throughout the 1950s. In 1957 Professor Edwin O. Reischauer observed:

> We are in a particularly delicate position in our relations with Japan because of the occupation period, so fresh in Japanese memories, and the overwhelming influence the United States still exercises. . . . The Japanese are naturally sensitive about the inequalities of their partnership with us. Influence seems to extend only in one direction. The policies of the United States come close to determining Japan's whole position in the world. In return the Japanese exercise little control over us. At most, they can only drag their heels. American influence runs strong in all sectors of Japanese life.[87]

The preponderant influence of the United States was felt particularly in security arrangements and also was evident in the diplomatic and economic areas.

While Japan undertook a modest program for rearmament after 1952, U.S. ground troops and base facilities in Japan were reduced during the 1956-57 period. Nevertheless, the United States continued to maintain a security shield for Japan and between 1953 and 1961 supplied military aid valued at $955 million. Meanwhile, the U.S. China policy was directed to diplomatic isolation, military containment, and economic embargo of the PRC. During the Dulles years, Washington's ongoing search for ever-better vehicles with which to hasten the fall of the communist regime was grounded on the secretary of state's conviction that communist rule was a transitory phenomenon.[88] The Mutual Defense Treaty with Taiwan (1954) and the Congressional resolution on Formosa (1955) reflected the prevailing assumptions. In 1956 Japanese Prime Minister Hatoyama Ichiro normalized diplomatic relations between Tokyo and Moscow.[89] However, his diplomatic flirtation with the PRC provoked a strong protest from Washington. Since Japan was still unsure of its proper role and status in the postwar international community, this U.S. reaction to Hatoyama's initiative reinforced Japanese timidity in developing relations with any state the United States disapproved of.

During the 1950s, United States-Japanese economic relations were also conducted in the context of the cold war bipolar system. A sense of shared economic interests prevailed among the political influentials in both countries. A U.S. perception of these interests was well expressed by Senator Albert Gore in 1954:

> Our reliance on Japan as the major bastion of free-world strength in the Far East demands our attention and concern. The problem of integrating the Japanese economy into that of the free world and of making Japan economically viable must be regarded as a major test of our economic statesmanship. This problem presents a special challenge to our leadership of the free world.[90]

In order to foster Japan's emergence as a stable and viable member of the Asian alliance, the United States assisted Japan's economic recovery and reconstruction by granting $377 million in aid between 1953 and 1961, stimulated Japan's export-oriented industries, such as textiles, and opened up the vast U.S. domestic market to Japanese goods. While compelling Japan's adherence to the Coordinating Committee (COCOM) and the China Committee (CHINCOM) restrictions,[91] Washington also championed within Europe a free trade policy beneficial for Japan and sponsored Japan's admission to the General Agreement on Tariffs and Trade (GATT). In addition to providing Japan with a major market for its growing exports, the United States aided Japan directly through sales of new U.S. technology and indirectly, by providing military protection, thereby permitting Tokyo to divert a larger share of its financial resources into sustaining economic growth.

For Japan, the objective of economic rehabilitation was achieved by 1955, when its annual industrial production reached the prewar level. In subsequent years, the Japanese economy continued to grow rapidly. Between 1956 and 1958 the average annual percentage increase in the GNP was 7.8 percent. Even higher growth rates followed in the next two years: 17.7 and 11 percent respectively. The bilateral trade balance was favorable to the United States. In 1956-60, the United States exported $6.4 billion in goods to Japan, while importing goods valued at $3.9 billion. Viewed broadly, these multiple links to the United States enabled Japan to achieve rapid economic growth, while maintaining its external security with moderate rearmament and, hence, with modest cost.

Across the Sea of Japan, the Korean War had been inconclusive. With some minor territorial shifts the Demilitarized Zone (DMZ) replaced the 38th parallel as the de facto boundary between North and South. The ceasefire ushered in a period of "neither war, nor peace," during which South Korea's utter dependency on the United States as protector and guarantor of its survival was confirmed repeatedly. U.S. generals continued to head the U.N. Command for Korea, which was moved from Tokyo to Seoul in 1957, and to represent the U.N. side at Military Armistice Commission meetings in Panmunjom. U.S. advisors, military aid, and supplies strengthened the Republic of Korea armed forces. However, between the time of the truce accords and 1960, the U.S. forces in South Korea were reduced from 360,000 to 60,000 personnel. Yet even after 1958, when the last of the CPV had been withdrawn from North Korea, Washington refrained from undertaking a complete military withdrawal from South Korea as pledged in the armistice agreement. After 1953, the diplomats made no more progress in reconciling the conflicting goals of the two Koreas than the generals had made. The 1954 Geneva Conference on the peaceful unification of Korea was an exercise in futility. A declaration by the 16 nations participating in the Security Council's collective security measures referred the Korean question back to the United Nations.[92]

Since neither North nor South Korea was a U.N. member, the United States and the Soviet Union continued to represent and protect the diplomatic interests of their respective clients at the annual U.N. debates on the Korean question. North Korea's allies, led by the Soviet Union, repeatedly denounced both the UNC and the seven-member United Nations Commission for the Unification and Rehabilitation of Korea (UNCURK), which had replaced UNCK in October 1950 for the purpose of "bringing about the establishment of a unified, independent and democratic government of all Korea."[93] As had been done for postwar Japan, the United States provided massive economic aid for the relief and reconstruction of its Korean ally (see Table 1.2), which experienced nonmilitary war damages totaling more than $3 billion or the equivalent of the country's GNP over two years.[94] With this economic patronage, Washington sought to enhance South Korea's political stability and to underwrite its huge defense expenditures. For the 1953-61 period, U.S. total direct assistance to South Korea exceeded $4 billion — $2.6 billion in economic aid and $1.8 billion in military aid. The United States allocated the same amount of economic aid to Japan from 1945 through 1961, but a considerable portion of U.S. economic aid to South Korea was used indirectly for defense purposes. Almost all U.S. assistance to South Korea was given in the form of grants-in-aid because South Korea's economic capabilities were too limited to sustain the burdens of loan repayment. As measured by the per capita amount of aid, South Korea ranked as one of the major recipients of U.S. economic and military assistance in the world throughout the 1950s and early 1960s. South Korea's very extensive economic dependence gave the United States a dominant voice in that country's domestic and foreign economic activities. Even though the binational Combined Economic Board, established by the Agreement on Economic Cooperation (May 1952), was charged with making decisions regarding the implementation of U.S. aid policy in South Korea, the United States Operations Mission (USOM)

TABLE 1.2
U.S. Assistance to South Korea: 1946-80

(in million dollars)

	Economic Assistance			Military Assistance			Total Assistance		
	Total	Loans	Grants	Total	Loans	Grants	Total	Loans	Grants
1946-48	181.2	24.9	156.3	–	–	–	181.2	24.9	156.3
1949-52	485.6	–	485.6	12.5	–	12.5	498.1	–	498.1
1953-59	1,857.7	19.5	1,838.2	1,215.3	–	1,215.3	3,073.0	19.5	3,053.5
1960	215.9	1.1	214.8	256.5	–	256.5	529.2	1.1	528.1
1961	270.4	6.8	263.6	276.4	–	276.4	526.9	6.8	520.1
1962	202.1	25.4	176.7	210.5	–	210.5	478.5	25.4	453.1
1963	201.3	30.9	170.4	158.2	–	158.2	411.8	30.9	380.9
1964	222.2	29.7	192.5	123.4	–	123.4	380.4	29.7	350.7
1965	185.3	49.2	136.6	237.1	–	237.1	309.2	49.2	260.0
1966	261.8	80.5	181.3	277.1	–	277.1	498.9	80.5	418.4
1967	177.8	63.5	114.3	422.7	–	422.7	454.9	63.5	391.4
1968	171.8	34.7	137.1	563.9	–	563.9	594.5	34.7	559.8
1969	235.4	113.5	121.9	354.8	–	354.8	799.3	113.5	685.8
1970	140.7	64.1	76.6	354.8	–	354.8	495.5	64.1	431.4
1971	169.9	122.9	47.0	680.0	15.0	665.0	849.9	137.9	712.0
1972	252.2	230.7	21.5	745.0	17.0	728.0	997.2	247.7	749.5
1973	188.5	171.3	17.2	367.7	24.2	343.5	556.2	195.5	360.7
1974	37.1	25.0	12.1	167.9	56.7	111.2	205.0	81.7	123.3
1975	36.7	27.2	9.5	142.6	59.0	83.6	179.3	86.2	93.1
1976	124.7	121.8	2.9	188.1	126.0	62.1	312.8	247.8	65.0

TQ*	13.8	13.3	0.5	135.6	134.1	1.5	149.4	147.4	2.0
1977	77.4	75.1	2.3	155.0	152.4	2.6	232.4	227.5	4.9
1978	58.6	56.3	2.3	276.9	275.0	1.9	335.5	331.3	4.2
1979	41.0	38.0	3.0	238.4	225.0	13.4	279.4	263.0	16.4
1980	30.9	28.5	2.4	130.5	129.0	1.5	161.4	157.5	3.9
Total	5,840.5			7,649.4			13,489.9		

*Transitional Quarter

Source: Agency for International Development.

in Seoul had virtual veto power in the event of policy conflicts with its South Korean counterparts. USOM rejected frequent South Korean proposals for using U.S. aid funds in import-substitution industries and continued to promote social overhead investments, for example, roads, electricity, and water resources. In assessing U.S. aid administration, President Rhee complained of interagency confusion, an excess of well-intentioned, but useless, reports and surveys, high personnel costs, and the purchase of nonessential goods.[95] USOM made sure that South Korea practiced a strict policy of buying U.S. goods and developed close links with the United States-dominated international economic order.

The United States favored the development of mutual economic and diplomatic assistance between Japan and South Korea. When meeting with President Rhee in 1953, Secretary of State Dulles pointed out the strategic importance of the anticommunist arc, stretching from Japan and Korea to Taiwan, the Philippines, and Indochina, and emphasized that the security interests of the Western Pacific area required a close cooperative relationship between South Korea and Japan. Rhee's reaction was predictably negative. He indicated that the Korean people were worried more about Japan than about the Soviet Union because Japanese policies were designed to revive Tokyo's old colonial ideas. Rhee asked that Washington stop building up Japan militarily and economically and refrain from allocating ECA funds to buy Japanese goods for South Korea's use. The State Department minutes summarize Dulles's response:

> If Japan goes Communist, Korea will be lost. Since Japan is essentially an industrial economy without adequate resources of its own, it must live on its manufactures and manufacturing capabilities. Unless this process continues under the auspices of the United States and the free world, it will inevitably come under Soviet Communism, which desires to control Japan as a workshop for war. The Secretary suggested to President Rhee that he must recognize as a problem of ROK national security the necessity for keeping the Japanese economy viable and strong. . . . Otherwise, Japan might become Communist, for it would starve without trade with the free world.[96]

Neither the secretary of state's efforts at persuasion, nor U.S. sponsorship of the Tokyo-Seoul negotiations diminished Rhee's stubbornly held anti-Japanese feelings. In his draft letter addressed to Dulles in 1954, Rhee stated that if the United States attempted to build up Japan, all the Oriental peoples "would rather join with the Soviets to resist the Japanese." However, if the United States pledged not to do so and if Japan accepted South Korea's conditions for diplomatic normalization, he would be willing to form a three-nation pact with the United States and Japan.[97] (Unlike Rhee, Generalissimo Chiang Kai-shek was quite eager to work with Japan in joint economic and diplomatic undertakings despite Japan's long colonial domination of Taiwan.) In the case of Japanese-Korean relations, interbloc conflict did not necessarily improve intrabloc cooperation. Although Washington's design for an intimate and harmonious trilateral relationship among the United States, Japan, and South Korea remained unrealized, the United States sustained the two sets of its bilateral, patron-client relations — namely, with Japan and South Korea — throughout the 1950s.

EROSION OF U.S. INFLUENCE: 1960s

In the 1950s, implementation of Washington's containment policy in East Asia and actions taken by the U.S. government in the role of patron vis-à-vis its client states, especially Japan and South Korea, generated intermittent tensions. During the 1960s, structural change in the international and regional political systems produced a substantial modification of U.S. containment policy and its relations with East Asian allies. The principal requirements and constraints of the loose bipolar system, which prevailed in the 1950s, had eroded irrevocably: intrabloc cooperation, alliance rigidity, compromise of domestic political integrity, and primacy of ideological and security issues. No longer was the Sino-Soviet bloc seen as a viable monolith; the Soviet Union and China openly displayed an irreconcilable cleavage in their perceptions of and approaches to the United States and Asia. The spillover effects of this Sino-Soviet rift were manifest in the U.S. Asian policy.

At the same time, U.S. influence in Asia gradually declined for a variety of reasons. First, the United States lost its overwhelming strategic superiority as the Soviet Union achieved approximate strategic parity during the 1960s. The situation was further complicated by China's (and France's) independent nuclear development. Second, as U.S. allies in Europe and Asia became self-confident, nationalistic, and self-assertive, they grew increasingly reluctant to submit unquestioningly to U.S. leadership. Anticommunist exhortations for collective action on the ideological and strategic fronts proved increasingly less effective in the face of the Sino-Soviet split and international communist polycentrism. Western Europe and Japan displayed a greater concern with the tangible economic component of their national interests, which was a bias intensified by the growing difficulties of the U.S. economy. Third, the inability of the United States to bring the Vietnam conflict to a prompt and favorable resolution caused deep domestic divisions and erosion in the postwar foreign policy consensus and demonstrated the limits of U.S. military power and political wisdom. Fourth, after the Cuban missile crisis, the United States and the Soviet Union improved their own bilateral relations selectively in the areas of nuclear nonproliferation, trade, and cultural exchange. As a consequence of these factors, Washington and Moscow found it increasingly difficult to dominate their erstwhile client-state allies and to determine the direction of Asian affairs.

Indeed, during the 1960s there emerged a close, general correlation between the decrease in interbloc conflicts and the increase in intrabloc misperceptions and tensions. Toward the end of the decade, the United States witnessed a growing conflict in its economic relations with Japan and, to a lesser extent, with South Korea. Conflict was much less evident in diplomatic and military areas, but the United States faced potential policy tension in Japan's diplomacy toward China and in South Korea's military posture.

Diplomatic Issues

In 1965, when Japan and South Korea entered into normal diplomatic relations, Washington had evidence that its long-pursued aim, a strategically vital, triangular coalition in East Asia, was on the verge of being realized. For more than a decade after Dulles's futile efforts to bring Japan and South Korea into direct ongoing cooperation, the United States prodded and promoted the tortuous negotiations between Tokyo and Seoul. Finally, the persistence of the United States paid off.

As mentioned earlier, General MacArthur invited President Rhee to Japan twice — in October 1948 and February 1950. Under the aegis of the GHQ, Japanese and South Korean diplomats held two rounds of negotiations during 1951 and 1952. The U.S. mediators attributed the failure of these meetings to South Korea's "unreasonable" and "most intransigent" behavior.[98] After the signing of the peace treaty with Japan, General Mark Clark, U.N. commander, invited Rhee to Japan for a January 1953 meeting with Prime Minister Yoshida in which Robert D. Murphy, the U.S. ambassador to Japan, took part.[99] Clark and Murphy agreed that Japanese-South Korean cooperation was imperative to the conduct of the war in Korea. Although the two Asian leaders intensely disliked each other, they pledged their support to common efforts against communism and to continuing bilateral negotiations.[100] In the mid-1950s, Japan asked John M. Allison, the U.S. ambassador to Japan, to intercede with Seoul and to facilitate the resumption of the stalemated talks between Tokyo and Seoul.[101] However, these and subsequent talks failed to produce any tangible results due to lingering mutual distrust and substantive policy differences.

The ouster of President Rhee in April 1960 paved the way for a renewal of South Korea's diplomatic contacts with Japan, first by the new Chang Myon government, then by General Park Chung-hi who engineered a successful coup d'etat against Chang in May 1961. Unlike Rhee, General Park, who had been an officer in the Imperial Japanese Army, seemed to have no intrinsic anti-Japanese hostility. As an ardent admirer of the Meiji leaders' modernization model, Park felt that diplomatic and economic cooperation with Japan was important to South Korea's rapid economic development and to the anticommunist campaign in Asia.[102] The Kennedy Administration, which disavowed its hastily issued public protest against Park's coup, seized the new opportunity to mediate between Tokyo and Seoul.[103] Like Dulles, Secretary of State Dean Rusk, who had years of experience in Asian politics, was convinced that the peace and security of East Asia required Tokyo-Seoul solidarity. The Task Force Report on Korea, prepared in June 1961 for the National Security Council decision, paid special attention to Japanese-South Korean relations. It recommended:

> Discuss with the Japanese Prime Minister during his forthcoming visit, the U.S. planning for Korea and the ways in which economic and political differences between Korea and Japan can be bridged, despite the recent changes of government. It should be understood that while the U.S. will not participate actively in negotiations, it should be prepared to act as a catalyst in seeking a settlement. The Prime Minister should be encouraged to continue efforts recently begun to develop Japanese trade with Korea, and to provide economic assistance for Korean development coordinated with American programs. . . . (The U.S. should also urge the SCNR [Supreme Council for National Reconstruction in South Korea] to be responsive to Japanese overtures.)[104]

With the virtually identical Soviet-North Korean and Sino-North Korean defense treaties negotiated in the summer of 1961, the task of promoting Japanese-South Korean cooperation required urgency. Moreover, Rusk wanted an economically dynamic and prosperous Japan to join with the United States in sharing the economic burden for South Korea's ambitious developmental programs.

At the summit meeting with Japanese Prime Minister Ikeda Hayato in June 1961, President Kennedy and Secretary Rusk stressed the importance of Tokyo-Seoul rapprochement.[105] During Rusk's visit to Asia in November 1961, he urged the Japanese prime minister to seek an early diplomatic settlement with South Korea and to resolve the highly controversial issues of property and claims, thereby assisting South Korea's forthcoming five-year economic plan. The secretary of state conveyed a similar message to General Park in Seoul.[106] The timing of these representations was fortuitous. In the wake of the security treaty crisis, Ikeda had already decided to adopt a "low posture" in domestic politics. More importantly, the prime minister had concluded that an aggressive international economic policy would best serve his public commitment to "income-doubling" plans. A few days after Rusk's visit, Ikeda and Park met in Tokyo and agreed on a broad policy framework for diplomatic and economic normalization. Specifically, they concurred that property and claims issues would be conceptualized as a method of economic cooperation rather than as a form of postcolonial restitution.[107] During President Kennedy's meeting with Park that same month, the president evidently offered the United States' assistance in Tokyo-Seoul discussions.

Conceivably, the United States exercised considerable influence on the negotiated settlement of property and claims issues dividing Tokyo and Seoul. Although the Japanese government initially insisted on a maximum of $70 million for settling South Korean property and other claims, it finally accepted an economic aid package of $800 million distributed over a ten-year period (1966-75): $300 million in grants, $200 million in long-term low-interest government loans, and more than $300 million in commercial loans. During the period from 1964 to 1965, a number of top-level U.S. officials — notably, Secretary of State Rusk, Ambassadors Edwin O. Reischauer, Samuel D. Berger, and Winthrop G. Brown, and Assistant Secretaries of State for Far Eastern Affairs W. Averell Harriman and William P. Bundy — made a variety of individual and collective contributions to the resolution of Tokyo-Seoul conflicts.[108] Rusk offered assurance that "the basic policy of the United States military and economic assistance to the Republic of Korea would not be affected by normalization of relations between Korea and Japan."[109] And Ambassador Brown told South Korean Foreign Minister Lee Dong-won that the United States would assist in an "appropriate way" in bringing about the earliest possible settlement between Tokyo and Seoul.[110] Bundy recalls that "after I became Assistant Secretary in March of 1964, I did play an active role in mediating between the two nations at the time when they were trying to work out normalization."[111] Depicting the discreet approach adopted by the U.S. government, he states that:

It was to try to encourage reasonable communication between the parties, but not to inject ourselves directly. We would try to explain Japanese attitudes in Korea, and by the same token try to explain Korean attitude in Japan. But we did not involve ourselves, at any stage . . . in the direct negotiations. All we did was to say that we thought normalization would be constructive if it could be achieved on a mutually agreeable basis.

In addition to these communication and mediation functions, Bundy appears to have articulated Washington's strategic perspective and assessment of regional developments to Tokyo and Seoul.[112] Moreover, in urging the South Korean public in October 1964 to recognize the national interest "on a supra-partisan basis," he attempted to help the South Korean government, which was beset by popular demonstrations and partisan attacks against diplomatic normalization with Japan.[113]

In spite of mounting political turmoil in both countries, the Japanese and South Korean governments followed through with their diplomatic normalization in 1965.[114] In the seven-article Treaty on Basic Relations, both sides, professing their adherence to the principles of "good neighborliness" and "mutual respect for sovereignty," agreed to establish diplomatic and consular relations. Upon Japan's strong request, they affirmed in Article 3 that "the Government of the Republic of Korea is the only lawful Government in Korea as specified in the Resolution 195 (III) of the United Nations General Assembly." South Korea interpreted the Resolution 195 (III) of December 1948 as definitely establishing its legal representation over the entire Korean peninsula. However, Japan subtly dissociated itself from this unqualified, South Korean claim and acknowledged that South Korea's territorial sovereignty was limited to the area under its effective control. Other agreements, protocols, and notes on property claims and economic cooperation, fisheries, cultural assets, and the legal status of Korean residents in Japan were adopted to the mutual satisfaction of the signatories.[115] Also, at the time of diplomatic normalization, both sides exchanged notes pledging themselves to peaceful resolution of an extremely sensitive, but still unresolved, territorial dispute over Takeshima or Dokto Island (as it is called in Japanese and Korean respectively).

As the patron of both Japan and South Korea, the United States was enormously satisfied with this diplomatic milestone, which was achieved 14 years after the GHQ-sponsored first direct negotiations between Japan and South Korea. However, with normalization, Japan had taken a definite formal step to align itself with one of Korea's two rival governments. The North Korean government termed the Tokyo-Seoul rapprochement "criminal" and "invalid" and argued that normalization was designed to revive Japanese militarism, form the United States-controlled Northeast Asia Treaty Organization, and sabotage Korea's unification. The Soviet Union and China echoed North Korea's condemnatory pronouncements. Throughout the late 1960s, Japan had never deviated from its staunch pro-Seoul diplomatic position; it never seriously entertained the notions of a "two-Korea" solution and an "equidistant" policy. The Japanese government decidedly favored those Korean residents (about 400,000 out of 650,000) in Japan who registered as citizens of the Republic of Korea. The government prevented the exchange of persons between Japan and North Korea (except for strictly humanitarian cases and permanent repatriation) and denied Pyongyang's request for governmental trade agreements and resident economic missions in Japan. Japan cooperated with South Korea in the United Nations, the Asian and Pacific Council (ASPAC), and other international organizations. These cooperative efforts were reinforced by annual ministerial meetings, beginning in 1967, and by various organizational networks that embraced the members of the top political and business circles in both countries. Some of these organizations lobbied for policies favorable to South Korea's interests both in Japan and in the United States. The expansion of diplomatic and economic ties between Japan and South Korea was accompanied by reaffirmation of a shared strategic outlook. In August 1968, the Second Annual Ministerial Meeting declared that "the security and prosperity of [South] Korea have important influence on that of Japan."[116] This clear identification of a security linkage between the two countries preceded the celebrated Nixon-Sato joint statement of November 1969 in which the same point was explicated more forcefully.

Although the United States and Japan exhibited a high degree of mutual reinforcement in their diplomatic approaches toward the Korean peninsula, they were not always effective in coordinating their respective policies toward China. Signs of their actual and potential policy differences regarding China appeared gradually in three areas — diplomatic styles, economic contacts, and "people's diplomacy." While Japan consistently supported the U.S. policy of denying diplomatic recognition and U.N. membership to China during the

1960s, it did so in a subdued, somewhat apologetic manner. After the security treaty turmoil in 1960, Prime Minister Ikeda declared a policy of "friendly diplomacy" (*zenrin gaiko*) with all countries, including China and the Soviet Union. He secretly proposed to China to open ambassadorial talks, similar to the Chinese-United States Warsaw talks. China rejected Ikeda's proposal, insisting that since Chinese-Japanese and Chinese-United States relations differed fundamentally, a comprehensive political settlement should be negotiated at the ministerial level.[117] The Chinese also rebuffed the Kennedy Administration's conciliatory proposals for the release of prisoners, exchange of journalists, and renunciation of force. In Warsaw, U.S. Ambassador John M. Cabot was instructed to inform his Chinese counterpart that no U.S. support would be given to any Nationalist Chinese attempt to invade the mainland.[118]

In December 1961, Japan and the United States cosponsored a U.N. resolution declaring that any proposal to change the representation of China was an "important question" and thus required support by two-thirds of those voting rather than a simple majority. This resolution was intended to make it difficult for the PRC to replace Taiwan in the United Nations. The Ikeda government called it a transitional measure for admitting the PRC to the General Assembly and the Security Council, while ensuring a General Assembly seat for Taiwan. Whereas Japan publicly espoused a long-term "two-China" policy, the Kennedy Administration could not because of the fear of the powerful China lobby. Speaking to the United Nations, Japanese Ambassador Okazaki Katsuo reminded members that Japan and China had a 2,000-year history of intimate, cultural interaction.[119] Okazaki's mild style was sharply contrasted with that of Ambassador Adlai E. Stevenson, who maintained that if China were admitted to the United Nations, it would favor nuclear proliferation, advocate the "rule of the gun," and exert a "demoralizing effect" upon the United Nations itself. Subsequently, the United States decided to revise Dulles's conception of China as a passing phenomenon. In 1963 Assistant Secretary of State Roger Hilsman declared that "we have no reason to believe that there is a present likelihood that the Communist regime will be overthrown."[120] However, this realistic appraisal did not significantly alter the U.S. diplomatic posture toward China. Nor did it abate the continuous anti-Peking rhetoric repeated by the U.S. delegation to the United Nations, especially during the Chinese Cultural Revolution. For example, in November 1967, Representative L. H. Fountain, a U.S. delegate to the United Nations, said that "there cannot be any more widely known fact in international affairs today than the warlike and aggressive manner in which the Peking regime has conducted itself all around its periphery from Tibet to Korea." Confronted with Albania's defense of China's peaceful policy, he rhetorically asked: Can this possibly be said of the regime that committed or assisted an aggressive act in Korea, India, Laos, and Vietnam and that intervened to promote subversion as far away as Africa and Latin America? Citing instances of China's irrational behavior, Fountain urged other member-states to reject U.N. membership for "this rigidly fanatical and violence-prone regime."[121] The Japanese delegates, too, pointed out China's dogmatic and disruptive foreign policy but refrained from joining the emotional, anti-Peking denunciations. They pledged to expand economic and cultural exchanges with China and to resolve the diplomatic issues "in a fair manner, consistent with world opinion."

In contrast to the U.S. policy of interdicting all ties with China, Japan's policy separated economic from diplomatic matters. Reflecting Prime Minister Ikeda's vigorous foreign economic policy, Japan and China resumed commercial ties (suspended since 1958) under the friendship trade formula, whereby trade was channeled through certain Japanese companies that China had designated as "friendly" to its positions. Further, Ikeda gave a wholehearted support to Dietman Matsumura Kenzo — a senior leader of the Liberal Democratic Party — who in 1962 initiated the semiofficial memorandum trade formula with China. The two sides agreed to exchange resident trade liaison offices between Tokyo and Peking and to apply the methods of deferred payments and medium-term credits to finance China's import of Japanese industrial plants. When in August 1963 the Ikeda government allowed the use of Export-Import Bank funds for selling a $22 million vinylon plant to China, it received a barrage of protests from the LDP's pro-Taipei members, Taipei, and Washington. Assistant Secretary of State Hilsman suggested that Japan's deferred payment method, as applied to transactions with the PRC, amounted to foreign aid for the "enemy."[122] The growing pressure from foreign and domestic sources forced the Ikeda government to prohibit any further use of Export-Import Bank funds for financing projects in China. Yet, despite Washington's and Taipei's explicit displeasure, Prime Minister Ikeda carried out the exchange of trade liaison offices with China in 1964. Each office was staffed by government personnel on leave, and they enjoyed quasi-diplomatic status. The United States was uneasy about the possibility that the trade liaison offices might lead to Japan's de facto recognition of China, especially after French President Charles de Gaulle's diplomatic switch from Taipei to Peking.

The political controversies in Japan over the trade liaison office and deferred payment, Japan-South Korea diplomatic negotiations, and the Vietnam War did not inhibit the expansion of Japanese-Chinese trade, which increased sharply between 1963 and 1967. Stimulated by the combination of friendship and memorandum trade formulas, two-way commercial transactions registered a 126 percent increase between 1963 and 1964, and the value of two-way trade ($470 million) during 1965 was three times the amount of the previous postwar peak attained during 1956. This value exceeded that of the dwindling Sino-Soviet trade and the moderately rising Japanese-Soviet trade. When this figure jumped by 32 percent in 1966, China became Japan's fourth largest trading partner after the United States, Australia, and Canada. Even when trade declined in 1967, Japan remained China's number-one trading partner.

Emphasis on economic cooperation between Japan and China was conducive to the development of "people's diplomacy." While the doors to

Chinese-United States exchange remained firmly closed throughout the 1960s, a variety of Japanese groups and individuals were engaged in "people's diplomacy" with their Chinese counterparts. The activities ranged from cultural exchanges and mutual visits to joint declarations and political rallies. The political tactics of "people's diplomacy" were used against U.S. policy in Asia. "People's diplomacy" served as a powerful tool by which China gained access to Japan's policy-making processes and attempted to provoke dissension between Japan and the United States.

The Chinese used "people's diplomacy" adroitly to encourage an increasingly serious policy cleavage between the pro-Peking and pro-Taipei members of the ruling LDP. The Asian-African Problems Study Group (AAPSG), a coalition of about 80 pro-Peking LDP Dietmen, formed in 1965, advocated a forward-looking approach for Japan's China policy and promoted a variety of economic ties and "people's diplomacy" with China. Influential AAPSG leaders, such as Matsumura Kenzo, favored an autonomous Japanese foreign policy that dissociated itself from the U.S. containment policy and promoted Japan's Asian identity by restoring traditional brotherhood between Japan and China. They considered it absurd and unrealistic for the Japanese government to recognize the Republic of China as representing all the people on the mainland. In a proposal supported by Japanese public opinion, the AAPSG urged the government not to join the United States in cosponsoring the "important question" resolution at the United Nations but to vote for PRC membership. By the end of the 1960s, the vocal, active, and increasingly influential proponents of diplomatic normalization with the PRC (the AAPSG, the opposition parties, business circles, and various "people's organizations") had substantially undermined the domestic support base for continuing Japanese-United States cooperation regarding China.

Economic Relations

The difficulty the United States and Japan faced in coordinating their policies on China trade was a harbinger of the economic frictions that the two allies were to experience in the 1960s. In the early part of that decade, there was an air of hope and optimism in both countries as each welcomed a new political leader. Japan continued its high rate of economic growth, and this trend was given further impetus by the "income-doubling plan" espoused by Ikeda Hayato, who became prime minister in 1960 in the wake of the bilateral crisis over the revision of the mutual security treaty. The new U.S. president, John F. Kennedy, accepted Japan as an "equal partner" in the alliance and instituted a system of regular bilateral cabinet-level consultations on economic affairs. The United States continued to champion the cause of free trade in the free world and allowed Japan to steadily increase its exports to U.S. markets.

At the same time, however, the U.S. government began to make concessions to protectionist pressures in specific domestic industries threatened by growing imports. This tension between trade liberalism and protectionism was reflected in the fact that the administration negotiated a multilateral, cotton textile, import-control arrangement in 1961-62, while pushing the Trade Expansion Act that initiated the Kennedy Round for across-the-board tariff reductions. The protectionist trend became even more evident in the latter half of the 1960s when the U.S. economy began to have its own serious difficulties (exacerbated by its heavy financial burden of continuing a war in Vietnam) and the United States came to face increasing trade competition from abroad, particularly from Japan. The year 1965 was significant in that the bilateral trade balance shifted in favor of Japan for the first time in postwar history. Moreover, as the cold war tension subsided toward the end of the decade, the United States became less benevolent and magnanimous toward Japan (and other U.S. allies) over bilateral economic disputes. This was especially true because Japan was rapidly emerging as a major economic power in its own right. In 1967, for instance, Japan replaced West Germany as the second largest economic power in the non-communist world.

During 1967-68 the United States haggled with Japan (and the European Economic Community) over steel imports. A major trade war was launched in 1969, when the Nixon Administration pressed Japan to limit synthetic and wool textile exports to the U.S. markets, but the Japanese, increasingly proud and self-assertive, but still expecting U.S. benevolence, adamantly resisted. The executive branch's slant toward protectionism was complemented by an even stronger protectionist shift in the U.S. Congress. Chairman Wilbur Mills of the House Ways and Means Committee commented in 1970 that Kennedy's Trade Expansion Act would not have attracted even 50 votes on the House floor in that year.[123] This situation foreshadowed stormy economic relations between the United States and Japan in the 1970s.

By the early 1960s, when South Korea's economic recovery from the war had been assured, the United States redirected its aid efforts to the challenge of helping its client build a viable, self-reliant economy. South Korea's readiness for economic modernization coincided roughly with a basic change in Washington's approach to foreign aid and in the character of the Seoul government. Seeking the reduction of international payments deficits, the Foreign Assistance Act (1961) established that future U.S. aid in the form of loans rather than grants would be concentrated on economic instead of military projects. With this shift in emphasis and with U.S. assistance and encouragement, the new military government in South Korea adopted its first Five-Year Plan (1962-66), which set ambitious goals for economic development. The plan envisaged a 7.1 percent average annual growth rate in the gross national product that was projected to reach $2.5 billion (in terms of the 1961 constant price) by the target year.[124] It gave high priority to the development of coal and other energy sources and called for a 99.3 percent increase of labor-intensive, secondary industries during the period of the plan. Foreign sources (aid, capital investments, and foreign exchange earnings) were to provide 27.8 percent of the total funds, and the value of commodity exports during the target year was set at $137 million. For both external funds and export expansion, South Korea relied primarily on the United States, and secondarily, on Japan and Europe.

In spite of early difficulties and some downward adjustments, the plan was overfulfilled by 1966. The GNP grew at an average annual rate of 9.4 percent and by 1966 totaled $3.6 billion.[125] Commodity exports reached $255 million, thereby showing an average annual growth rate of 44 percent; labor-intensive, light industries (textiles, plywood, wigs, etc.) constituted 62.4 percent of all exports. During the period of the plan, the United States played a major role in South Korea's successful campaigns to expand exports and to attract foreign capital ($322 million). South Korea's export-led growth policy made it one of the most rapidly developing less developed countries (LDCs) in the world in terms of the growth rates of the GNP and exports. Through the Agency for International Development (AID), the United States took a "very active and direct interest" in formulating and implementing the Second Five-Year Plan (1967-71).[126] This plan produced results even more impressive than the first one: by 1971 the GNP had grown to $9.4 billion (a 10.5 percent average growth rate per year), and exports climbed to $1.1 billion (35.2 percent average growth rate per year). South Korea had received $2.2 billion in total foreign capital inducements.

Throughout the 1960s, the United States supported and guided South Korea's economic development programs. AID, in particular, directly and effectively employed its economic leverage and technical expertise to elicit changes in a wide range of South Korean economic policies — such as tax reform, floating exchange rate, import liberalization, stabilization program, and currency devaluation. The blunt, adversarial way in which some AID personnel pressured the South Korean government (for example, by withholding support assistance for nine months to effect tax reform in 1963) created policy cleavage and personal tension on both sides.[127] Also, the United States failed to pay much attention to the question of social and political reforms in South Korea. Nevertheless, AID's varied activities were crucial to South Korea's enormously successful economic performance.

The broad U.S. policy objectives in the Asian-Pacific region had a beneficial effect on South Korea's economic growth. The normalization of relations between Japan and South Korea had significant effects on the course of Washington-Seoul economic relations. By the end of 1969, Japan provided South Korea with $123 million in grants and $75 million in government loans. The amount of commercial loans ($380 million by the end of 1969) exceeded the original Japanese pledge of $300 million over ten years. Japan was also active in the areas of direct investments, technology transfer, technical training, and, above all, trade.[128]

Securing South Korean military participation in the Vietnam War was another U.S. policy objective that yielded handsome economic and military dividends for South Korea. The Vietnam venture during the 1965-70 period enabled South Korea to receive from the United States more than $1 billion in the form of security assistance funds, military procurements, development loans, cash allowances, and arms transfer. Various business activities associated with the Vietnam War earned another billion dollars, which constituted about 10-20 percent of current account receipts during this period.[129] The infusion of at least $2 billion considerably stimulated South Korea's economic growth, but it was much less than what Japan earned from either the Korean or Vietnam Wars. Finally, the continuing U.S. policy of giving military assistance to South Korea and of maintaining military presence in the Korean peninsula afforded South Korea a security guarantee and permitted Seoul to moderate the growth of defense costs.

Critics of U.S. economic policy in South Korea, especially liberal Senators J. William Fulbright and Mike Mansfield and economy-minded Congressmen Otto Passman and Wilbur Mills, argued that much of U.S. foreign aid to South Korea was wasteful or ineffective. Other critics contended that the United States and Japan imposed upon South Korea "dependent industrialization" and "negative contributions" — such as labor exploitation, political repression, corruption, income disparity, and pollution-prone industries. Spokesmen for the U.S. government vehemently defended the United States' positive contributions to South Korea's economic and military well-being. Often, the debates between critics and defenders of U.S. Korean policy were acrimonious and hyperbolic, as the following exchange between Fulbright and Winthrop G. Brown (deputy assistant secretary of state) illustrated:

> Senator Fulbright. We have already given them [South Koreans] money. What has happened to the money there? Have we poured it down a rat hole? What has happened to the $7 billion? That is an awful lot of money. . . .
> Mr. Brown. What has happened is a country that was totally devastated, full of refugees, land, homes, and schools destroyed, no earning power of foreign exchange, a problem of no fuel, no real means of earning a livelihood has changed into a vigorous country which is beginning to earn its own way and which will not require any grant economic aid after this year, which is increasing its exports, which is participating responsibly in the affairs of Asia, and which is one of the fastest, if not the fastest, growing nations in the world. That, sir, is what has happened as a result of our aid.[130]

While one may hesitate to accept Brown's categorical claim at face value, it is nonetheless undeniable that U.S. aid programs had a positive impact on the South Koreans' conscious and tenacious efforts for rapid economic growth. A key South Korean economic official readily identified a number of areas in which U.S. aid had helped South Korea: to provide essential budget support for the postwar government lacking an adequate tax base; to ease the burden of defense costs (through PL 480 and other programs); to free South Korea from the necessity of massive agricultural investments, thus permitting the concentration of investments on industrialization; and to improve human, educational, and scientific resources.[131] Conspicuously absent in his catalog was AID's dominant policy-making role. The official admitted that U.S. aid policy forced South Korea to solidify its economic ties with the United States and to internationalize its economic policy orientations. Although the U.S. overall economic policy in South Korea was relatively successful, it produced incipient strains that emerged in their bilateral trade relations. The United States and Japan also developed a mixture of collaboration and competitiveness in their economic relations with South Korea.

Military Relations

The year 1960 was a watershed in the politics of the United States-Japanese military alliance. In January, after long and difficult negotiations, the United States and Japan signed the revised security treaty in Washington. In June, the signatories exchanged the instruments of ratification in Tokyo. Even though the new treaty accommodated much of Japan's desire for sovereign independence and reciprocal obligations, it aroused what Professors Scalapino and Masumi called the "greatest mass movement" in Japan's political history.[132] In expressing opposition to the treaty and to Prime Minister Kishi's arrogant and tactless handling of its ratification in the National Diet, millions of Japanese people from all walks of life demonstrated in Tokyo's streets, signed petitions, and paralyzed governmental and parliamentary processes. Common to this emotional explosion was the shared perception that the new treaty violated Article 9 of the Japanese Constitution, maintained Japan's subservience to U.S. regional military interests, and increased the probability of Japan's involvement in the U.S. Asian war. During this political trauma, President Eisenhower's Press Secretary James Hagerty and Ambassador Douglas MacArthur II were once surrounded and harassed by Japanese demonstrators at the Haneda airport. Finally, they were taken to Tokyo by military helicopter.[133] The incident forced Kishi to cancel President Eisenhower's planned state visit to Japan (in contrast to his successful trip to Seoul) and to resign from the prime ministership when the treaty entered into force. After the tumultuous treaty crisis, the new security arrangements contributed to the stabilization of the United States-Japanese alliance.

Whereas the original 1952 treaty was imposed upon Japan at the time of the U.S. occupation, its revision was negotiated on the basis of equal legal status between the two nations. Consequently, from the Japanese viewpoint, the revised treaty was an improvement in several major aspects.[134] Most important, the 1960 treaty made the U.S. defense commitment to Japan more explicit and reciprocal. Article 5 stated:

Each party recognizes that an armed attack against either party in the territories under the administration of Japan would be dangerous to its own peace and safety and declares that it would act to meet the common danger in accordance with its constitutional provisions and processes.[135]

This promise of reciprocal collective security was common in other defense treaties between the United States and its Asian allies. Here, its application was strictly limited to either party in Japanese territories because Article 9 of the constitution has been interpreted as prohibiting Japanese military actions abroad. In treaties with the Philippines, South Korea, and Taiwan, the United States and the other signatories designated larger geographical range, namely, either party in the Pacific or Western Pacific area.

As Japan wished, the revised treaty absolved the United States from any responsibility for Japan's internal security, which normally is the exclusive responsibility of an independent nation. The clause of "prior consultation" was another important innovation requested by Japan. Articles 4 and 6 required both countries to consult together from time to time regarding the implementation of the treaty. In the exchange of notes with Prime Minister Kishi, Secretary of State Christian A. Herter promised that "major changes" in the deployment or use of U.S. armed forces, equipment, and facilities in Japan would be subject to prior consultation with Japan.[136] The Eisenhower-Kishi joint communiqué, issued in January 1960, added that "the United States government has no intention of acting in a manner contrary to the wishes of the Japanese government with respect to the matters involving prior consultation under the treaty."[137] In the course of the Senate debates, Herter made it very clear that prior consultation meant "prior approval."[138] In addition, the new treaty placed great emphasis on the signatories' economic collaboration and their adherence to the Charter of the United Nations. Through an exchange of notes, Japan assumed an indirect, partial security responsibility for the peoples of the Ryukyus and Bonin Islands, based on its "residual sovereignty" over these territories. The treaty was to be in force for an initial period of ten years; afterwards, either party could exercise the right to terminate it by giving one year's notice.

All these revisions and clarifications notwithstanding, there was no change in the essential features of the United States-Japanese military alliance and in Japan's ultimate security dependency on the U.S. protective shield. The United States enjoyed the same military base rights in Japan as before. Similarly, the Herter-Kishi notes reaffirmed Japan's intention to permit the use of U.S. facilities in Japan for the United Nations Command in South Korea. The high-level "Japanese-American Committee on Security," established in 1957 for bilateral security consultations, was renamed the "Security Consultative Committee."

The net result of the revised treaty was to freeze the United States-Japanese alliance for one decade at least. Yet, in the 1960s, the alliance was exposed to constant challenges and controversies in Japan. Opposition political parties and

other antitreaty forces, notably pacifists and neutralists, challenged the consti-
tutionality of Japan's Self-Defense Forces and the Japanese-United States
military alliance, but the Japanese Supreme Court was not prepared to make an
authoritative decision on these matters. Treaty opponents protested joint military exercises, the U.S. continual military use of Japanese territory, and Japan's
contingency plans, particularly the top secret "Three Arrow Study" (*Mitsuya
Kenkyu*).[139]

The transfer of U.S. forces or equipment (such as tanks, ships, and aircraft)
from Japan in conjunction with the Vietnam War and the Pueblo incident
provoked heated public controversy over the application of the prior consultation clause.[140] Emotional, allergic protests were frequently organized against
any nuclear-related action; for example, the port calls of U.S. nuclear-powered
naval vessels and the U.S. decision to provide a nuclear umbrella for Japan in
the aftermath of China's atomic tests.

One of the most persistent and disruptive irritants in United States-Japanese
security relations during the 1960s evolved around the continuous U.S. control
of the Okinawa (Ryukyus) Islands. (The Bonin Islands were returned to Japan's
control in 1968.) Many Japanese viewed Okinawa not only as a forward base
for U.S. nuclear and military policy in Asia, but also as a symbol of Japan's
postwar dependence on U.S. influence. In 1969, after a series of summit
meetings and other top-level discussions, President Nixon agreed to revert the
administrative rights over Okinawa to Japan by 1972, so long as this constituted
no detriment to the peace and security of the Far East. In return, Prime Minister
Sato expressed his intentions to extend the security treaty automatically after
1970, to apply the treaty's terms to postreversion Okinawa, and to assume the
responsibility for Okinawa's future defense. The Nixon-Sato communiqué
issued on November 21, 1969 added:

> The President and the Prime Minister specifically noted the continuing
> tension over the Korean peninsula. The Prime Minister deeply appre-
> ciated the peace-keeping efforts of the United Nations in the area and
> stated that the security of the Republic of Korea was essential to
> Japan's own security. The President and the Prime Minister shared
> the hope that Communist China would adopt a more cooperative and
> constructive attitude in its external relations. The President referred
> to the treaty obligations of his country to the Republic of China which
> the United States would uphold. The Prime Minister said that the
> maintenance of peace and security in the Taiwan area was also a most
> important factor for the security of Japan.[141]

Moreover, Sato said at the National Press Club that if South Korea or
Taiwan were under an armed attack, Japan would regard it as a threat to the
peace and security of the Far East, including Japan, and would take prompt and
positive measures so that the United States would use its military bases and
facilities within Japan to meet the armed attack. He pledged to make "active

contributions" to the peace and prosperity of Asia, especially, in economic fields.[142] The Sato statements were promptly and enthusiastically endorsed by South Korean President Park.[143]

Sato's open identification of Japan's security linkage with South Korea and Taiwan represented an overstated inducement for Okinawa's reversion, but it provoked scathing attacks from China and North Korea. Premier Chou En-lai asserted that "abetted by U.S. imperialism and drunk with rabid ambition," the Sato government was attempting to "step up the revival of militarism and realize its old dream of a Greater East Asia Co-Prosperity Sphere."[144] Later, in April 1970, he joined North Korea's Kim Il-song in justifying their common struggle against Sato:

> Actively shielded by U.S. imperialism, Japanese militarism has revived and has become a dangerous force of aggression in Asia. . . . The Japanese militarists are directly serving U.S. imperialism in its war of aggression against Vietnam, actively taking part in the U.S. imperialist new scheme of war in Korea and wildly attempting to include the Chinese people's sacred territory Taiwan in their sphere of influence.[145]

Chou warned that China would sever economic relations with those Japanese companies that had heavy trade or large investments in South Korea or Taiwan or had assisted U.S. war efforts in Vietnam.

Contrary to the Chinese and North Korean condemnation of Sato's militaristic policy, critics in the U.S. Senate — such as Senators Stuart Symington, J. W. Fulbright, and Mike Mansfield — complained that Japan's inadequate defense budget ($1.3 billion vs. $600 million for U.S. military expenditures in Japan during 1969) amounted to a "free ride" at the expense of U.S. taxpayers. The U.S. government leaders emphasized the vital, strategic interdependence between the United States and Japan and explained that the United States gradually reduced the number of its troops and facilities in Japan, terminated its military assistance programs to Japan by 1965, and sold arms to Japan (valued at $450 million through 1969), while Japan's defense expenditures showed a moderate annual growth during the 1960s. Yet Washington reiterated its unswerving commitment to retain U.S. military bases in Japan proper and in postreversion Okinawa for U.S. regional strategic interests. Testifying before the Senate in early 1970, Under Secretary of State U. Alexis Johnson admitted that:

> Our position in our facilities, bases in Japan as well as in Okinawa, are not so much related directly to the defense of Japan and Okinawa as they are to our ability to support our commitments elsewhere . . . in Korea and Taiwan.[146]

In order to "maintain a presence and a force in Korea," he argued, "it seems to me important that we have a back-up or presence in . . . Japan and Okinawa."[147]

Thus, Johnson and Sato reflected the shared view that there existed an intimate, mutually reinforcing trilateral security relationship among the United States, Japan, and South Korea.

The United States and Japan became increasingly sensitive to Korean security issues during the 1960s when conflicts and tensions intensified between the two hostile and well-armed rivals in the peninsula, backed by competitive international security coalitions. Pyongyang secured almost identical bilateral defense treaties from the Soviet Union and China apparently because he thought that the open escalation of the Sino-Soviet dispute and the 1961 military take-over of South Korea were real threats to North Korean security.[148] Both treaties, which entered into force on the same day in September 1961, contained the same language defining reciprocal security obligations:

> Should either of the contracting parties suffer armed attack by any state or coalition of states, and thus find itself in a state of war, the other contracting party shall immediately extend military and other assistance with all the means at its disposal.[149]

This language was a carbon copy of the Sino-Soviet Treaty (Article 1). Unlike the U.S. security treaties with Japan and South Korea, neither treaty with North Korea referred to the "common danger." Further, the North Korean treaties were categorical regarding mutual defense responsibilities (without any escape clause such as "in accordance with its constitutional provisions") and broad in the geographical scope to which the treaties applied. The Soviet and Chinese treaties with North Korea had a few minor semantic and procedural differences,[150] but the Soviet Union and China were equally committed to the military protection of North Korea. In this sense, both North Korea and South Korea were formally well integrated into opposing international military coalitions.

The international aspects of the intra-Korean rivalry were manifest in the late 1960s when opposing policies were adopted regarding the Vietnam War. The United States initiated, financed, and directed South Korea's large-scale armed intervention in Vietnam. Started as a modest dispatch of noncombat troops in 1964-65, the number of South Korean military personnel in South Vietnam grew to about 50,000 by the end of 1969. President Park defended this military expedition as the discharge of moral obligation to the free-world's collective security against Chinese-supported Vietnamese guerrillas. Since he thought that a communist victory in South Vietnam would subject the whole Asian region to the spreading communist threats, his decision was an "indirect national defense" for South Korea. Pointing out that South Korea had been saved by the United States and its free-world allies during the Korean War, he declared, "we cannot sit on our hands and see one of our friendly allies become prey to Communist invasion."[151] However, beneath this anticommunist rhetoric was a pragmatic concern for the economic and security benefits, which Park was extracting from the United States. As a *quid pro quo* for South Korea's military support, the United States agreed to underwrite all expenses for South Korea's military operations in Vietnam and to provide substantial military equipment for South Korea.[152] In addition, Washington decided to procure South Korean supplies and services for United States' and South Vietnamese use and to increase AID loans for South Korea's economic programs. Further, U.S. leaders profusely reaffirmed their defense obligation to South Korea and promised not to reduce U.S. troops stationed in South Korea without prior consultation. Vice President Hubert H. Humphrey, during his Seoul visit in February 1966, unequivocally stated that: "As long as there is one American soldier on . . . the demarcation line, the whole and entire power of the United States of America is committed to the defense of Korea."[153] The Johnson-Park summitry held at Seoul in November 1966 produced a joint statement, which said:

> The two Presidents acknowledged the need to ensure that the forces of aggression do not again menace the peace and tranquility of the Republic of Korea. They agreed that the growing strength of the Communist forces in the northern part of Korea and of the Chinese Communists remained a major threat to the security of the Republic of Korea and neighboring areas. President Johnson reaffirmed the readiness and determination of the United States to render prompt and effective assistance to defeat an armed attack against the Republic of Korea. In accordance with the Mutual Defense Treaty of 1954, President Johnson assured President Park that the United States has no plan to reduce the present level of United States forces in Korea, and would continue to support Korean armed forces at levels adequate to ensure Korea's security. They agreed that their two Governments would continue to consult closely to ensure that the Korean forces are strengthened and modernized within the limitations imposed by legislative and budgetary considerations.[154]

Critics of the United States-South Korean military undertaking in South Vietnam contended that Park had agreed to supply and sacrifice the South Korean troops solely for economic benefits. Senator Fulbright labelled Park's venture as a "good business deal at our request and urging."[155] Others argued that by spearheading the anticommunist crusade in another foreign country, South Korea enhanced its image as a fierce, cold war warrior, thus increasing Seoul's alienation from the third world. The fact that a vast number of South Koreans (about 340,000 altogether) had direct combat experience in Vietnam and that the United States strengthened and modernized the South Korean forces was considered provocative to North Korea, which supported the communist cause in Indochina.

The United States greatly appreciated and materially rewarded South Korea's military cooperation in Vietnam, but this did not prevent a potentially explosive policy disagreement with South Korea in regard to the appropriate response to North Korea's extreme militancy in the late 1960s. When North

Korea dispatched a 31-member commando team to attack President Park's official residence (Blue House) in Seoul and seized the U.S.S. Pueblo in January 1968, the South Koreans were enraged by Washington's failure to meet the North Korean challenge with a response. President Park urged the United States to launch air strikes against North Korean military installations and offered South Korea's armed reprisals against North Korea. In Congressional testimony, Ambassador William Porter recalled Park's angry remarks:

> Mr. Fraser: How did the Korean Government perceive these two events in relation to its ongoing concern about its security?
>
> Mr. Porter: With great concern. It was a very severe shock. Both items were very severe shocks for the President, the Cabinet, and the people as a whole. President Park was quite intent on striking back. He told me he could be in Pyongyang within 2 days' time, and I had to tell him that if he tried that, he would have to do it alone.[156]

In spite of Park's requests, the United States decided not to escalate the Pueblo incident and open a second war front in Asia. Instead, Washington sought the peaceful release of the Pueblo crewmen through direct bilateral negotiations with North Korea at Panmunjom. Upon the U.S. request, Japanese Foreign Minister Miki Takeo instructed Japanese embassies in Eastern Europe to contact North Korean diplomatic personnel and to press for the Pueblo settlement.[157] U.S. and South Korean perceptions of the two incidents diverged sharply. Whereas the United States was preoccupied with the release of Pueblo crewmen, the South Koreans viewed the status of Pueblo personnel as a side issue and felt strongly that the United States should take extraordinary retaliatory measures to prevent a recurrence of North Korea's commando raids.[158] The South Korean frustration was eased somewhat by former Deputy Secretary of Defense Cyrus R. Vance, President Johnson's special envoy, who visited Seoul in February 1968. The Vance mission persuaded President Park to refrain from independent military retaliation against North Korea and agreed to a $100 million aid package for South Korean military modernization (including F-4 aircraft to combat North Korea's MIG-21) and to equip South Korean reserve forces with improved small arms such as the M-16.[159] The two sides decided to initiate annual consultations between their defense ministers and to convene a meeting of military experts regarding assistance programs. U.S. commitments to South Korean security and military modernization were strengthened and expanded at the Johnson-Park summit of April 1968 and the first Annual Consultative Meeting of United States-South Korean defense ministers in May 1968.

Despite all these meetings and commitments to strengthen the military alliance between the United States and South Korea, elements of strain and misperception persisted. These neuralgic points were irritated again in 1969 by the EC-121 incident in April and the Guam Doctrine announced by President

Nixon (July). When two North Korean MIG aircraft shot down an EC-121 (unarmed propeller-driven reconnaissance aircraft) with 31 crew members over the Sea of Japan, President Nixon considered a number of possible retaliatory actions against North Korea — such as air strikes, a torpedo attack against the North Korean navy, mining of the North Korean harbors, and seizure of merchant ships. On the recommendations of Secretary of State William Rogers, Secretary of Defense Melvin Laird, and CIA Director Richard Helms, Nixon decided against any direct military action.[160] Once again, the South Koreans were disturbed by the emerging pattern of U.S. self-restraint, which they felt could only encourage North Korean belligerency. Seoul began to question seriously whether the United States, bogged down in the Vietnam War and undergoing an erosion in its global influence, had the resolve to protect South Korea effectively in the event of an armed attack. The Guam Doctrine further fed South Korean doubts about the U.S. military reliability. While reaffirming U.S. security treaty commitments in Asia, President Nixon asked the Asian allies to assume greater responsibility for their own internal and external security, especially by mobilizing their ground forces.[161] During the course of the 1970s, the full meaning of this doctrine came painfully clear to the South Koreans.

NOTES

1. See Akira Iriye, "The United States as an Asian-Pacific Power," in Gene T. Hsiao, ed., *Sino-American Detente and Its Policy Implications* (New York: Praeger, 1974), pp. 3-21.

2. For the background of United States-East Asian relations before and during the Pacific War, see Dorothy Borg and Shumpei Okamoto, eds., *Pearl Harbor as History: Japanese-American Relations, 1931-1941* (New York: Columbia University Press, 1973); Robert J. C. Butow, *Tojo and the Coming of the War* (Stanford: Stanford University Press, 1961); John K. Fairbank, *The United States and China* (Cambridge, Mass.: Harvard University Press, 1979); Akira Iriye, *Across the Pacific* (New York: Harcourt, Brace and World, 1967); Tang Tsou, *America's Failure in China: 1941-50* (Chicago: University of Chicago Press, 1963); John Toland, *The Rising Sun: The Decline and Fall of the Japanese Empire, 1936-1945* (New York: Random House, 1970); U.S. Department of State, *United States Relations with China* (Washington, D.C.: USGPO, 1949). For the most popular Japanese textbook, see *Taiheiyo Senso* [Pacific War], 37th ed. (Tokyo: Chou koronsha, 1974).

3. Iriye, "Asian-Pacific Power."

4. For the Yalta agreement on Japan, see U.S. Department of State, *Occupation of Japan: Policy and Progress* (Washington, D.C.: USGPO, n.d.), pp. 52-53.

5. Ibid., pp. 73-81. The document issued on August 29, 1945 by the Far East Subcommittee of the State, War, and Navy Coordinating Committee (SWNCC).

6. Robert E. Ward, "Reflections on the Allied Occupation and Planned Political Change in Japan," in Robert E. Ward, ed., *Political Development in Modern Japan* (Princeton, N.J.: Princeton University Press, 1968), pp. 520-21. For the opposing view expressed by the then State Department representative in Japan, who called the Washington instructions "loose and unclear" and "ambivalent and often contradictory," see William J. Sebald, *With MacArthur in Japan: A Personal History of the Occupation* (New York: W. W. Norton,

1965), pp. 41, 47. For a similar view, see Justin Williams, Sr., *Japan's Political Revolution under MacArthur: A Participant's Account* (Athens: University of Georgia Press, 1979).

7. See Edwin O. Reischauer, *The United States and Japan*, rev. ed. (New York: Viking Press, 1957), p. 224. For descriptions of MacArthur's intimate knowledge of Japan and the Orient, see memoirs written by his longtime military aides – Courtney Whitney, *MacArthur: His Rendezvous with History* (New York: Alfred A. Knopf, 1956); and Charles A. Willoughby, *MacArthur: 1941-1951* (New York: McGraw-Hill, 1954).

8. See Hans H. Baerwald, *The Purge of Japanese Leaders under the Occupation* (Berkeley: University of California Press, 1959).

9. Reischauer, *The United States and Japan*, p. 351.

10. See Whitney, *MacArthur*, pp. 257-62. For the origin, development, and controversies of Article 9, see Fukase Tadakazu, ed., *Senso no hoki* [Renunciation of War] (Tokyo: Sanseido, 1977).

11. Reischauer, *The United States and Japan*, p. 326. For U.S. reform measures, see Kazuo Kawai, *Japan's American Interlude* (Chicago: University of Chicago Press, 1960).

12. As samples of criticism, see George F. Kennan, *Memoirs 1925-1950* (Boston: Little, Brown, 1967), pp. 388-89; Harold S. Quigley, "Revising the Japanese Constitution," *Foreign Affairs* (October 1959), p. 140; Takayanagi Kenzo (chairman of the Japanese Constitutional Commission), "Making the Japanese Constitution," *Japan Times* (March 16, 1959); Sodei Rinjiro, *Makasano nisennichi* [MacArthur's Two Thousand Days] (Tokyo: Chou koronsha, 1974); Sodei Rinjiro's comments in L. H. Redford, ed., *The Occupation of Japan: The Proceedings of a Seminar on the Occupation of Japan and its Legacy to the Postwar World* (Norfolk: MacArthur Memorial, 1976), pp. 149-58; and Richard H. Minear, *Victor's Justice: The Tokyo War Crimes Trial* (Princeton, N.J.: Princeton University Press, 1971).

13. For one of the most recent and popular biographies of MacArthur, see William Manchester, *American Caesar: Douglas MacArthur, 1880-1964* (New York: Dell, 1978). However, it contains some serious factual errors.

14. For General MacArthur's relationship with the emperor, see Douglas MacArthur, *Reminiscences* (New York: McGraw-Hill, 1964); and Sodei, *MacArthur's Two Thousand Days*, pp. 89-96.

15. Kennan, *Memoirs 1925-1950*, pp. 374-75.

16. The most prominent examples – Prime Ministers Hatoyama Ichiro and Kishi Nobusuke, Foreign Minister Shigemitsu Mamoru (Class-A war criminal sentenced to seven years of imprisonment), and Finance Minister Kaya Okinori (Class-A war criminal sentenced to life imprisonment).

17. E. J. Lewe van Aduard, *Japan: From Surrender to Peace* (The Hague: Martinus Nijihoff, 1953), pp. 75-82.

18. Martin Bronfenbrenner, "The American Occupation of Japan: Economic Retrospect," in Grant K. Goodman, ed., *The American Occupation of Japan: A Retrospective View* (Lawrence, Kans.: Center for East Asian Studies, 1968), p. 14.

19. See Redford, *Occupation of Japan*, p. 93.

20. See Frank Baldwin, ed., *Without Parallel: The American-Korean Relationship since 1945* (New York: Pantheon Books, 1973), pp. 5-6.

21. For the Cairo Declaration, see *Occupation of Japan: Policy and Progress*, pp. 51-52.

22. See George M. McCune, *Korea Today* (Cambridge, Mass.: Harvard University Press, 1950), p. 43.

23. See Soon Sung Cho, *Korea in World Politics, 1940-1950: An Evaluation of American Responsibility* (Berkeley: University of California Press, 1967), pp. 17, 23. Also see Carl Berger, *The Korea Knot: A Military-Political History* (Philadelphia: University of Pennsylvania Press, 1957), p. 36.

24. See, for example, *Foreign Relations of the United States, 1944*, vol. 5 (Washington, D.C.: USGPO, 1965), pp. 1224-42.

25. The proposal was recommended by two colonels – Dean Rusk (later, secretary of state) and Charles H. Bonesteel, III (later, U.S. commander in Seoul, Korea). See Rusk's recollection in *Foreign Relations of the United States, 1945*, vol. 6 (Washington, D.C.: USGPO, 1969), p. 1039; also see Bonesteel's correspondence dated February 12, 1972, in James K. Terry, *The Republic of Korea and the United States: The Occupation Years, 1945-1948*, M.A. thesis, University of Kansas, 1977, p. 49.

26. As discussed in Terry, *Occupation Years*, pp. 62-64.

27. See Bruce Cumings, "American Policy and Korean Liberation," in Frank Baldwin, ed., *Without Parallel*, pp. 39-108.

28. McCune, *Korea Today*, p. 47. For the U.S. policy and implementation, see E. Grant Meade, *American Military Government in Korea* (New York: King's Crown Press, 1951.)

29. John M. Allison, *Ambassador from the Prairie: or Allison Wonderland* (Boston: Houghton Mifflin, 1973), p. 143. As head of the Japan-Korean Division of the State Department, he visited Japan and South Korea in December 1948.

30. See the joint communiqué issued on December 27, 1945, in Se-Jin Kim, ed., *Korean-American Relations, 1943-1976* (Seoul: Research Center for Peace and Unification, 1976), pp. 30-31.

31. See *Foreign Relations of the United States, 1946*, vol. 8 (1971), pp. 693-99.

32. See the new U.S. proposal, in Kim, *Korean-American Relations*, pp. 39-41.

33. *Public Papers of the Presidents of the United States, Harry S. Truman, 1947* (Washington, D.C.: USGPO, 1963), pp. 178-79.

34. See U.S. Department of State, *United States Relations with China* (Washington, D.C.: USGPO, 1949), p. xvi.

35. U.S. Department of State, *Policy Statement: Korea*, January 31, 1949 (top secret document declassified), p. 3.

36. See Gregory Henderson, *Korea: The Politics of the Vortex* (Cambridge, Mass.: Harvard University Press, 1968), p. 150.

37. *Policy Statement: Korea*, p. 3.

38. See Sebald, *With MacArthur in Japan*, pp. 180-81; and W. Averell Harriman's recollection, in Francis H. Heller, ed., *The Korean War: A 25-Year Perspective* (Lawrence: Regents Press of Kansas, 1977), p. 16. As to Rhee's special envoy, Cho Byong-ok, and Ambassador Chang Myon, who attempted to gain military aid from Secretary Acheson and other U.S. leaders, see Yi Hyo-jae, *Hanguk woegyo jongchekui yisang gwa hyonsil* [Ideals and Reality of Korean Diplomatic Policy], 3rd ed., (Seoul: Bommunsa, 1975), pp. 286-307.

39. As recalled by J. Lawton Collins (then Army chief of staff), in Heller, *The Korean War*, p. 16.

40. Cho, *Korea in World Politics*, pp. 252-55.

41. As quoted in Dean Acheson, *The Korean War* (New York: W. W. Norton, 1971), p. 2.

42. For U.S. economic aid, see Cho, *Korea in World Politics*, p. 243; and Yi, *Korean Diplomatic Policy*, pp. 333-49.

43. *Yuen hangukmunjae kyoluijip* [Collection of United Nations Resolutions on Korea] (Seoul: Woemubu, 1976), pp. 58-59.

44. *Policy Statement*, pp. 7-8.

45. See Tang Tsou, *America's Failure in China: 1941-50* (Chicago: University of Chicago Press, 1963).

46. See Roderick MacFarquhar, ed., *Sino-American Relations, 1949-71* (New York: Praeger, 1972), pp. 70-71.

47. Ibid., pp. 71-75.
48. For the text, see *Oppose the Revival of Japanese Militarism* (Peking: Foreign Languages Press, 1960), pp. 1-4.
49. MacFarquhar, *Sino-American Relations*, pp. 71-75.
50. The widely held conventional view is that in the early morning of June 25, 1950, North Korea started a massive, well-coordinated armed attack across the 38th parallel, although there had been numerous previous military clashes between North and South Korea. For the revisionist views, which challenge the conventional interpretation, see I. F. Stone, *The Hidden History of the Korean War* (New York: Monthly Review Press, 1952); D. F. Fleming, *The Cold War and Its Origins: 1917-1960* (New York: Doubleday, 1961); David Horowitz, *The Free World Colossus* (New York: Hill and Wang, 1965); Joyce and Gabriel Kolko, *The Limits of Power: The World and United States Foreign Policy, 1945-1954* (New York: Harper and Row, 1972); Karunakar Gupta, "How Did the Korean War Begin?" *China Quarterly*, October-December 1972, pp. 354-68. For an important new historical perspective, see Bruce Cumings, *The Origins of the Korean War: Liberation and the Emergence of Separate Regimes, 1945-1947* (Princeton, N.J.: Princeton University Press, 1981).
51. Acheson, *The Korean War*, p. 20.
52. Harry S. Truman, *Memoirs: Year of Trial and Hope* (Garden City, N.Y.: Doubleday, 1956), pp. 334-37.
53. Glenn D. Paige, *The Korean Decision, June 24-30, 1950* (New York: Free Press, 1968), p. 117.
54. See the minutes of this meeting, in U.S. Department of State, *Memorandum of Conversation*, June 25, 1950 (top secret document declassified in August 1972), in *Foreign Relations of the United States, 1950*, vol. 7 (1976), pp. 157-61.
55. See *Memorandum of Conversation*, June 26, 1950 (top secret document declassified in August 1972), in ibid., pp. 178-83.
56. Paige, *The Korean Decision*, pp. 204-5.
57. For this trip, see Whitney, *MacArthur*, pp. 322-33.
58. See this Taejon agreement of July 15, 1950, in Kim, *Korean-American Relations*, p. 119.
59. See *Transcript of Interview with Muccio* (in the Truman Library); and Harold J. Noble, *Embassy at War*, ed. Frank Baldwin (Seattle: University of Washington Press, 1975).
60. For MacArthur's plans, the JCS opposition, and the Inchon operation, see Whitney, *MacArthur*, pp. 354-67; and David Rees, *Korea: The Limited War* (Baltimore: Penguin Books, 1970), pp. 77-97.
61. The U.S. government seriously considered a plan for permanent neutralization of unified Korea. See *Foreign Relations of the United States, 1950*, vol. 7 (1976), pp. 720, 972, 981.
62. See ibid., p. 953. For the conflicting interpretations of the Wake Island encounter, see Whitney, *MacArthur*, pp. 384-95; Truman, *Memoirs*, pp. 364-67; and Muccio's *Transcript*.
63. As to China's participation in the Korean War, see Allen S. Whiting, *China Crosses the Yalu* (Stanford: Stanford University Press, 1968); and Robert R. Simmons, *The Strained Alliance: Peking, P'yongyang, Moscow and the Politics of the Korean Civil War* (New York: Free Press, 1975).
64. Acheson, *The Korean War*, pp. 119-22.
65. See C. Turner Joy, *How Communists Negotiate* (New York: MacMillan, 1955). For Joy's detailed diary, see Allan E. Goodman, ed., *Negotiating While Fighting: The Diary of Admiral C. Turner Joy at the Korean Armistice Conference* (Stanford: Hoover Institution, 1978).
66. See Dwight D. Eisenhower, *The White House Years: Mandate for Change, 1953-1956* (Garden City, N.Y.: Doubleday, 1963), p. 180. For President Eisenhower's preference to use tactical nuclear weapons against the Kaesong sanctuary, see the Memorandum of the

National Security Council meeting of February 11, 1953 (declassified in December 1979 in the Eisenhower Library).

67. W. D. Reeve, *The Republic of Korea: A Political and Economic Study* (New York: Oxford University Press, 1963), p. 103.

68. Rees, *Korea: The Limited War*, p. 460.

69. *Journal of Korean Affairs*, July 1974, p. 41.

70. Martin E. Weinstein, *Japan's Postwar Defense Policy, 1947-1968* (New York: Columbia University Press, 1971), p. 50.

71. See Rees, *Korea: The Limited War*, p. 85; and Sebald, *With MacArthur in Japan*, pp. 197-99.

72. See Chae-Jin Lee, *Japan Faces China: Political and Economic Relations in the Postwar Era* (Baltimore: Johns Hopkins University Press, 1976), pp. 135-37.

73. George P. Jan, "Japan's Trade with Communist China," *Asian Survey*, December 1969, p. 904.

74. This discussion of the San Francisco system is based on Lee, *Japan Faces China*, pp. 23-26.

75. Ibid.

76. For the texts of both treaties, see Reischauer, *The United States and Japan*, pp. 363-80.

77. Ibid.

78. For the residual sovereignty issue, see Frederick L. Shiels, *America, Okinawa and Japan* (Washington, D.C.: University Press of America, 1980), pp. 123-48.

79. See the text of Yoshida's letter in Dean Acheson, *Present at the Creation* (New York: W. W. Norton, 1969), pp. 963-64. For Dulles-Yoshida discussions, see *Foreign Relations of the United States, 1951*, vol. 6, pt. 1 (Washington, D.C.: USGPO, 1977), pp. 1416-21, 1431, 1437-39, 1443-50, and 1466-67.

80. For the security treaty negotiations conducted between President Rhee and Assistant Secretary of State Walter Robertson, see the Department of State's "secret security information" (declassified in 1974).

81. Interview with Ambassador Kim Yong-shik, June 26, 1978, Washington, D.C. He assisted President Rhee during the security treaty negotiations in 1953.

82. For this contingency plan developed by General Clark in May 1953, see the JCS Memorandum for Record dated June 1, 1953 (declassified in 1976). Also see Robert T. Oliver, *Syngman Rhee and American Involvement in Korea, 1942-1960: A Personal Narrative* (Seoul: Panmun, 1978), p. 413. A similar contingency plan had been considered in June 1952 when President Rhee declared a martial law to suppress domestic political opponents. For the threatening letters from Eisenhower and Dulles, see Oliver, *Syngman Rhee*, p. 412.

83. For President Eisenhower's attitudes toward these issues and President Rhee ("this fiercely patriotic but recalcitrant old man"), see Eisenhower, *White House Years*, pp. 171-91.

84. See the text in Kim, *Korean-American Relations*, pp. 185-86.

85. For a participant's account of the Dulles-Rhee meeting, see Oliver, *Syngman Rhee*, pp. 425-31. However, Oliver is wrong in his contention that the Dulles-Rhee joint statement was not issued due to policy differences.

86. As quoted in Roger Hilsman, *To Move a Nation* (Garden City, N.Y.: Doubleday, 1967), p. 296.

87. Reischauer, *The United States and Japan*, p. 333.

88. See Dulles's speech of June 28, 1957, in MacFarquhar, *Sino-American Relations*, pp. 134-42.

89. See Donald C. Hellmann, *Japanese Foreign Policy and Domestic Politics: The Peace Agreement with the Soviet Union* (Berkeley: University of California Press, 1969).

90. *Congressional Record*, 83rd Cong., 2d sess., June 23, 1954, p. 8723.

91. The United States and Western European nations organized in November 1949 at Paris a consultative group to regulate exports of strategically relevant items to the communist bloc and set up a Coordinating Committee (COCOM) as its executive arm; Japan joined it later. COCOM established a special China Committee (CHINCOM) in 1952 but abolished it in 1957.

92. For the Geneva Conference on Korea, see *The 1954 Geneva Conference: Indo-China and Korea* (New York: Greenwood Press, 1971).

93. The UNCURK was originally composed of Australia, Chile, the Netherlands, Pakistan, the Philippines, Thailand, and Turkey, but Chile and Pakistan withdrew in 1970 and 1972, respectively. It was dissolved in 1973. The commission submitted its annual report to the General Assembly. For its last report, see *Report of the United Nations Commission for the Unification and Rehabilitation of Korea, General Assembly Official Records: Twenty-eighth Session Supplement*, no. 28 (A/9027) (New York: United Nations, 1973).

94. For the economic consequences of the Korean War, see Kwang Suk Kim and Michael Roemer, *Growth and Structural Transformation* (Cambridge, Mass.: Council on East Asian Studies, Harvard University, 1979), pp. 30-33.

95. See the Department of State Memorandum for Records concerning Rhee-Dulles meetings held in August 1953 (declassified in 1974).

96. Ibid.

97. Oliver, *Syngman Rhee*, pp. 468-69.

98. See Sebald, *With MacArthur in Japan*, pp. 287-88.

99. Interview with Ambassador Kim Yong-shik, June 26, 1978, Washington, D.C.; he took part in the 1953 Yoshida-Rhee meeting.

100. When Ambassador Murphy arranged a U.S. Embassy luncheon for Rhee and Yoshida, Yoshida conveyed his regrets at the last moment and sent Foreign Minister Okazaki Katsuo on his behalf. Yoshida explained that his personal dislike of Rhee was so intense that he felt he could not conceal it at the luncheon. Later, Yoshida and Rhee met in General Clark's Tokyo office. See Robert D. Murphy, *Diplomat among Warriors* (Garden City, N.Y.: Doubleday, 1964), p. 351. In 1958 Rhee told Yatsugi Kazuo how untrustworthy Yoshida had been. See Yamamoto Tsuyoshi, *Nikkan Kankei* [Japan-South Korean Relations] (Tokyo: Kyoikusha, 1978), p. 53.

101. Kimura Shusan, "Nikkan Kosho no keii" [The Circumstances of Japanese-South Korean Negotiations], in *Kokusai Seiji* [International Relations], vol. 2 (Tokyo: Nihon Kokusai Seiji Gakkai, 1963), p. 117. Allison is extremely critical of South Korea's "unreasonable" posture, but he recalls that the U.S. "did manage to keep the incipient fire [between Japan and South Korea] from bursting into flames." See Allison, *Ambassador from the Prairie*, pp. 258-59.

102. Asked how he intended to lead South Korea, General Park told Japan's senior conservative politicians – Kishi Nobusuke and Ishii Mitsujiro – in November 1961 that he would attempt to build a nation in the same way that the Meiji patriots ('*ishin no shishi*") had done for Japan. He expressed his complete agreement with *ishin no shishi*; he was to use the same concept "ishin" (*yushin* in Korean) for his reform measures in October 1972. See Ishii Mitsujiro, *Kaiso hachijuhachinen* [Reminiscences – Eighty-eight years] (Tokyo: Karucha shupansha, 1976), pp. 441-42.

103. For the U.S. role in Rhee's downfall and its reaction to the coup, see John Kie-chiang Oh, "Role of the United States in South Korea's Democratization," *Pacific Affairs*, Summer 1969, pp. 164-77. For Ambassador Walter McConaughy's aide-mémoire dated April 21, 1960, which precipitated Rhee's downfall, see Oliver, *Syngman Rhee*, p. 486.

104. See House Committee on International Relations, *Investigation of Korean-American Relations: Appendixes to the Report of the Subcommittee on International Organizations*,

vol. 1 (Washington, D.C.: USGPO, 1978), p. 46. The Task Force Report also authorized the U.S. ambassador "to invite the Chief of [South Korean] Government to Washington for an informal visit including conferences with the President and the Secretary of State."

105. See the Kennedy-Ikeda joint statement in *Waga gaiko no kinkyo* [Recent State of Our Diplomacy] (Tokyo: Gaimusho, 1962), pp. 104-5; or *Department of State Bulletin*, July 10, 1961, pp. 57-58.

106. Yamamoto Tsuyoshi, *Nikkan kankei*, pp. 67-68. For the Rusk-Kosaka joint communiqué of November 4, 1961, see *Department of State Bulletin*, November 27, 1961, pp. 891-93.

107. *Waga gaiko no kinkyo* (1962), pp. 77-79. The Ikeda-Park meeting was preceded by the exchange of high-level emissaries between Japan and South Korea. The South Korean emissaries to Japan included Kim Yu-taek (minister of the Economic Planning Board), Kim Jong-pil (director of the Central Intelligence Agency), Choe Dok-sin (future foreign minister), and Yi Yong-hi (professor of Seoul National University). A number of Japan's influential conservative leaders – such as Yasuoka Masaatsu and Kishi Nobusuke – promoted the Ikeda-Park meeting. See Yaki Nobuo, *Fusei aika* [World Elegy] (n.p., 1971), pp. 506-13.

108. Terao Koro et al. "Nikkan kaidan" [Japanese-South Korean talks], in *Nihon to Chosen* [Japan and Korea] (Tokyo: Keiso shobo, 1965), pp. 47-118.

109. See the Rusk-Park joint communiqué of January 29, 1964, in Kim, *Korean-American Relations*, pp. 283-84.

110. See the Brown-Lee joint communiqué of August 17, 1964, in Kim, *Korean-American Relations*, p. 284.

111. William P. Bundy's letter (dated February 6, 1980) to Chae-Jin Lee.

112. Yamamoto Tsuyoshi, *Nikkan kankei*, p. 69.

113. See the joint communiqué issued on October 3, 1964, between Bundy and Foreign Minister Lee Dong-won, in Kim, *Korean-American Relations*, pp. 284-85.

114. See Hans H. Baerwald, "Nikkan Kokkai: The Japan-Korea Treaty Diet," in Lucian W. Pye, ed., *Cases in Comparative Politics: Asia* (Boston: Little, Brown, 1970), pp. 19-57.

115. For the collections and explanations of these accords, see *Nikkanjoyaku to Kokunaiho no Kaisetsu* [Commentaries on Japan-South Korea Treaty and Domestic Laws] (Tokyo: Okurasho, 1966); and *Hanilhoedam Baekso* [White Paper on South Korean-Japanese Conferences] (Seoul: Woemubu, 1965).

116. See the text of the joint communiqué, *Asahi Shimbun*, August 30, 1968.

117. See Lee, *Japan Faces China*, pp. 42-43.

118. See Kenneth T. Young, *Negotiating with the Chinese Communists: The United States Experience, 1953-1967* (New York: McGraw-Hill, 1968), pp. 240-41; and Hilsman, *To Move a Nation*, p. 319.

119. Lee, *Japan Faces China*, pp. 43-45.

120. Hilsman, *To Move a Nation*, p. 351.

121. Lee, *Japan Faces China*, pp. 61-63.

122. See Takahashi Shogoro and Tanaka Shujiro, *Nitchu boeki kyoshitsu* [A Classroom for Japan-China Trade] (Tokyo: Seinen shuppansha, 1968), pp. 179-81.

123. C. Fred Bergsten, "Crisis in U.S. Trade Policy," *Foreign Affairs*, July 1971, p. 619.

124. See *Summary of the First Five-Year Economic Plan 1962-1966* (Seoul: Economic Planning Board, 1962).

125. P. W. Kuznets, "Korea's Five-Year Plans," in Irma Adelman, ed., *Practical Approaches to Development Planning: Korea's Second Five-Year Plan* (Baltimore: Johns Hopkins University Press, 1969), p. 66.

126. David C. Cole and Young Woo Nam, "The Patterns and Significance of Economic Planning in Korea," in Adelman, ed., *Practical Approaches*, p. 14. See *The Second Five-Year Economic Development Plan 1967-1971* (Seoul: Economic Planning Board, 1966).

127. See House Committee on International Relations, *Investigation of Korean-American Relations: Report of the Subcommittee on International Organizations* (Washington, D.C.: USGPO, 1978), p. 166.

128. *Waga gaiko no kinkyo* (1970), pp. 82-87.

129. Paul W. Kuznets, *Economic Growth and Structure in the Republic of Korea* (New Haven: Yale University Press, 1977), p. 71.

130. See Senate Committee on Foreign Relations, *United States Security Agreements and Commitments Abroad — Republic of Korea: Hearings before the Subcommittee on United States Security Agreements and Commitments Abroad* (Washington, D.C.: USGPO, 1970), pp. 1562-63. For other criticisms of U.S. and Japanese economic policy, see *Conference for a New Direction in U.S. Korea Policy* (New York: Committee for a New Direction for U.S. Korea Policy, 1977), pp. 155-61; Herbert P. Bix, "Regional Integration: Japan and South Korea in America's Asian Policy," in Frank Baldwin, ed., *Without Parallel*, pp. 179-232; and Jon Halliday and Gaven McCormack, *Japanese Imperialism Today* (New York: Monthly Review Press, 1973).

131. Interview with Kim Jae-ik, director-general, Bureau of Economic Planning, Economic Planning Board, June 22, 1979, Seoul.

132. Robert A. Scalapino and Junnosuke Masumi, *Parties and Politics in Contemporary Japan* (Berkeley: University of California Press, 1962), p. 1.

133. See George R. Packard, III, *Protest in Tokyo: The Security Treaty Crisis of 1960* (Princeton, N.J.: Princeton University Press, 1966).

134. For the comparison of the two, see *Nichibei Anpojoyaku no shoten* [The Focal Points of Japanese-American Security Treaty] (Tokyo: Asahi Shimbunsha, 1967), pp. 76-110.

135. See Senate Committee on Foreign Relations, *United States Security Agreements and Commitments Abroad: Japan and Okinawa: Hearings before the Subcommittee on United States Security Agreements and Commitments Abroad* (Washington, D.C.: USGPO, 1970), p. 1434.

136. Ibid., p. 1436.

137. See the text in *Department of State Bulletin*, February 8, 1960, pp. 179-80.

138. Weinstein, *Japan's Postwar Defense*, p. 97.

139. See Tsukasa Matsueda and George Moore, "Japan's Shifting Attitudes toward the Military: *Mitsuyakenkyu* and Self-Defense Forces," *Asian Survey*, September 1967, pp. 612-25.

140. Weinstein, *Japan's Postwar Defense*, p. 98.

141. See the text in *United States Security Agreements* (Japan and Okinawa), pp. 1425-28.

142. Ibid., pp. 1428-33.

143. Interview with Kanayama Masao (former Japanese ambassador to Poland and to South Korea), July 6, 1979, Tokyo; as ambassador, he personally travelled from Seoul to Tokyo to assist the exchange of letters between Sato and Park.

144. *Peking Review*, December 5, 1969, pp. 10-12.

145. Ibid., April 10, 1970, p. 5.

146. *United States Security Agreements* (Japan and Okinawa), p. 1166.

147. Ibid., p. 1242.

148. See Byung Chul Koh, *The Foreign Policy of North Korea* (New York: Praeger, 1969), pp. 61-63.

149. As translated in *United States Security Agreements* (Korea), p. 1577. For the texts of both treaties, see *Voice of Korea* (Washington, D.C.), August 1961.

150. Unlike the Soviet-North Korean treaty, the Sino-North Korean treaty has an intimate reference to their relationship as "brothers" and emphasizes the principle of mutual nonaggression. The Soviet treaty is effective for the first ten years, can remain in force for

the next five years if no one-year advance denunciation is made by either party, and can be further extended in accordance with the five-year rule; the Chinese treaty can continue its effectiveness unless both sides agree on its amendment or termination.

151. See Park's speech in *United States Security Agreements* (Korea), p. 1543.

152. See the Brown letters in ibid., pp. 1529-30.

153. Ibid., p. 1525.

154. Ibid., p. 1720-22.

155. Ibid., p. 1552.

156. *Investigation of Korean-American Relations* (pt. 4, 1978), p. 37.

157. Interview with Kanayama Masao, July 6, 1979, Tokyo.

158. *Investigation of Korean-American Relations* (Report, 1978), pp. 56-57.

159. See the Vance-Park joint communiqué in Kim, *Korean-American Relations*, pp. 350-51.

160. For a critical view of Nixon's indecision, see Henry Kissinger, *White House Years* (Boston: Little, Brown, 1979), pp. 312-21. For Nixon's view, see Richard M. Nixon, *RN: The Memoirs of Richard Nixon* (New York: Grosset and Dunlap, 1978), pp. 382-85.

161. For the text of Nixon's impromptu pronouncement of this strategic doctrine in Guam on July 25, 1969, see *Public Papers of the Presidents of the United States, Richard Nixon, 1969* (Washington, D.C.: USGPO, 1971), pp. 544-56.

2

DIPLOMATIC RELATIONS

The preceding historical discussions suggest that the changing patterns of United States-Chinese relations often constituted a major determinant of the U.S. traditional approach to Asia and that the Korean War crystallized the U.S. policy of containing and isolating the PRC in military, diplomatic, and economic areas. Although subjected to a mild, indirect challenge by Japan's growing economic cooperation and people's diplomacy with China, the containment policy remained an essential feature of the conceptual framework of U.S. relations with Japan and Korea during the 1960s. Governed by the rigid cold war principle, the United States effectively influenced the diplomatic posture of Japan and South Korea; neither of these Northeast Asian allies was allowed to deviate from the U.S. staunch anti-Peking leadership.

However, in the early 1970s, under President Richard M. Nixon, who had been intimately associated with the Dullesian hard-line policy against China, the United States initiated a dramatic transformation in the policy of containment and isolation of China. The secret journey of Henry Kissinger, Nixon's assistant for national security affairs, to Peking in July 1971 was followed by Nixon's own visit to China in February 1972. The fundamental change so initiated in the U.S. Asian diplomacy throughout the 1970s and early 1980s evolved around detente with China, which had profound effects not only on Washington's policy toward Japan and South Korea but also on relations between East Asian countries.

The key diplomatic issues that emerged in the context of U.S. influence relationships with Japan and South Korea were both the substantive direction of the United States' new China policy and the way in which the United States formulated and executed this policy. As far as Japan was concerned, the progressive unfolding of Washington-Peking detente conclusively proved the passing of the regional containment structure and raised a serious question about U.S. diplomatic leadership and policy credibility. Consequently the Japanese gradually assumed an assertive diplomatic approach, especially in regard to China, and showed a sign of resistance in accommodating the U.S. influence in diplomatic, economic, and security matters. The U.S. pursuit of policies of diplomatic reconciliation with China and of partial military disengagement in the Korean peninsula during the 1970s caused considerable strain and uncertainty within the Washington-Seoul alliance. While the South Koreans remained dependent upon the guarantee of U.S. military and diplomatic protection, they aggressively expanded their influence-seeking activities in the United States. They apparently concluded that to assure U.S. support for Seoul's vital interests they must use all possible means, legitimate and other, to penetrate the political power structure of the United States. In retrospect, the Koreagate scandals epitomize a significant shift in the underpinnings of bilateral relations. In the case of Korea, this emerged from the superimposition of a nascent but misdirected national self-assertiveness onto a lingering dependency mentality. Indeed, the entire Koreagate affair, coupled with the human rights issues, dominated the diplomatic controversies agitating Washington and Seoul during the latter half of the 1970s and appreciably changed the direction of their future relations.

UNITED STATES-CHINA DETENTE AND JAPAN

United States-Chinese Detente

In January 1969, President Nixon promised at his first inauguration to enter an "era of negotiation" and to seek "a world in which no people, great or small, will live in angry isolation."[1] "When I spoke those lines," Nixon recalled three years later, "I had the People's Republic of China very much in mind."[2] Less than two weeks after Nixon's inauguration, the new president instructed the National Security Council under Kissinger's leadership to undertake a comprehensive review of the U.S. China policy.[3] Soon the United States implemented a "phased sequence of unilateral measures" favorable to China, progressively relaxed trade and travel restrictions, and through the secret channels of Pakistan and Rumania explored the possibility of Kissinger's secret visit to China.[4]

The U.S. initiatives and peace feelers developed primarily from Nixon's and Kissinger's shared view that the United States should adjust its Asian policy to the reality of China and the emerging multipolar international order. They argued:

So long as we were not dealing with the People's Republic of China, our foreign policy could not truly reflect the emerging multipolar world. The isolation of one-fourth of the human race, partly self-imposed and partly the result of the policies of others, distorted the international scene. It also tended to reinforce China's own sense of insecurity. There could be no stable world order if one of the major powers remained outside it and antagonistic toward it.[5]

Increasing multipolarity offered an opportunity for the United States to cultivate China as a counterweight to the Soviet Union. Nixon and Kissinger also felt that Peking's understanding and cooperation were necessary to the success of their efforts to end the Vietnam War and to implement the Guam Doctrine elsewhere in Asia, for instance, in Korea. Other possible secondary reasons for the China overtures were the U.S. desire to enter the potentially profitable China market, to avoid its own diplomatic isolation vis-à-vis China, and to give a "shock treatment" to Japan, which was increasingly arrogant and recalcitrant in its economic rivalry with the United States. Nixon bitterly complained:

> Japan also benefited greatly from the liberal trade policies of the United States. But Japan's insistence on restricting its own markets contributed to a growing imbalance in our trade, and was an anachronism, inconsistent with its economic strength and symbolizing a lack of economic reciprocity which could not be long sustained.[6]

The president's personal fascination with China's culture and people, coupled with his tepid feelings toward Japan developed in part as a result of the prolonged textile dispute, may have also played a role in his opening to China.[7]

Sharing some parallel interests with the United States, the Chinese were quite receptive by the early 1970s to Nixon's peace feelers and exchanged mutually reinforcing signals with Washington. In the immediate aftermath of the bloody border clashes with the Soviet Union in 1969, the Chinese developed an overriding concern with counterbalancing the Soviet strategic superiority. Reconciliation with the United States presented the only possibility to that end. As shown by the April 1970 joint statement of Premier Chou En-lai and Premier Kim Il-song,[8] the revival of Japanese militarism was also a Chinese concern, though much less serious or pressing than the Soviet threat. Peking reasoned that any relaxation in United States-Chinese relations might minimize the chance for Japanese military buildup or regional political influence. Finally, China's receptivity was an outgrowth of Premier Chou's attempt: to restore China's diplomatic respectability after the disastrous Cultural Revolution; to seek U.S. trade and technology for China's economic development; and to further weaken Taiwan's diplomatic and military position. The convergence of basic interests between the United States and China made it possible for Kissinger to make his historic trip to Peking in July 1971.[9]

Nixon's unanticipated announcement of Kissinger's trip and of his own planned visit to China shocked and embarrassed Japan, even though Japan was not a primary factor in U.S. detente with China. Ironically, only hours before

Nixon's televised announcement on the evening of July 15, 1971 (the morning of July 16, Japanese time), Japanese Prime Minister Sato Eisaku had begun discussion with his cabinet on the draft of a speech to the National Diet.[10] The prime minister had removed the customary reference to Japan's cooperation with Taipei and Seoul and inserted a policy statement endorsing "friendly relations" with Japan's neighbors, meaning the PRC. As a result of disagreements within the cabinet, Sato dropped the proposed statement and restored the reference to Taipei and Seoul. While this discussion was underway, Secretary of State William P. Rogers, who had not been privy to the details of the Nixon-Kissinger negotiations with China, tried to deliver to Japanese Ambassador Ushiba Nobuhiko notification of Nixon's scheduled announcement. Ushiba could not be reached then. When, finally, Ushiba received Rogers's notification and conveyed it to Deputy Foreign Vice Minister Yasukawa Takeshi in Tokyo, Sato's cabinet meeting was about to adjourn. This was a few minutes before Japanese national television flashed an Associated Press bulletin on Nixon's statement.[11] The U.S. ambassador to Japan, Armin H. Meyer, casually heard the news from a local U.S. military radio station. When Nixon mentioned Kissinger's visit to Peking, Meyer thought that it was a slip of the tongue and that the president meant Vietnam.[12]

While Nixon rejoiced over what he called "one of the greatest diplomatic surprises of the century," his shock produced deep feelings of diplomatic betrayal among Sato and his associates because Washington had violated its repeated commitment to prior consultation with Japan regarding the Chinese question. In October 1970, Nixon and Sato had specifically agreed to keep in close communication and consultation on China. In June 1971, Secretary Rogers reaffirmed this agreement to Foreign Minister Aichi Kiichi. Immediately after the celebrated "ping-pong diplomacy" and one month prior to Nixon's announcement, Ambassador Meyer reassured Sato that the United States would not move toward recognition of China without prior consultation with Japan. Only ten days before the announcement, Defense Secretary Melvin Laird gave the same reassurance to his Japanese counterpart, Nakasone Yasuhiro.[13] These top-level promises notwithstanding, the Nixon Administration called the secrecy of Kissinger's China trip "unavoidable" and argued that, despite Peking's preference for open diplomacy, advance public disclosure might have generated inflated expectations, created pressures on China and the United States, and frozen both countries into extreme and irreconcilable positions.[14] Viewing this issue philosophically, Nixon observed that "no major step in international relations is taken without some painful adjustments and potential costs."[15]

It was indeed painful for Sato, having lost face in the eyes of his countrymen, to adjust his China policy to what Ambassador Meyer called a "diplomatic Pearl Harbor." Speaking to the National Diet the day after Nixon's announcement, Sato gracefully welcomed Nixon's planned visit to China as a measure to ease world tensions and declared:

It is most important for our country to maintain and promote friendly and amicable relations with the Republic of Korea, the Republic of China, and other neighboring countries. In particular, the China problem is one of the biggest issues facing our country's diplomacy in the 1970s. . . . Recently, exchanges between Japan and China have also shown signs of becoming more active; it is strongly hoped that in the future, these will develop into intergovernmental talks.[16]

Sato's adjusted stance on China concealed his deep apprehension that the United States and China might strike a diplomatic bargain at the expense of Japanese national interests or might collude in an economically motivated campaign to stop Japan. The prime minister regretted Japan's complacent diplomatic dependency on the Department of State and its negligence of the policy dispositions of the White House and the National Security Council. Also, in terms of the deepening distrust in the United States-Japanese alliance and Sato's plummeting political fortunes, costs of the U.S. diplomatic coup were high. Sato's critics in the ruling Liberal Democratic Party (LDP) and the opposition parties assailed his China policy as bankrupt, and his popularity sank to an all-time low.

In retrospect, Kissinger admitted:

We could have chosen a more sensitive method of informing the Japanese even though Meyer's considerations [such as Japan's inability to maintain confidentiality] precluded earlier consultation. It would have surely been more courteous and thoughtful, for example, to send one of my associates from the Peking trip to Tokyo to brief Sato a few hours before the official announcement. This would have combined secrecy with a demonstration of special consideration for a good and decent friend. In the pressure of events the thought occurred to no one; it was a serious error in manners.[17]

He asserted that Sato, a devoted friend of the United States, did not deserve the "ill fortune" inflicted by the Nixon shock. In addition to those mistakes occasioned by the "pressure of events," Kissinger confessed that he made many others, because "neither I nor my colleagues possessed a very subtle grasp of Japanese culture and psychology."[18] However, Kissinger emphasized the compatibility between the United States' new China policy and its close alliance with Japan. This gave little comfort to Sato, who was disappointed primarily with the procedural aspects of U.S. accommodation with China, not the substantive matters.

Nixon's domestic critics also denounced the unconventional style of his China diplomacy. While former Under Secretary of State George W. Ball criticized Nixon's unnecessary extravagance and its "corrosive consequences," former Ambassador to Japan Edwin O. Reischauer was contemptuous of the flamboyant, reckless, and even quixotic Nixon-Kissinger "histrionics." He added:

The Japanese Government was humiliated, and the Japanese as a whole were deeply disturbed to see that the United States could be so unmindful of the Japanese on an issue of such crucial importance to them. It was a clear signal that the United States either did not regard its relations with Japan as very important or else did not have the ability or possibly even the intention, to treat Japan as an equal. Beyond that the United States seemed very unpredictable and therefore unreliable. Japanese confidence in the reliability of the American defense commitment and Japanese hopes that the United States could learn to treat Japan as a full equal were both seriously damaged.[19]

Except for economic conflicts, Nixon and Kissinger did not attach a high priority to United States-Japanese relations in the context of global balance-of-power politics. In sharp contrast to many pages devoted to Nixon's summitry with Leonid Brezhnev and Chou En-lai, the meetings that Nixon had with Sato in 1969, 1970, and 1972 and with Prime Minister Tanaka Kakuei in 1972 are scarcely mentioned in either Nixon's or Kissinger's voluminous memoirs. If Sato and Tanaka wrote their memoirs, they would have discussed at length their meetings with Nixon. This suggests that the United States and Japan had substantially different perceptions of each other's relative importance.

Even after the "serious error in manners" associated with the initial Nixon shock was fully recognized, Washington persisted in its insensitive approach to Japan. In August 1971, Secretary of State Rogers gave Sato less than 30 minutes notice of Nixon's other shocking pronouncement of a "New Economic Policy," which included a 10 percent import surcharge and restricted the dollar's convertibility to gold.[20] In addition, Kissinger postponed his scheduled visit to Japan several times. To soothe Japan's bitterness, Nixon hosted a White House dinner for Foreign Minister Fukuda Takeo and other Japanese cabinet members during their Washington visit and made a long trip to Alaska to greet the emperor and empress of Japan, who were on their first postwar trip to Europe. However, the U.S. attitude toward the China issue at the United Nations further disillusioned Japan's policy makers.

China at the United Nations

With a rapid increase in the number of new pro-Peking member-states, the 20-year-old U.S. policy of opposition to U.N. membership for the PRC was increasingly untenable in the early 1970s. In preparation for the inevitable, the Department of State, in consultation with Japan, worked out a dual-representation formula for China, even before Kissinger's first Peking trip. The Nixon-Kissinger strategy called for procrastination on any decision involving the proposed formula until after Kissinger's trip. In early August, Secretary Rogers was allowed to announce the new U.S. sponsorship of two resolutions: one (commonly known as the "reverse important question" resolution) for defining the expulsion of the Republic of China from the General Assembly as an important issue, which would thus require a two-thirds vote; and the other for accepting the PRC as a U.N. member with a permanent seat in the Security Council. The United States asked Japan to cosponsor both resolutions, but the Japanese government and the LDP were deeply divided over the issue. When Prime Minister Sato finally decided to follow the U.S. lead at the United Nations, he became the target of public protest from not only opposition parties and business circles but members of his own cabinet and the LDP. The Chinese reaction was blunt and harsh. According to China's *People's Daily* (September 26, 1971), the Sato decision "has further exposed his reactionary features as a docile accomplice of U.S. imperialism." He was further accused of providing anti-Chinese tactical advice to the United States.

The Japanese U.N. delegates made a more concerted and extensive effort than did their U.S. counterparts in the futile campaign to retain the General Assembly seat for the Republic of China. The U.S. government was divided over the Chinese question at the United Nations. Secretary Rogers and U.N. Ambassador George Bush worked hard on Taiwan's behalf, but Kissinger, a realist, was critical of the notion of dual representation because the PRC rejected it vehemently.[21] Sensing a defeat in the United Nations, Nixon adopted an opportunistic stance and refrained from making too strong an effort to retain Taiwan's representation in the General Assembly.[22] Nixon's deliberate ambiguity was in sharp contrast with Sato's unstinting support for Taiwan's diplomatic interests. The Japanese prime minister wrote personal letters to leaders in ten key countries that were undecided on the Chinese question, sent emissaries to Mexico and other countries that were wavering, and utilized economic leverage to the maximum extent. In New York, the Japanese U.N. representative Aichi Kiichi (the former foreign minister) conferred with more than 40 U.N. delegations within a week.[23] Aichi agreed to accept the PRC as a member of both the General Assembly and the Security Council but argued against the pro-Peking Albanian resolution, which he called "irrational" and "irresponsible." He joined with George Bush in contending that the expulsion of the Republic of China would violate the principle of universality, upset the balance of power in the Far East, and set a bad precedent.[24]

In October 1971, the General Assembly defeated the "reverse important question" resolution by a four-vote margin and then passed the Albanian resolution overwhelmingly. The U.S. government publicly deplored the undiplomatic behavior of some pro-Peking delegates who danced and cheered in the United Nations after the defeat of the "reverse important question" resolution. Nixon, in anticipation of his planned China journey, was relieved by the vote. Within the Japanese government the prevailing mood was different. Prime Minister Sato and Foreign Minister Fukuda were surprised by their unexpected diplomatic failure at the United Nations. The setback inflicted irreparable damage to their domestic and foreign influence. The domestic political predicament of Sato and Fukuda was so critical that a telegram from the U.S. Embassy in Tokyo erroneously predicted that the Sato government would fall within a matter of days.[25] Sato and Fukuda were particularly unhappy about the timing of Kissinger's greatly publicized second visit to Peking, during the U.N. China debates. The picture of Kissinger and Chou smiling during their meeting, displayed prominently in the *New York Times*, may have weakened the effectiveness of U.S. diplomatic efforts on behalf of Taipei and helped the pro-Peking movement in the United Nations. In Japan, it was rumored that the U.S. government's public efforts to retain Taiwan's seat were calculated mainly to blunt the charge by pro-Taipei forces that Nixon had adopted a "sell-out" policy.

Nixon's Visit to China

The PRC's accession to the right of exclusive representation in the United Nations removed a longstanding symbol of the U.S. anti-Peking containment and isolation policy and facilitated preparations for Nixon's scheduled visit to China. Acting on Ambassador Meyer's face-saving recommendation, President Nixon had a summit meeting with Prime Minister Sato at San Clemente in early January 1972. The lingering effects of the Nixon shocks considerably strained their personal rapport, but they intensely discussed China, the Okinawa reversion, and economic matters. Sato expressed his desire to establish intergovernmental contacts with China but told Nixon that Japan wished to resolve the Taiwan issues, including the Japan-Taiwan Peace Treaty, at the time of, but not prior to, intergovernmental negotiations.[26] In the joint statement, both leaders committed themselves "to consult closely on their respective Asian policies."[27] However, Sato declared somewhat defiantly in his press conference that as an independent nation, Japan did not necessarily agree with the United States in regard to the Chinese issue.[28] In spite of diplomatic tensions over China, Nixon's foreign policy report, issued a week before his departure for Peking, reaffirmed the overriding importance of the United States-Japanese alliance. Nixon stated:

> Japan is our most important ally in Asia. It is our second greatest trading partner. It is an essential participant, if a stable world peace is to be built. Our security, our prosperity, and our global policies are therefore intimately and inextricably linked to the U.S.-Japanese relationship. The well-being of both countries requires cooperation and a shared commitment to the same fundamental goals.[29]

At summit meetings with Premier Chou En-lai, Nixon repeated the same theme. He told Chou that the United States-Japanese alliance was also in China's interest, because the alliance was a major factor in deterring the designs of others (presumably the Soviet Union) in the Western Pacific and in preventing the revival of militaristic nationalism in Japan.[30] Nixon argued that "if we were to leave Japan naked and defenseless, they would have to turn to others for help or build the capability to defend themselves."[31] In the joint communiqué, issued at Shanghai on February 27, 1971, Nixon stated that "the United States places the highest value on its friendly relations with Japan; it will continue to develop the existing close bonds."[32] In a parallel statement, Chou En-lai expressed his opposition to "the revival and outward expansion of Japanese militarism" and his support for "an independent, democratic, peaceful and neutral Japan." Nevertheless, Chairman Mao Tse-tung and Chou made it clear during their summit discussions that China did not pose any threat to Japan or South Korea and that they strongly supported close relations between the United States and Japan.[33]

The Japanese government's reaction to the Nixon-Chou joint communiqué was conspicuously cool, although LDP Secretary-General Hori Shigeru noted its contribution to world peace.[34] Aware of Japan's heightened sensitivity, President Nixon, returning from China, sent a telegram to Sato that stressed friendly relations between their countries. He also dispatched to Tokyo members of his China delegation: Assistant Secretary of State for East Asian and Pacific Affairs Marshall Green and John Holdridge (a staff member of the National Security Council, who had accompanied Kissinger to Peking in July 1971). Earlier, Kissinger hinted that there would be a visit to Tokyo, but neither he nor Secretary Rogers had a direct opportunity to inform Japanese leaders. Although Nixon deliberately excluded Rogers and Green from the most important meetings in China due to his prejudice against the Department of State, Green assured Prime Minister Sato and Foreign Minister Fukuda that the president had explained to China's leaders the United States' continuing security commitments to Japan and that no secret deal had been made in China.[35] In Washington, Kissinger had a long briefing session with Japanese Ambassador Ushiba.

Japanese-Chinese Diplomatic Normalization

Nixon's move meant a drastic reversal of the U.S. policy of diplomatic isolation and military containment of the PRC, which Japan had been compelled to follow since the San Francisco conference. Even though this reversal did not produce an instant diplomatic rapprochement between the Sato government and China, it prompted a huge outpouring of pro-Peking sentiment, which had grown steadily among Japan's political and economic circles. Widely disparate groups, ranging from the mainstream business organizations to all opposition parties, demanded Japan's immediate diplomatic reconciliation with China. A coalition of pro-Peking forces predominated over the pro-Taipei elements within the LDP. Public opinion tilted overwhelmingly toward Peking. This irresistible trend in favor of normalizing relations with China, coupled with a growing desire for independent Japanese diplomacy, imposed stringent limitations on the freedom of Sato's successor to resolve the Chinese question.

When in July 1972 Tanaka Kakuei succeeded Sato and Ohira Masayoshi became foreign minister, the new Japanese cabinet pledged to attach top priority to the issue of Tokyo-Peking diplomatic normalization. At the new prime minister's first press conference, Tanaka reaffirmed this pledge, which was promptly welcomed by Premier Chou En-lai.[36] It is likely that Chou viewed the governmental transition from Sato to Tanaka as an unparalleled opportunity for opening direct communications with the Japanese government, especially before Tanaka hardened his position on Taiwan or the Soviet Union sabotaged negotiations between Peking and Tokyo. Tanaka intended to settle the chronic Chinese problem in his characteristic straightforward style. Unlike the processes of accommodation between Washington and Peking, both Tanaka and Chou deemphasized their respective governmental bureaucracies and relied heavily on a few nongovernmental individuals for communications and mediation.

Having completed preliminary negotiations and preparations for his China trip, Tanaka met Nixon in Honolulu on August 31 and September 1, 1972. The prime minister reportedly confided to his U.S. host that if Japan failed to normalize diplomatic relations with China, Japanese public opinion, aroused by the United States-Chinese detente, might bring down his new cabinet. Nixon showed his understanding of the domestic political pressure on Tanaka.[37] Conscious of Chou En-lai's earlier request that the United States support detente between Peking and Tokyo, Kissinger explained to Tanaka that as long as Japan's new China policy did not undermine United States-Japanese security ties, the United States would not oppose it. Nixon and Kissinger were unenthusiastic about Tanaka's decision to establish full diplomatic relations with China before the United States, but they knew that Tanaka's move was an inevitable consequence of their own bold initiatives. Hence, while praising the president's visits to Peking and Moscow as a "significant step forward," Nixon and Tanaka expressed their hope that the prime minister's upcoming trip to China "would also serve to further the trend for the relaxation of tension in Asia."[38] A day after returning from Honolulu, Foreign Minister Ohira went to Seoul to explain Tanaka's imminent China visit to President Park Chung-hi, while LDP Vice President Shiina Etsusaburo undertook a similar, though more difficult, mission to Taipei.

On September 25, 1972, Tanaka and Ohira reenacted Nixon's journey to Peking. After a series of summit sessions, Tanaka and Chou signed a joint statement on September 29, which declared:

> China and Japan are neighboring countries separated only by a strip of water, and there was a long history of traditional friendship between them. The two peoples ardently wish to end the abnormal state of affairs that has hitherto existed between the two countries. The termination of the state of war and the normalization of relations between China and Japan — the realization of such wishes of the two peoples will open a new page in the annals of relations between the two countries.[39]

The two countries agreed to end the "abnormal state of affairs" and to establish diplomatic relations. While China reaffirmed that Taiwan was an "inalienable part" of its territory, Japan recognized the PRC as the sole legal government of China. Although Japan suspended diplomatic relations with Taiwan and unilaterally abrogated the Tokyo-Taipei Peace Treaty of 1952, Tanaka indicated that Japan would continue to maintain nondiplomatic ties with Taiwan. The Chinese did not challenge this indication. Following the precedent of the Nixon-Chou joint communiqué, the Japanese easily accepted Chou's proposal for the antihegemony clause — a commitment not to seek hegemony in the Asian-Pacific region and to oppose efforts by any country or group of countries to establish such hegemony. As the two key members of the Tanaka delegation recalled, the Japanese did not fully anticipate at that time that the antihegemony clause would prove a major stumbling block in the subsequent peace and friendship treaty negotiations between Tokyo and Peking.[40]

The normalization of diplomatic relations between Japan and China was more than a new important phase in their postwar relations. It also reflected a fundamental shift in Asia's multipolar regional order. It was more than a simple extension of United States-Chinese detente because Japan had taken a step ahead of the United States. Tanaka and Ohira, in the light of the Nixon shock, intended to outgrow the policy constraints of the San Francisco system and to transcend the residual influence of the containment-cum-isolation structure. They were anxious to make Japan an active participant, rather than a passive object, of the balance-of-power game as played by Nixon and Chou. Although the Japanese leaders were not seeking to weaken Japan's vital security linkage with the United States, they learned an important lesson from the Nixon shock episode: they needed to reduce, if not eliminate, the remaining U.S. patronage in Japanese diplomacy. The experience inspired Japan's nationalistic assertiveness. Tokyo's success in negotiating diplomatic normalization with China was instructive for U.S. observers, but the so-called "Japan formula," which allowed the continuity of nondiplomatic relations between Tokyo and Taipei, had limited applicability to the U.S. situation. Unlike Japan, the United States had a security commitment to Taiwan and assumed global as well as regional responsibilities. Thus, it took six more years for the United States to enter into full diplomatic relations with China.

Effects of China Policy on Korea

The rapidity with which the United States and Japan redirected their China policy had an unsettling effect on the Korean peninsula.[41] While North and South Korea attempted to adjust their external positions to their shifting environments and to reinforce internal political regimentation, they were equally apprehensive about such big-power diplomacy, which might disregard or sacrifice the vital interest of small governments like their own. In order to mitigate this apprehension, Nixon and Chou publicly reaffirmed in the Shanghai communiqué support for their respective Korean allies. Nixon promised to maintain the

United States' "close ties with and support for" South Korea, and Chou endorsed North Korea's peaceful unification policy. Chou had already dispatched his top-level emissaries — Vice Premier Li Hsien-nien and Li Te-sheng (director of the PLA General Political Department) — to Pyongyang the day before Nixon's announcement of the first Kissinger visit, and Marshall Green traveled to Seoul after Nixon's visit to China.[42] Even though the initial Nixon shock had given President Park and his associates "one hell of a jolt" because they were not consulted at a time when 50,000 South Korean troops were fighting "China-supported" guerrillas in Vietnam, by March 1972 Green found Park "quietly confident."[43] Park welcomed Nixon's China initiative, expressed appreciation for its utility to peace in Korea, and indicated his understanding that there were no secret deals with China. Still, Park's deep suspicion of big-power politics and the euphoria over detente was never dissipated. The Tanaka-Chou summitry was also followed by the explanatory missions of Chinese Foreign Minister Chi Peng-fei and former Japanese State Minister Kimura Toshio to Korea's rival capitals.

The opening of a North-South dialogue in Korea was the most significant and tangible effect of detente between the United States and China.[44] Just a month after Kissinger's secret visit to China, the president of the South Korean Red Cross proposed to his North Korean counterpart that both sides start negotiations to reunite an estimated ten million families separated since the end of the Korean War. Soon, in historic meetings at Panmunjom, representatives from each side arranged full-dress Red Cross conferences in Seoul and Pyongyang. When these conferences were stalemated during 1972, both sides in a dramatic political initiative after Nixon's trip to China exchanged secret visits by South Korea's Central Intelligence Agency Director Lee Hu-rak and North Korea's Second Vice Premier Pak Song-chol. As a result of direct North-South negotiations, on July 4, 1972, both sides issued a joint communiqué, in which they agreed to seek the peaceful, independent unification of Korea without foreign interference and to realize national unity by transcending differences in ideologies and systems. They also pledged to end armed provocations, to promote various exchange programs, and to establish a "hot-line" between Seoul and Pyongyang. The new North-South Coordinating Committee, cochaired by Lee Hu-rak and Kim Yong-ju (director of the powerful Organization and Guidance Department of the Korean Workers' Party and Kim Il-song's younger brother), was entrusted with the implementation of these agreements and related matters. This unprecedented breakthrough in intra-Korea relations was exuberantly acclaimed in both North and South Korea and abroad. Duly notified of Korea's secret exchanges, the United States and Japan welcomed the joint communiqué as a contribution to peace and stability in Asia. China and the Soviet Union voiced similar sentiments.

The joint communiqué paved the way for the exchange of Red Cross delegations between Seoul and Pyongyang in the first such large-scale visit since the Korean War. Also, the North-South Coordinating Committee met alternately in the two capitals. However, as these rounds of talks progressed during 1973, there appeared a fundamental cleavage in the parties' perceptions and policies regarding the future course of North-South relations. Whereas North Korea advocated a comprehensive, drastic political solution of all unification problems, including mutual arms reduction, South Korea adopted an incremental and functionalist approach, stressing practical cooperation in humanitarian, cultural, and economic areas rather than difficult political and military issues. Mutual distrust was still deep-seated, and political propaganda overshadowed the promise of reciprocal compromises. The negotiations became deadlocked in August 1973, and each side blamed the other for violating the 1972 joint communiqué.

Without doubt, the detente between opposing international coalitions, exemplified in the Kissinger and Tanaka visits to China, stimulated and encouraged intra-Korea contacts, but in the end it proved insufficient for sustaining fruitful dialogue. Still, the big-power detente lessened the intensity of international controversies over Korea, notably in the United Nations. Both in 1971 and 1972, the U.N. General Assembly decided to postpone substantive discussion of the Korean question on the ground that it would interfere with intra-Korea negotiations. Even after negotiations were suspended in the fall of 1973, the U.N. First Committee abandoned the 12-year-old "Stevenson formula," which had prevented North Korea's participation in the U.N. debates, and extended to both North and South Korea an unconditional invitation to take part in discussion of the Korean question.[45] Close, behind-the-scenes Chinese-United States cooperation was instrumental in the tabling of two rival resolutions on Korea and in producing a compromise, consensus statement.[46] The statement urged North and South Korea to continue their dialogue in accordance with the 1972 joint communiqué, and endorsed the self-dissolution of UNCURK. For the sake of the Chinese-United States diplomatic reconciliation, both Washington and Peking preferred to avoid a confrontation over the pro-Pyongyang resolution, which would have disbanded the United Nations Command and requested the withdrawal of U.S. forces from South Korea. However, as conflict between North and South Korea intensified and their U.N. strategies were further differentiated, the spirit of compromise on Korea did not last long in the United Nations. The South Koreans proposed the simultaneous admission of both Koreas, but their northern rival flatly denounced the proposal as a device for permanent national division. Pyongyang opposed Seoul's idea of cross-recognition— namely, that in return for Moscow's and Peking's diplomatic recognition of South Korea, the United States and Japan would recognize North Korea. Meanwhile, North Korea opened its doors slightly to U.S. journalists, scholars, and other visitors. South Korea's overtures to establish direct communications with China remained unanswered because Peking did not want to test North Korea's extreme sensitivity or to drive it into Moscow's embrace. The United States and Japan used their new diplomatic entrée to China on South Korea's behalf but with no visible result.

United States-Chinese Diplomatic Normalization

The Nixon shock to Japan's and South Korea's complacent and unimaginative diplomacy gradually subsided over a couple of years, and U.S. diplomatic relations with these two East Asian allies resumed a semblance of calm and normalcy. No serious diplomatic *faux pas* or perceptual dissonance troubled United States-Japanese relations. Pursuing varied approaches to China, both nations cooperated reasonably well. In accordance with the Chou-Tanaka joint statement, Japan and China exchanged their first ambassadors — Ogawa Heishiro and Chen Chu — in 1973 and conducted negotiations on trade, civil aviation, navigation, and fisheries. Negotiations were not always easy, but both sides were prepared to make concessions in their common effort to sustain the newly generated momentum for diplomatic accommodation. Trade grew rapidly, and a variety of cultural exchange programs flourished. The Chinese stopped their hostile rhetoric against the revival of Japanese militarism and publicly supported the important regional role of United States-Japanese security ties. In East Asia, the last vestiges of rigid cold war bipolarity were disappearing.

Unlike Japan, the United States did not yet enjoy full diplomatic relations with China, but it sought purposefully the incremental realization of rapprochement with China. A year after Nixon's visit to China, both sides agreed to abandon the use of their diplomatic channels in Paris and to establish liaison offices in their respective capitals. Although the liaison offices were no substitute for embassies in a strict diplomatic sense, their actual functions included governmental representation, diplomatic negotiations, and consular service. The U.S. Liaison Office in Peking was headed by a person with ambassadorial rank and was staffed by governmental employees, primarily from the Department of State. A mutual sense of warm friendship and genuine cooperation prevailed in Washington-Peking relations. Top-level policy consultations and coordination were sustained through the liaison offices and at direct top-level meetings, such as Kissinger's frequent visits to China. A number of private organizations, including the National Committee on U.S.-China Relations, the Committee on Scholarly Communication with the People's Republic of China, the China Council of the Asia Society, and the National Council of U.S.-China Trade, were set up or strengthened to promote educational, cultural, scientific, and/or economic cooperation between the two nations. Trade showed a phenomenal increase, from $5 million in 1971 to $93 million in 1972. Yet, in subsequent years, the two-way trade volume remained much less than Sino-Japanese trade, in part because the United States faced persisting obstacles in pursuing its China trade, for example, the legal complications of frozen assets and unsettled property claims, the absence of most-favored-nation status, the unavailability of Export-Import Bank loans, and the constraints of partial diplomatic relationship.[47]

Two basic factors continued to prevent the United States and China from normalizing their diplomatic relations — namely, the inability to find a mutually acceptable solution on the future status of United States-Taiwan relations and the absence of the respective domestic political conditions permitting a decisive initiative for diplomatic breakthrough. Nixon found it difficult to make a deal that would guarantee Taiwan's future security, since the PRC adamantly insisted that as a precondition of diplomatic normalization, the United States must sever diplomatic relations with Taiwan, immediately abrogate the 1954 security treaty with Taiwan, and completely withdraw its military forces and installations from Taiwan. Nixon wanted to obtain Peking's explicit promise to refrain from using force against Taiwan and from opposing U.S. arms sales to Taiwan. Nixon's diplomatic difficulty was complicated further by his declining political fortunes. Despite a landslide reelection, the Nixon presidency was crippled, then destroyed by the spreading Watergate investigations. Nixon lost the psychological as well as the political leverage for consummating his historic diplomacy with China. His successor, Gerald Ford, endorsed the Shanghai joint communiqué by paying a state visit to China in December 1975.[48] Even if Ford had intended to normalize diplomatic relations with China, it is doubtful whether he would have succeeded. Throughout 1976 his diplomatic capability was severely limited by the politics of presidential election, especially the challenge of his conservative, intraparty rival Ronald Reagan, who was critical of the U.S. pro-Peking tilt. The Indochinese debacle in 1975 continued to have a sobering effect on Ford's diplomatic assertiveness.

Moreover, the Chinese experienced a series of traumatic political changes during 1976, which continued to reverberate in 1977. Confusion caused by the successive deaths of Premier Chou En-lai, Marshal Chu Teh, and Chairman Mao Tse-tung was intensified by the tumultuous Tien-an-men Square riot, the dismissal of Vice Premier Teng Hsiao-ping, and the massive Tangshan area earthquake. After Mao's funeral, the "Gang of Four," led by Mao's widow (Chiang Ching), was arrested in the struggle for succession. In October, Premier Hua Kuo-feng became CCP Chairman, but Teng was not reinstated formally until July 1977. This protracted political instability, coupled with the replacement of Foreign Minister Chiao Kuan-hua by U.N. Ambassador Huang Hua, immobilized China's diplomacy.

In early 1977, the new Carter Administration committed itself to extending the Nixon-Ford China policy. President Carter clearly stated:

> It is important that we make progress toward normalizing relations with the People's Republic of China. We see the American-Chinese relationship as a central element of our global policy, and China as a key force for global peace. We wish to cooperate closely with the creative Chinese people on the problems which confront all mankind, and we hope to find a formula which can bridge some of the difficulties that still separate us.[49]

Yet, Carter did not seem to be in any hurry to normalize diplomatic relations with China. As Richard C. Holbrooke, assistant secretary of state for

East Asian and Pacific Affairs, suggested, the United States was generally satisfied with the status quo in relations between Washington and Peking and saw
no short-range benefits from the immediate establishment of diplomatic relations with China.[50] In the absence of a politically tolerable compromise on
Taiwan, Carter apparently shared Secretary of State Cyrus Vance's moderate
view that any precipitous move toward China might upset the United States'
delicate SALT negotiations with the Soviet Union and might antagonize some
senators prior to the Senate ratification of the highly controversial Panama Canal
treaties. The Carter Administration also gave top priority to having full consultations with Japan "in all matters of mutual concern," including China. During
his global tour in January 1977, Vice President Walter Mondale conveyed
Carter's assurance to Japanese Prime Minister Fukuda Takeo that there would
be no surprises (meaning the Nixon shocks) in United States-Japanese relations.[51]

Initially, in 1977, the United States was unenthusiastic or, at least, "neutral"
about Prime Minister Fukuda's professed intention to negotiate with China
a treaty of peace and friendship, which might include the antihegemony clause
and thereby irritate the Soviet Union.[52] Secretary Vance's exploratory trip to
China in August produced no appreciable progress in diplomatic discussions.
The Chinese leaders, especially Teng Hsiao-ping, showed no inclination to assure
that no force would be used regarding Taiwan or to agree with Vance's suggestion that the United States, after diplomatic normalization with Peking,
exchange the liaison offices with Taipei.[53] At Tokyo, Vance fully briefed
Japanese Prime Minister Fukuda and other officials in regard to his visit to China
and stated that "of all of our allies and old friends, none is more important to us
than Japan."[54] However, the Carter Administration, in the spring of 1978
following the passage of the Panama Canal treaties, adopted Assistant to the
President for National Security Affairs Zbigniew Brzezinski's manipulative view
that the United States should establish relations with China and encourage
Japanese-Chinese cooperation in a concerted attempt to counterbalance the
rapid Soviet military ascendancy in the Asia-Pacific area. This change occurred
as the Soviet Union balked at the SALT negotiations and accelerated its military
and political thrusts into Africa by means of Cuban surrogates. In April 1978,
the Carter Administration counselled restraint and reconciliation between Tokyo
and Peking, which were engaged in a potentially explosive dispute over the
Senkaku (or Tiaoyutai) Islands. The United States, which ceased its naval
shelling practices over one of the islands, succeeded in defusing the conflict,
which was soon resolved temporarily to mutual satisfaction.[55]

At the Carter-Fukuda summit meeting in early May, the president gave his
unmistakable blessing to the prime minister's expected treaty negotiations with
China.[56] A couple of weeks later, Brzezinski repeated his anti-Soviet and anti-
Cuban rhetoric in Peking, assailing the "international marauders who masquer-
ade as nonaligned to advance big power ambitions in Africa." He also declared,
"We recognize — and share — China's resolve to resist the efforts of any nation
which seeks to establish global or regional hegemony."[57] Brzezinski clarified

President Carter's determination to normalize diplomatic relations with Peking and briefed the Chinese on U.S. foreign and security policy, including the contents of SALT II and top-secret Presidential Review Memorandum No. 10 regarding global military assessment.[58] Returning from Peking via Tokyo, Brzezinski urged Prime Minister Fukuda to conclude a treaty of peace and friendship with China at an early date. Since Fukuda understood from Brzezinski that the United States was moving rapidly toward diplomatic normalization with China, the prime minister sought to stay one step ahead of the United States, thus averting adverse domestic political fallout similar to the Nixon shock. In Peking, on August 19, 1978, Japan and China signed a ten-year treaty of peace and friendship, which prominently included the article against hegemonism "in the Asia-Pacific region or in any other region."[59] While the Soviet Union angrily condemned the treaty as the prelude to a NATO of the East, the United States was very satisfied with the treaty's successful conclusion, which was the culmination of the process begun by the Chou-Tanaka joint statement of 1972. Even before the treaty was actually signed in Peking, the Department of State issued an unprecedented statement endorsing the aims of the treaty and the principle of antihegemonism. U.S. ambassador to Japan, Mike Mansfield, was quoted as saying: "In a certain sense, China is occupying the position of NATO in Asia by holding down the Russian divisions along the Chinese border." In Mansfield's view, the treaty was "another indication that Japan is breaking out of its insularity and becoming a part of the world in a political as well as an economic sense."[60]

The breakthrough achieved by the Japanese-Chinese treaty negotiations was soon followed by intensified Chinese-United States discussions concerning their diplomatic normalization. On December 15, 1978, President Carter announced that the United States and China had agreed to recognize each other and to establish diplomatic relations, which would be effective on January 1, 1979.[61] It took more than seven years after Kissinger's secret Peking journey for both nations to find a mutually acceptable formula for final diplomatic rapprochement. The timing of China's decision was probably linked to the signing of the Soviet-Vietnamese friendship treaty of November 1978, which was in turn partly a response to the Sino-Japanese peace and friendship treaty.[62] Asked why the United States decided to normalize diplomatic relations with China in December 1978, Deputy Secretary of State Warren Christopher said that it was not until that month that the Chinese made a number of important concessions concerning Taiwan's security.[63] However, critics argued that given the deterioration of the Iranian situation, the stalemate in Middle East peace negotiations, and the problems with SALT II, the Carter Administration urgently needed a major foreign policy announcement toward the end of 1978 to bolster its sagging image.[64]

As Japan had done in 1972, the United States recognized the PRC as the sole legal government of China, acknowledged the PRC position that "there is but one China and Taiwan is part of China," and defined as its policy the maintenance of nondiplomatic relations with "the people of Taiwan" in cultural, commercial, and other fields. The Carter-Hua joint communiqué, issued simultaneously in Washington and Peking, reiterated their respective governments' opposition to any form of hegemonism. Unlike the Japanese formula, however, the United States-Chinese compromise contained various provisions about Taiwan's security. The United States rejected the Chinese request for an immediate abrogation of its Mutual Defense Treaty with Taiwan but agreed to give Taiwan one-year notification regarding nullification, which would be effective January 1, 1980 (in accordance with Article 10 of the treaty). The United States also agreed to withdraw its military personnel from Taiwan within four months (by April 30, 1979); the size of the U.S. military personnel stationed in Taiwan had already decreased from 10,000 in 1972 to 700 in 1978. However, President Carter stated:

> The United States is confident that the people of Taiwan face a peaceful and prosperous future. The United States continues to have an interest in the peaceful resolution of the Taiwan issue and expects that the Taiwan issue will be settled peacefully by the Chinese themselves.[65]

The Chinese agreed not to contradict this statement. Although they rejected Washington's request for assurance that they would not use force in resolving the Taiwan issue, they publicly expressed their policy preference to deal with the Taiwan situation by peaceful means. Over China's manifest protest, President Carter made it clear that the United States would continue to sell defensive weapons to Taiwan.[66] Yet he decided to impose a one-year moratorium on new arms sales commitments to Taiwan. The Chinese-United States agreement to disagree on the issue of arms sales remained a potential source of serious disputes between Washington and Peking.

Unlike the Japanese National Diet, which had overwhelmingly supported the Chou-Tanaka joint statement and the Sino-Japanese peace and friendship treaty, the U.S. Congress was highly critical of the way in which President Carter negotiated with China. As summarized in a report prepared by the Senate Committee on Foreign Relations, many senators and congressmen, irrespective of party or ideological affiliations, expressed their disappointment about:

> the haste with which the Administration had moved late in 1978, the lack of consultation with Congress despite the provision in the International Security Assistance Act of 1978 which said the President should consult Congress before making policy changes which might affect the Mutual Defense Treaty, and the lack of adequate consultation between the United States and its Asian allies.[67]

Other sources of Congressional criticism included Carter's failure to extract China's explicit commitment not to use force, his unilateral abrogation of the

United States-Taiwan security treaty, and its adverse psychological effects on Japan and South Korea. Moreover, Senator Barry Goldwater (Rep., Arizona) and 25 other members of Congress brought an unusual lawsuit against President Carter on the ground that it was unconstitutional for the president to unilaterally abrogate the security treaty without the Senate's advice and consent.[68]

The critical Congressional mood was clearly manifested in the legislative maneuvers over the administration-drafted "Taiwan Relations Act," which Senator Frank Church (Dem., Idaho), chairman of the Senate Committee on Foreign Relations, bluntly characterized as "woefully inadequate to the task, ambiguous in language, and uncertain in tone."[69] Despite Carter's threatened veto, the Congress substantially altered the administration's draft and specifically articulated the U.S. policy toward Taiwan. The final "Taiwan Relations Act" stated:

> It is the policy of the United States . . . to consider any effort to determine the future of Taiwan by other than peaceful means, including by boycotts or embargoes, a threat to the peace and security of the Western Pacific area and of grave concern to the United States . . . and to maintain the capacity of the United States to resist any resort to force or other forms of coercion that would jeopardize the security, or the social or economic system, of the people on Taiwan.[70]

The act instructed the government to provide Taiwan with "arms of a defensive character." It also determined the legal and financial terms for the American Institute in Taiwan, which, as a nongovernmental nonprofit corporation, incorporated in the District of Columbia, was responsible for unofficial relations with "the people on Taiwan." Similarly, Taiwan set up its Coordination Council for North American Affairs in the United States. Equipped with semidiplomatic immunities, the two organizations were patterned after the Japan-Taiwan model, whereby, all relations were handled by Japan's Interchange Association and Taiwan's East Asian Relations Association. For all practical purposes the American Institute and the Coordination Council were functional equivalents of the liaison offices, which had operated in Washington and Peking from 1973 to 1978.

Contrary to Nixon's dramatic diplomatic style, Carter, who as a member of the Trilateral Commission had developed a keen awareness of Japan's sensitivity, took extreme care to inform Japan's leaders of the progress in the Washington-Peking negotiations. On the day Carter announced diplomatic normalization with China, he talked personally to Japanese Prime Minister Ohira Masayoshi, who as foreign minister had engineered diplomatic normalization between Tokyo and Peking in 1972. The Ohira government was fully supportive of Carter's diplomatic success, although it had some reservations about the timing of Carter's announcement. As Brzezinski correctly noted, for the first time in decades the United States simultaneously enjoyed good relations with both China and Japan.[71] One may contend that the emerging regional diplomatic configuration amounted to a very loose anti-Soviet protocoalition between the United States, Japan, and China, but it was certainly far from a trilateral military alliance.

The U.S. action to abruptly terminate its defense treaty with Taiwan for the sake of diplomatic normalization with China left some Japanese uneasy about the reliability of the U.S. security commitment to Japan.[72] Other Japanese, especially those in industry and commerce, expected some economic competition with the United States in the potentially lucrative Chinese market. The South Koreans, too, were concerned about the dependability of U.S. security policy in the peninsula, and the possibility that China's aggressive economic policy might hurt South Korea's trade (particularly textiles) and construction contracts in the United States, Europe, the Middle East, and Southeast Asia. Seoul ostensibly welcomed Washington's and Tokyo's rapprochement with Peking as a contribution to detente in East Asia. However, the South Koreans were apprehensive that in the process of increasing cooperation with China, the United States and Japan might become too flexible toward North Korea.[73] Yet they hoped that both the United States and Japan would continue to represent South Korea's diplomatic interests to China and to encourage the latter's moderating influence over North Korea. The United States' and Japanese officials maintained frequent policy consultations with their Chinese counterparts in regard to the Korean questions.[74] On the other hand, the North Koreans, in the light of China's new friendship and cooperation with the United States and Japan, took the opportunity to experiment with the variety of methods aimed at diplomatic isolation of South Korea. The U.S. government consistently rebuffed North Korea's direct and indirect feelers toward bilateral political talks on the grounds that such talks without South Korea's full participation would serve no useful purpose and could only create difficulties for Washington-Seoul relations.[75] However, the United States, with South Korea's approval, proposed a meeting on Korea among three, four, or six parties, but this has not been successful so far.[76] While both the United States and Japan successfully consummated diplomatic normalization with China and made a significant progress in mutually beneficial economic, scientific, and cultural interactions during the 1970s, this detente had a limited impact on the Korean peninsula.[77]

DIPLOMACY OF KOREAGATE DISPUTES AND HUMAN RIGHTS

Development of Koreagate Scandals

While the systematic South Korean scheme for buying influence in the United States evidently was implemented first in the fall of 1970, its operational antecedents can be identified in the late 1960s. For example, in 1968, South Korea's Prime Minister Chung Il-kwon and KCIA Director Kim Hyong-wook decided to assist U.S. Congressman Richard Hanna (Dem., California) and South Korean businessman Park Tong-son, who both agreed to share the commissions from U.S. rice sales to South Korea and to use them to elicit favorable policies from the Congress. Hanna told Chung and Kim that unlike the National Assembly in South Korea, Congress played a very significant role in U.S. foreign policy and advised them how to lobby the Congress effectively, along the successful models used by Taiwan and Israel.[78]

As the exclusive rice sales agent for South Korea, Park quickly reaped huge commissions and distributed some of them to Hanna, Kim, and perhaps Chung.[79] In Washington, Park started entertaining congressmen, Cabinet members, generals, and other influentials at the George Town Club, which he had taken over from his social patron, Mrs. Anna Chennault, with the KCIA's financial support. In addition, Park and Hanna actively organized a series of well-publicized Congressional junkets to Seoul. After heading a 25-member mission to South Korea in March 1969, House Majority Leader Carl Albert (Dem., Oklahoma) told the House that "we can make no better investment than investing in the strength and prosperity of a friend and ally like Korea."[80] Other members of the Albert delegation profusely praised South Korea's achievements and President Park's political leadership. In particular, House Majority Whip Thomas P. O'Neill, Jr. (Dem., Massachusetts) publicly defended the controversial constitutional amendment allowing President Park to run for a third term.[81] O'Neill characterized the parliamentary maneuvers of the ruling Democratic Republican Party, secretly initiating the constitutional referendum in the absence of opposition party members, as a "very commendable course of action." The majority whip categorically rejected the view that President Park sought the imposition of a kind of personal rule.

In addition to these tangible effects of "delegation diplomacy,"[82] Park Tong-son joined Hanna and other like-minded congressmen in lobbying for the South Korean government. A case in point is the December 1969 campaign for passage of a military aid bill, earmarking $50 million for South Korea. Representative Hanna's Congressional testimony illuminates the tactics of the influence peddlers:

Mr. Nields. What sorts of efforts did you make in that connection?
Mr. Hanna. Well, I submitted a statement in the debate process, I talked with other people who I thought had the same kind of attitude about it and they, after my discussions and maybe would have in spite of my discussions, or maybe [for] whatever reasons, added their comments to this debate.
Mr. Nields. Did Tongsun Park also participate?
Mr. Hanna. Yes, he said he was talking to some of his friends relative to the Korean position at the same time.
Mr. Nields. Was this effort ultimately successful?

Mr. Hanna. I believe that it was.

Mr. Nields. And did you write a letter to Chung Il Kwon on December 11, 1969, detailing the efforts you and Tongsun Park had made and the successes you had achieved?

Mr. Hanna. Yes, I did.[83]

Hanna reported to Chung that members of the Albert delegation were helpful in passing the aforementioned legislation and noted his own success in soliciting cooperation of Secretary of Defense Melvin Laird, Carl Albert, Gerald Ford (Rep., Michigan), and other Congressional leaders.[84]

Angered by President Nixon's unilateral 1970 decision to withdraw the Seventh Infantry Division (20,000 combat troops) from South Korea, Seoul felt the urgent need for countermeasures. The demonstrated effectiveness of Park's and Hanna's lobbying practices suggested an attractive model for a more ambitious influence-peddling scheme. The Park government resolved to build a position of influence in the United States, especially within Congress, to preserve the remaining U.S. military presence on the Korean peninsula. With the knowledge that Congressional approval and appropriations were necessary to effectuate the Nixon Administration's pledge of $1.5 billion for South Korea's five-year (1971-75) military modernization plan, Seoul sought to buy off sympathetic members of the Democratic leadership and of the key Armed Services, Foreign Affairs, and Appropriations Committees. Constant reminders from top administration figures (for example, Vice President Spiro Agnew, Defense Secretary Melvin Laird) and various congressmen regarding the legislative branch's crucial foreign policy-making role, coupled with a strong tradition of State Department and Pentagon support for military aid programs, further reinforced Seoul's preoccupation with Congress.[85]

Beyond furthering the Korean interest in ensuring consistent and favorable policies from the United States, the scheme that produced the Koreagate scandals was launched to blunt the growing U.S. criticism of President Park's repressive policies and human rights violations. Not only Congress but the whole White House, academia, the media, business, religious groups, and the Korean community in the United States were evidently targeted for South Korean penetration, manipulation, and monetary seduction. In the opinion of the Senate Select Committee on Ethics:

> The Government of the Republic of Korea went well beyond the practices ordinarily used by friendly foreign nations and adopted a scheme to influence the United States Government . . . that relied expressly upon improper and illegal methods.[86]

Seoul's resort to extraordinary influence-building practices stemmed from impatience with its own professional diplomats, whose efforts appeared markedly less effective than those of Park Tong-son and the KCIA.

In close cooperation with the KCIA, Park Tong-son made cash payments and campaign contributions or provided services to at least 32 congressmen and 7 senators.[87] The amounts of Park's alleged payments per person ranged from $100 to more than $100,000 (for Richard Hanna, Otto Passman, and Cornelius Gallagher). Not all payments or services were illegal or improper, but many members of Congress accepted and used the money and services in unethical ways. Park gave expensive gifts and favors freely and hosted lavish social events for Washington dignitaries: in 1973 a dinner honoring Senator Birch Bayh (Dem., Indiana) cost at least $3,979; in 1973 a party for Congressman John McFall (Dem., California) cost about $2,000; in 1973 and 1974, birthday parties for House Majority Leader O'Neill cost $1,978 and $5,597 respectively; and in 1975 a farewell party for Attorney General William Saxbe cost $3,599. The recipients of Park's largess proclaimed their innocence. Yet it was strange that these experienced politicians did not question the intentions of their alien benefactor.

The South Korean government sought influence not only through Park's flamboyant activities but apparently relied upon other individuals and organizations as well: Kim Han-jo (or Kim Hancho), Park Bo-hi (or Park Bohi), Kim Kwang, Suzi Park Thomson, and the Unification Church.[88] The exact extent to which this concerted lobbying scheme shaped and perhaps redirected U.S. Korean policies remains unclear. Conceivably, it contributed to the articulation and promotion of South Korea's interests in the United States.

A number of legislators entered pro-Seoul statements in the *Congressional Record*, sometimes at Park Tong-son's urging. They exchanged mutually laudatory communications with President Park. At the time of Park's narrow electoral victory in 1971, 14 members of Congress sent congratulatory letters.[89] For example, Senator Jack Miller (Rep., Iowa) wrote, "First, my warmest congratulations on your magnificent reelection. Second, be assured of my continued active and personal interest in your country and its future."[90] Each letter spoke highly of Park Tong-son's activities. In response, President Park expressed his appreciation for each congressman's support for South Korea's military modernization programs and acknowledged Park Tong-son's contribution in this respect.[91]

The pro-Seoul congressmen articulated South Korea's military, diplomatic, and economic interests publicly. For example, Representative Otto Passman (Dem., Louisiana) declared that since U.S. security was linked directly to that of South Korea, Washington should increase military aid to this vital ally.[92] He labeled criticism of the human rights situation in South Korea "unfair and illegitimate." Speaking in the U.S. Senate against further protectionist legislation, Jack Miller counselled patience with Seoul's opposition to U.S. restrictions on textile imports and identified voluntary Korean export limits as the best solution. House Speaker Carl Albert played a key role in blocking House adoption of a unanimous International Relations Committee resolution that criticized Seoul for sentencing 18 prominent dissidents, including former

President Yun Po-son.[93] Other pro-Seoul congressmen often spoke out in favor of military and economic aid programs for South Korea, for example, PL 480. Seoul's friends in the Congress also advised South Korean officials on legislative procedure and Congressional hearings. The chairman of the House Subcommittee on Asian and Pacific Affairs, Cornelius E. Gallagher (Dem., New Jersey), along with his assistant, Kim Kwang (Park Tong-son's cousin), initiated and conducted hearings on United States-Korean relations that upheld Seoul's interests. Gallagher received payoffs from the South Korean government for his help.[94]

While the explanation of all pro-Seoul activities in Congress solely by reference to the Koreagate scheme is unwarranted, their close association has been amply documented. Evidence of Park Tong-son's influence-buying operations is substantial and persuasive. The Senate Select Committee on Ethics unequivocally declared Park to be an "unregistered agent of the Republic of Korea." It further stated that "Park played an integral role in the plans prepared by the Government of the Republic of Korea, and particularly by the Korean Central Intelligence Agency, to influence United States foreign policy."[95]

If the Koreagate operations were as pervasive as the evidence suggests, and if indeed the State Department was fully aware of the compromising activities of Park Tong-son and others as early as 1970, then how is one to account for official inaction and the long period of six years that passed before these activities were seriously investigated by Congress and the Administration? A combination of factors seems to explain the belatedness of the Koreagate investigations: moral permissiveness, intra- and inter-bureaucratic conflict, and an executive-legislative cleavage.

The initial State Department reaction to Park Tong-son's Washington activities was registered in late 1970 when Donald Ranard, director of the Office of Korean Affairs (1970-74), informed the South Korean Embassy that Park's ubiquitous lobbying was "a liability" and "a poison."[96] Although South Korean ambassador to Washington, Kim Dong-jo, deeply resented Park's interference in South Korea's diplomacy as a case of infringement on the embassy's sphere of influence, the embassy found it difficult to restrain someone so well-connected politically in Seoul. A few months later, U.S. Ambassador William Porter tried repeatedly to persuade President Park and Prime Minister Chung that Park Tong-son's recall was necessary. President Park responded incredulously that many U.S. congressmen had told him that Park Tong-son was very effective in Washington.[97] U.S. pressure apparently led to Park's brief recall to Seoul, but he was soon back in his Washington circles. The South Korean government remained insensitive to the further presentations of Porter and Ranard.

In the early 1970s, the U.S. government moved against South Korea's other suspected Washington lobbyists. House Speaker Carl Albert was informed of the alleged KCIA connections of one of his secretaries, Suzi Park Thomson. The Justice Department and the Internal Revenue Service were asked to examine the tax-exempt status of Park Bo-hi's Radio of Free Asia. The Department of

Agriculture investigated Park Tong-son's status as rice sales agent for South Korea. Between September 1971 and February 1972, FBI Director J. Edgar Hoover sent three confidential memoranda to Attorney General John Mitchell and Presidential Assistant for National Security Affairs Henry Kissinger.[98]

The FBI reported that under KCIA direction, Park Tong-son had made payments to Congressman Gallagher, and it further noted that some Congressional staffers had ties with the KCIA. In a later inquiry neither Mitchell nor Kissinger could recall the FBI memoranda.[99] However, none of these cited investigations and disclosures resulted in any significant constraint on South Korea's lobbying activities. As Ambassador Porter later testified, the official U.S. response was characterized by a "great deal of permissiveness" primarily because Washington did not want to embarrass Seoul at a time when South Korea was the only ally helping the United States in South Vietnam.[100]

In 1972 the efforts of Porter's successor, Ambassador Philip Habib, to get Park Tong-son to register as a lobbyist for the South Korean government were similarly unsuccessful. In meetings with Ranard in Washington and with Political Counsellor Richard Peters and CIA Station Chief John Richardson in Seoul, Park denied any connection with the South Korean government and even threatened to bring a libel suit against Ranard and other State Department officials if they continued to accuse him of being a South Korean agent. Habib explicitly instructed all embassy personnel in Seoul that "without my express permission" they should have nothing to do with Park.[101] He also warned several visiting congressmen against associating with Park, but apparently the ambassador's advice was not taken very seriously. Generally, the Department of Justice was also not responsive to various State Department allegations regarding Park's influence-buying practices. Moreover, Attorney General William Saxbe, who maintained close, personal relations with Park, advised him that some individuals in the State Department were trying to get him.[102] In spite of the attorney general's knowledge of the allegations, Saxbe accepted Park's lavish farewell party honoring his appointment as ambassador to India.

When Habib returned from Seoul in late 1974 to the State Department post of assistant secretary for East Asian and Pacific Affairs, he was determined to take the initiative in collecting and presenting all possible evidence of Park Tong-son's influence-peddling activities.[103] In February 1975, Habib called Secretary of State Kissinger's attention to a number of sensitive intelligence reports documenting South Korea's bribery operations. Kissinger reported the matter to President Ford. The secretary of state remembered, "The President asked me whether the information was conclusive, and I told him it did not seem to be. He asked me to watch it, and when we had further information to come back to him."[104] At the end of October 1975, Kissinger received from Habib a more detailed intelligence report on South Korea's bribery scheme and, upon President Ford's instructions, turned it over to Attorney General Edward Levi.

Although it is not entirely clear why and how the Ford Administration finally decided to investigate the Koreagate scandals in 1975, the decision was unmistakably hastened by Habib's determination, pressure from Congressional critics (such as Fraser) and South Korean dissidents (such as Lee Jae-hyon), and aggressive investigative journalism. While Habib's "integrity" may account for his zealous probing of Koreagate ties, a long-held and intense animosity toward Park Tong-son suggests that a vendetta was also a factor. In 1975 Lee Jae-hyon, the former director of information (1970-73) at the South Korean Embassy in Washington, testified before the House hearings that in 1973 the KCIA had formulated a plan to buy off its supporters in the United States by seduction, payoff, and intimidation.[105] Fraser and other Congressional critics of the Park regime then called for a Justice Department inquiry into alleged KCIA operations and payoff schemes. Following the Watergate trauma and the Indochinese debacle, the dominant mood in Congress favored the reassertion of its role of overseeing administration foreign policy and moral posture. Finally, a number of reporters, particularly those from the *Washington Post* and the *New York Times*, pursued and exposed South Korean human rights violations and illegitimate lobbying activities in the United States. As a result, the Ford Administration wanted to avoid any appearance of obstructing justice — the issue that destroyed Nixon's presidency. Nevertheless, the Justice Department's investigations were deliberate and slow.

An October 24, 1976 *Washington Post* story, based on a leaked report from a secret grand jury investigation of the Koreagate scandals, triggered the diplomatic crisis between Washington and Seoul. The *Post* revealed that under the guidance of the South Korean government, Park Tong-son had used from half a million to one million dollars a year to bribe about 90 congressmen and other U.S. officials, that the U.S. CIA had eavesdropped on the Blue House and had tape recorded the planning sessions for Park's bribery scheme, and that President Park himself had taken part in some of these activities. Stunned by these sudden revelations, the South Korean government categorically stated that "Park has never been employed by the Korean government, nor does he have anything to do with President Park."[106] Seoul even denied President Park's personal knowledge of the name of Park Tong-son, despite the fact that the name had been prominently mentioned in President Park's communications with U.S. congressmen and during his meetings with Ambassador Porter. The Park government imposed a blackout on the *Post* story in South Korea and demanded clarification from the U.S. State Department. Consistent with established policy, the State Department refrained from commenting on the allegation of CIA bugging. Seoul then threatened to conduct its own investigation and to take "appropriate measures." The State Department sharply rebuked this threat as "not helpful."

There is considerable evidence to suggest that United States' and South Korean leaders mutually misperceived the stakes and constraints operating beyond the narrow substantive and procedural issues of the Koreagate investigations. Believing that an ally highly dependent on U.S. aid and protection could be compelled to cooperate with an investigation, U.S. officials adhered to a substantially legalistic approach with little heed to its possible psychological and diplomatic effects on Seoul. Their South Korean counterparts failed to understand Washington's true intentions or the importance of the Koreagate scandals within the context of U.S. political and judicial processes.

Many South Korean officials assumed that the Koreagate sensationalism was concocted by irresponsible journalists who, in collusion with liberal congressmen and anti-Park Korean residents, systematically exaggerated and distorted some minor cases of private gift giving, which was fully justified in Oriental custom.[107] They felt their ally's narrow, legalistic preoccupation and diplomatic arrogance to be the product of an anti-Park conspiracy. Still others, especially those at the South Korean Embassy in Washington, attributed the Koreagate investigations to President Ford's election strategy.[108] In this interpretation, Ford would neutralize Democratic exploitation of Watergate and the Nixon pardon as campaign issues by making a widely publicized probe, linking key Democratic congressmen to Koreagate.

Both explanations — conspiracy theory and election gimmickry — did nothing to challenge South Korea's complacent assumption that its persistent, flat denial of all untoward allegations would somehow dispose of the Koreagate fervor in time. It was inconceivable that the U.S. government would permit a minor scandal to embarrass its faithful ally in Asia. The primary concern of South Korea's top leaders was to assure President Park's dissociation from the alleged bribery of Park Tong-son and to await the passing of the president's extreme anger against the United States. Meanwhile, President Park dismissed KCIA Director Shin Jik-soo and other officials and appointed a veteran diplomat, Kim Yong-shik, to succeed Ambassador Hahm Pyong-choon in Washington.

Negotiations over Park Tong-son

In early 1977, contrary to Seoul's wishful thinking, both the House of Representatives and the Senate authorized their respective ethics committees to investigate the Koreagate allegations. John J. Flynt, Jr. (Dem., Georgia) chaired the House Committee on Standards of Official Conduct, and Adlai E. Stevenson, III (Dem., Illinois) headed the Senate Select Committee on Ethics. At roughly the same time, the new Carter Administration, fresh from its campaign for higher standards of public morality, accelerated the grand jury proceedings. In August 1977, the Department of Justice finally indicted Park Tong-son, who had returned home, on 36 counts of conspiring to bribe congressmen, defrauding the government, mail fraud, racketeering, and illegal campaign contributions.[109] Although the indictment did not link Park directly to the South Korean government, it strained still further bilateral diplomatic relations, which were already chilled by Carter's public criticism of human rights violations in South Korea and by his unilateral announcement of U.S. troop withdrawals from South Korea. In formal communications with the South Korean government during August 1977, both President Carter and Attorney General Griffin Bell requested Park Tong-son's extradition to the United States to face criminal charges; they unambiguously indicated that failure to comply with the request would have grave consequences for future bilateral relations.[110] The South Korean response was predictably negative and defiant.

As the Carter Administration and Congress increased political pressure on Seoul to permit Park's testimony before U.S. judicial and legislative bodies, the South Korean government showed signs of moderating its earlier defiant position. Seoul's willingness to negotiate a mutually acceptable compromise stemmed from its fear that the further deterioration in bilateral relations would irrevocably undermine U.S. support for South Korea's ambitious military build-up programs. This fear was given credence when, in November 1977, the House of Representatives rejected several amendments designed to cut U.S. aid to South Korea but passed a resolution calling on the South Korean government to cooperate "fully and without reservation" with the Koreagate investigations. After a series of intense governmental negotiations, Ambassador Richard Sneider and Foreign Minister Park agreed in December 1977 to cooperate for mutual prosecution assistance regarding Park Tong-son.[111] The agreement specified that in exchange for Park's "truthful testimony" in U.S. courts, the Department of Justice will grant him "full immunity."

Meanwhile, both the House Committee on Standards of Official Conduct and the Senate Select Committee on Ethics expressed their disappointment with the Washington-Seoul agreements, which, in effect, discouraged Park's appearance before the Congressional committees. The divergence of executive and legislative interests further complicated Washington-Seoul negotiations over Park. The House of Representatives, whose prestige was seriously damaged by Koreagate, insisted that Park himself must testify under oath before its Committee on Standards of Official Conduct. Leon Jaworski, special counsel of the committee, threatened to promote a House resolution calling on South Korea to produce not only Park, but former Ambassador Kim Dong-jo and others as witnesses. He implied that noncooperation might be met by cuts in U.S. military and economic aid to South Korea.[112]

In an attempt to head off a confrontation between Congress and Seoul, Assistant Secretary of State Richard Holbrooke and House Speaker O'Neill talked in February 1978 to Ambassador Kim Yong-shik and suggested that South Korea allow Park to appear at the Congressional hearings. The South Korean government grudgingly consented to permit Park's voluntary sworn testimony in secret sessions but not under subpoena. Although O'Neill insisted that "no conditions or restrictions" would be imposed on Park's questioning in Congress,[113] it seems likely that there was a tacit understanding to deemphasize questions regarding his alleged relations with South Korea's top public officials, especially President Park. Moreover, Seoul had become confident that the House leadership, particularly Speaker O'Neill and Majority Whip John Brademas, who were both recipients of Park's favors, would be able to restrain any extreme Congressional action against President Park and South Korea.

At last Park Tong-son, the focus of tremendous media attention, made several trips to the United States in 1978 to appear as a witness before the grand jury investigations and at the trials against Hanna, Passman, and Kim Han-jo. Both in executive sessions and public hearings, Park testified voluntarily before the ethics committees of both Houses. Speaker O'Neill persuaded Representative Fraser not to subpoena Park's appearance before the Fraser Subcommittee on International Organizations, which conducted a series of extensive investigations on United States-Korean relations.[114] The Department of Justice indicated its satisfaction with Park's "truthful testimony" in the criminal proceedings and honored its promise for his complete immunity.

Park's Congressional appearances received a mixed review. Accompanied by his U.S. lawyer, Park admitted that he had received over $9 million in rice sales commissions during the years 1969-75 and that he had dispensed less than $1 million in campaign contributions and cash payments to his personal friends in Congress.[115] He repeatedly denied any association with the South Korean government and insisted that although he had visited the Blue House, he had never met with President Park. (There is evidence, however, that the two Parks had first met in November 1961, during General Park's visit to Washington.)[116] Park portrayed himself as an "American success story on a small scale," and, because he had stood up against a big country's request for his extradition, as a "folk hero" in South Korea. He refused to admit that his lobbying efforts had been undertaken primarily as a shrewd and effective method for promoting his business interests, and not always as an expression of "patriotism." However, the report of the House Committee on Standards of Official Conduct suggested that "he was far more interested in paying Congressmen who would help him maintain his status as a rice agent than help the ROK on legislative issues affecting it."[117] Park's tendencies to show off his Rolls Royce and Cadillac, to date beautiful and influential women (including Humphrey's niece), to appear at high-society parties, and, above all, to be seen with distinguished political leaders reflected his great personal vanity. Nevertheless, the South Korean government was very pleased with Park's testimony, which met the basic requests of the Justice Department and Congress, yet did not directly establish Park's formal association with South Korea's public officials. Upon discharge of these obligations in the United States, Park returned safely and promptly to South Korea's exclusive jurisdiction.

Negotiations over Ambassador Kim Dong-jo

Although the State Department successfully obtained from the South Korean leaders conditional permission for Park Tong-son to testify to appropriate judicial and legislative bodies, it found the issue of securing former Ambassador Kim Dong-jo's testimony far more difficult due to sharp differences between Congress and Seoul and between Congress and the administration. Testimony presented to the House Committee on Standards of Official Conduct implicated Kim in the Koreagate scandals.[118] In addition, Jaworski evidently saw sensitive intelligence reports linking Kim's cash payments to about ten incumbent members of Congress. Thus, Jaworski regarded Kim as a more important target of his investigations than Park Tong-son and vigorously sought to bring Kim before the House ethics panel.

Although the South Korean government was finally persuaded to negotiate the terms of Park Tong-son's cooperation with the U.S. authorities, it adamantly opposed Jaworski's request that Kim testify in the United States. Viewing the underlying principle as nonnegotiable, Seoul maintained that accession to the request would violate South Korea's sovereign independence and the Vienna Convention, which established the immunity of diplomatic personnel from being compelled to testify in a foreign country.[119] Considering it unwise to establish a precedent in compromising diplomatic immunity for temporary expedience, the Department of State endorsed the South Korean position unequivocally. In fact, Jaworski did not deny the Vienna Convention's legal validity. Rather he urged a political solution by rhetorically asking:

> Is it asking too much of an ally, for whom our nation has done so much, to offer simple cooperation — truthful and upright cooperation — to make the facts known? I find it offensive not to have the cooperation plain comity dictates. I find it even more offensive to receive a cold shoulder from a country we have so handsomely befriended. . . . The failure by an ally — recipient of such bountiful largess — to cooperate in this pursuit is unpardonable.[120]

In retaliation for Seoul's uncooperative stance, some members of the House introduced resolutions to suspend PL 480 or reduce military aid. The resolutions failed, but the gesture indicated to South Korea that continuing defiance could prove costly. On May 31, 1978, the House adopted a mild resolution stating that if Kim Dong-jo were not available for "information" at an early date, it would be "prepared" to reduce or deny South Korea certain military funds. Speaker O'Neill warned publicly of grave consequences if South Korea refused to cooperate, but Samuel S. Stratton, Henry B. Gonzalez, Paul Findley, and other representatives rose to assail the resolution as "blackmail" and a "dangerous threat."[121] The State Department's public defense of Seoul's non-cooperation further frustrated Jaworski's negotiations with South Korea. On June 22, 1978, the House voted to eliminate U.S. economic aid to South Korea (PL 480), which was to be effective on October 1, 1978. Unsupported by the means to effectively influence the South Korean government, the House action was little more than a symbolic gesture. The Senate, the Department of Agriculture, farm belt legislators, and various farm organizations opposed the maneuver. The South Koreans were less impressed by a $56 million cut in economic aid than they would have been with an equivalent reduction in military aid. A high-ranking South Korean Embassy official privately ridiculed the vote as a gutless, preelection, public relations gimmick.[122] He added that other grain-exporting countries were offering better terms of trade and aid than those of PL 480.

The impasse over Kim's case required the concerted initiative of O'Neill and the Department of State. Congressional critics questioned O'Neill's seriousness about the Koreagate investigations and blamed the State Department for South Korea's recalcitrance. William Gleysteen, Jr., new U.S. ambassador to Seoul, joined O'Neill and Foreign Minister Park Tong-jin in finding a mutually acceptable resolution of the Kim issue. He actively promoted the formula that the ethics committees of both Houses would submit "written interrogatories" to Kim on the assumption that the South Korean government would give assurances that Kim "would supply new and concrete factual information regarding his financial transactions with Members of Congress."[123] While reserving the right to present follow-up questions, the Congressional ethics committees agreed to waive the requirement of an oath and to forego interrogation of any other South Korean officials. The South Korean Embassy in Washington apparently disliked the formula, but Gleysteen convinced Foreign Minister Park to agree to the plan. Thus the questions prepared by both ethics committees were transmitted to Kim through Ambassador Gleysteen and Foreign Minister Park. A month later, Kim's answers were delivered to both committees through the same diplomatic channels.[124]

In denying all the allegations made by various witnesses, Kim Dong-jo stated categorically that "I never offered or attempted to offer any money directly or indirectly to any U.S. Congressman or other public officials" with the single exception of Representative Jerome Waldie.[125] The Senate Select Committee on Ethics accepted the written interrogatories and found "no evidence" to contradict Kim's denial,[126] but the House Committee blasted them as "totally unsatisfactory and insulting" on the grounds that Kim's answers supplied no "new and concrete" information and were neither truthful nor complete.[127] This same committee charged also that the South Korean government had not acted in good faith.

An outspoken House Committee member, Bruce F. Caputo (Rep., New York), complained that the "fight for the most important witness [Kim] ended ignominiously, perhaps even humiliatingly, for the Committee."[128] Caputo charged that although the House Committee had obtained specific, detailed, convincing, and credible evidence that four sitting House members had received cash payments from South Korea's officials, it was concealing the names and the evidence on the grounds of "national security." The State Department drew criticism for resisting the House Committee's efforts to secure the testimony of former Ambassadors Kim Dong-jo and Hahm Pyong-choon and various KCIA officials such as former Director Lee Hu-rak.

While Caputo and other critics of the House Committee on Standards of Official Conduct remained profoundly dissatisfied, House Speaker O'Neill, the State Department, Ambassador Gleysteen, and the Senate Select Committee on Ethics were all relieved by the resolution of Kim's case. Its resolution allowed the House to restore the $56 million economic aid program for South Korea in September 1978. The House-Senate conference committee report on the FY79 International Security Assistance Act (including military aid to South Korea) passed in both Houses. The South Korean government relished its diplomatic victory and hoped that the House of Representatives and U.S. opinion leaders would soon forget about the disputes over Park Tong-son and Kim Dong-jo.

Koreagate's Effects

Despite Kim Dong-jo's noncooperation, the House Committee on Standards of Official Conduct, assisted by Park Tong-son's detailed testimony, in July 1978, decided to institute disciplinary proceedings against four sitting members: Edward R. Roybal, John J. McFall, Charles H. Wilson, and Edward J. Patten.[129]

The House voted to reprimand Roybal, McFall, and Wilson; Patten was exonerated. The House Committee on Standards of Official Conduct took no action against former members of the House, such as Hanna, Passman, Gallagher, and Edwards, and found "no impropriety" in the cases of other recipients of Park Tong-son's alleged payments, including John Brademas, John Murphy, Frank Thompson, Jr., William Minshall, and Nick Galifianakis. It also exonerated House Speaker O'Neill, finding that he did not commit any illegal act in his close association with Park, and there was no evidence of O'Neill's alleged request for campaign contributions or of his son's business connection with Park. The House Committee's report stated that the only action of "questionable propriety" was O'Neill's acceptance of two "large and expensive" birthday parties given by Park. However, the report added, "Although, judged by today's standards it may be unwise for an important Congressman to permit either a foreigner or a suspected lobbyist to give him a party, there appears to be no warrant for disciplinary proceedings."[130]

Although the Senate was less deeply implicated in the Koreagate scandals than the House, the Senate Select Committee on Ethics concluded that the South Korean government had adopted a scheme to influence the Senate by improper and illegal methods and that its "unregistered agent," Park Tong-son, had made substantial campaign contributions to seven or eight senators.[131] Yet the Senate Committee pronounced a rather generous verdict on those senators. Consequently, no past or incumbent senator was subjected to disciplinary action. Had the Senate followed the House rules and procedures, at least

two members — Birch Bayh and Joseph M. Montoya — might have been reprimanded. The Senate Committee established that these two senators had given
false information but recommended no disciplinary action.[132] The Senate
Select Committee on Ethics took note of the failure of Hubert H. Humphrey
and John McClelland to report, as required by law, campaign gifts of $5,000
and $1,000 respectively. It also noted Allen Ellender's admission that as a result
of Park's lobbying efforts, he had changed his position with regard to military
aid legislation for South Korea.

While the House was unhappy with the positions taken by the Departments
of Justice and State in regard to Park Tong-son, and with the State Department
in regard to Kim Dong-jo, the Senate Committee branded the Department of
Defense the "least cooperative" in the executive branch.[133] The Republican
Party leadership in Congress asked President Carter to name a special prosecutor,
but the request was rejected. The political and jurisdictional cleavages between
and within legislative and executive institutions not only confused and dupli-
cated the Koreagate investigations but also complicated Washington-Seoul
relations. Whereas the Department of State was often unable or unwilling to
articulate a unified view of U.S. pluralistic institutions, conflicting signals from
the United States were both a source of South Korea's frustration and an opportunity for self-serving, balancing maneuvers.

The Justice Department's much publicized and costly Koreagate investi-
gations proved anticlimactic. Despite Park's testimony before the grand jury and
criminal trials, the Justice Department succeeded in convicting only two persons
(Richard Hanna and Kim Han-jo). Its indictment of Otto Passman was defeated.
As Representative Caputo once remarked, the Justice Department as well as
Congress tended to establish that there were "only bribers and no bribees."[134]
The well-documented cases of campaign law violations were conveniently
ignored. The Justice Department, under Assistant Attorney General Benjamin R.
Civiletti's politically astute supervision, did not even interview the sitting
members of Congress who had allegedly received illegal cash payments from
Park Tong-son or Kim Dong-jo. Apparently, the Carter Administration decided
not to investigate or indict incumbent members of Congress for three main
reasons. First, it wanted to avoid a direct confrontation with Congress (and
particularly, members of the president's own party), which had already shown
an assertive attitude toward the president's legislative programs. Second, the
administration sought to protect key intelligence sources whose disclosure was
thought to be essential if convictions were to be obtained. Third, the administration sought to stop any further deterioration in diplomatic relations between
Washington and Seoul.

The State Department was anxious to put behind the agonizing and often
acrimonious two-year chapter in bilateral relations and to resolve certain persistent misunderstandings between Washington and Seoul. Speaking before the
United States-Korean Economic Council in Washington in December 1978,
Assistant Secretary of State Holbrooke explained:

Koreagate had its origins in misperceptions, misguided actions, and lack of timely or adequate remedial measures. Efforts to investigate the actions of Americans imposed a virtually unprecedented necessity for the full cooperation of foreigners and foreign institutions not subject to U.S. jurisdiction. Ultimately, the degree of assistance provided by the Korean Government, while substantial, fell short of what many had hoped. . . . There never was, nor can there ever be, any excuse for malfeasance in office. For the Executive Branch, for the Congress, for the Government of a close ally, this truly was a dark period. Although these abuses took place several years earlier, it fell to the Justice Department to pursue investigations in its own efforts. . . . Some aspects of these matters are not yet fully resolved. Additional actions may still occur in the courts and elsewhere. It will still take time to overcome the damage. But we believe that the issue is no longer threatening the very fabric of our alliance . . . and from the point of view of our national interest in stability in Northeast Asia, this is surely a good thing.[135]

Holbrooke observed optimistically that "our experience in recent years in coping with great difficulties in U.S.-Korea relations has revealed a reservoir of strength in the relationship that bodes well for our ability to solve the problems of the future."

William Clark, Jr., a political counsellor at the U.S. Embassy in Seoul, who had played a key role in the Koreagate negotiations, voiced similar optimism.[136] He said that while it was too early to have historical perspective on the Koreagate affair, its resolution attested to the basic soundness of United States-South Korean relations. He suggested that the relationship might have been strengthened because both sides solidified their importance in the processes of difficult diplomatic negotiations. Yet Clark noted that there was still a "little bit of schizophrenia" on both sides due in part to their cultural and institutional differences. He cited as examples a difference in viewing the giving or accepting of gifts and the South Korean confusion regarding relationships among diverse institutions in the United States — such as State, Justice, and Congress.

Although the Koreagate affair was a bilateral diplomatic matter between Washington and Seoul, the Japanese government leaders were concerned about its potential consequences. They hoped that the episode would not cause any irreparable damage to the United States-South Korean alliance system and that the United States would separate its influence-buying investigations from its security policy in Asia. Moreover, they felt uncomfortable about the possible spillover effects of the Koreagate scandals to Japan. While Donald Ranard repeatedly claimed that the influence-buying operations between Tokyo and Seoul were more extensive than those of Koreagate,[137] Kim Hyong-wook testified before the House Committee on Standards of Official Conduct:

Mr. Quillen. . . . did the government of South Korea, in its dealings with other nations, develop the same attitude, the same policy,

> trying to buy favoritism from other nations?
> General Kim. Yes, we do it to Japan.[138]

The Japanese government flatly denied Ranard's and Kim's allegations, and did not object to the proper U.S. investigations of Koreagate-related matters in Japan.[139] In the light of the Lockheed bribery scandals in Japan, some Japanese officials proposed to offer friendly advice and assistance to their South Korean colleagues, but the proposal was apparently rejected.[140] Yet the South Koreans were satisfied with the Japanese government's willingness to protect Seoul's diplomatic interests.[141] In the end, the Koreagate investigations left a few issues unanswered in Japan — notably, the extent of Park Tong-son's active financial and political involvement in Japan, the use of Japanese political kickbacks (as exemplified in the case of the $2.5 million Seoul subway scandals) for South Korea's influence-buying efforts in the United States, the entertainment of U.S. congressmen at South Korean restaurants and clubs in Japan, and the linkage of the Unification Church activities in the United States and Japan.

The summit meetings between Presidents Carter and Park held in Seoul on June 30 and July 1, 1979, presented an opportunity to transcend the ill will and confusion generated by Koreagate and to chart a return to their normal relations. Although Carter and Park did not discuss Koreagate-related issues, their joint communiqué upheld the Washington-Seoul solidarity as "traditional allies."[142] President Park was pleased with Carter's reaffirmation of U.S. commitment to South Korea's diplomatic, military, and economic interests. Park expressed his hope that Washington and Seoul would move beyond the recent period of "unfortunate relations."

Nevertheless, the Carter-Park summitry was not enough to dissipate the profound and far-reaching effects of the Koreagate issue in South Korea. President Park and his top lieutenants remained bitter about the way in which both the U.S. executive and legislative branches had sensationalized the influence-buying scandals and had publicly embarrassed them and pressured them against their will. The feeling that they had been thoroughly betrayed by a trusted ally was strong and pervasive. Asked to characterize recent bilateral relations, one of South Korea's principal negotiators in the entire Koreagate matters emphasized the U.S. display of "big-nation chauvinism" — a poignant contrast with Holbrooke's superficial optimism.[143] Other South Korean diplomats complained that Washington grossly underestimated South Korea's strong sense of nationalistic self-esteem and that complex negotiations with the United States were severely constrained by the diffusion of policy-making powers in Washington.[144] Conversely, they admitted that the diplomatic role of their own Ministry of Foreign Affairs was seriously handicapped because the KCIA was reluctant to make all intelligence data available to diplomats and because President Park had complete personal control over the Koreagate negotiations. Ultimately, they suggested, it was House Speaker O'Neill who greatly assisted Seoul at critical moments.

The intricacies of disputes and negotiations between Washington and Seoul were never fully revealed to the South Korean public. Seoul attempted to protect the legitimacy of President Park's leadership and foreign policy by selective reporting and by depicting U.S. demands as unfair and unreasonable. This tactic aroused South Korean nationalist feelings, which manifested some incipient hostility against the United States. Many, including opinion leaders, shared the emotionally charged view that the United States had tried to bully a small, weak country and had exaggerated the Koreagate scandals for its own internal political consumption. Public opinion of South Korea did not necessarily agree with Park Tong-son's self-characterization as a "folk hero," but it was more positive than negative about Park's contribution to South Korea's national interests.[145]

Not all South Koreans were so inclined to ignore the ugly implications of the Koreagate scandals. Critics of President Park's rule found in the scandals evidence of the bankruptcy of his domestic and foreign policies. A few courageous members of the opposition New Democratic Party (NDP) requested a parliamentary inquiry of Park Tong-son, Kim Dong-jo, and other persons allegedly involved in the Koreagate affair, but the governing Democratic Republican Party (DRP) quickly thwarted any meaningful investigation by the National Assembly. Some parliamentary interpellations and debates were allowed, but they were largely perfunctory because a number of powerful political leaders, including several NDP members, were deeply implicated in the influence-buying activities. At times, the nationalistic euphoria forced the NDP to join the DRP in passing various resolutions, for example, opposing former KCIA Director Kim Hyong-wook's testimony before the U.S. Congress and protesting the Fraser Subcommittee's investigations of United States-Korean relations. Similarly, the National Assembly demanded an apology from Washington in regard to former Ambassador William Porter's claim that the CIA had indeed eavesdropped on the Blue House.[146] In Seoul there were street demonstrations protesting the bugging episode, and pressure mounted for Porter's testimony before the National Assembly. Speaking before a group of foreign correspondents in Seoul, in June 1979, the newly elected head of the NDP, Representative Kim Yong-sam, offered the boldest public criticism against President Park. He stated that "the present government irreparably damaged our national prestige with the Kim Dae-jung kidnapping scandal . . . [and] also sullied the image of Korea throughout the world through the Park Tong-son affair."[147]

The text of Kim's speech was severely censored in South Korea's domestic press, but his courageous challenge to what he called President Park's "irrational, immoral, and dictatorial" policy marked the beginnings of a political crisis in South Korea. The implementation of Park's harsh retaliatory measures, including the police raid into the NDP headquarters and Kim's expulsion from the National Assembly, precipitated massive urban demonstrations that ended in the assassination of President Park by KCIA Director Kim Jae-kyu on October 26,

1979 — exactly three years after the first *Washington Post* report that had traced the Koreagate scheme into Park's Blue House and the KCIA.[148]

Human Rights

Added to the far-reaching effects of the Koreagate controversies were the human rights disputes, which strained Washington-Seoul diplomatic relations, notably during the Carter Administration. While the United States directly or indirectly attempted to influence Seoul's domestic policies so that human rights would be respected or political prisoners would be freed, the South Korean government resisted such an attempt as an unfair interference in sovereign domestic affairs. Although the Nixon and Ford Administrations were relatively reticent about this issue, the Carter Administration chose South Korea and the Philippines as the major Asian targets of its highly visible human rights diplomacy.

At a time when President Park feared that a further application of the Nixon Doctrine might eventually lead to total U.S. military pullout, he also faced growing criticism in the United States of his domestic political repression — criticism voiced by a number of liberal congressmen, media specialists, intellectuals, clergymen, and some Korean residents. An outspoken Congressional critic, Representative Fraser, presided over a series of House committee hearings on South Korea starting from July 1974 and categorically labeled Park's government as a "police state" practicing executions, torture, and arbitrary arrests and detentions. He suggested that "because the South Korean Government is increasingly oppressive and pays little heed to internationally recognized human rights for the Korean people, the military assistance to South Korea should be reduced or eliminated."[149] Other congressmen (such as Representative Robert N. C. Nix, Dem., Pennsylvania) who were influenced by a neo-isolationist mood and morality questioned the underlying premises of U.S. policy in the Asian mainland and urged that "all 38,000 of our men be brought home." Further, Professors Edwin O. Reischauer, Gregory Henderson, and Jerome Cohen publicly advocated a reduction in U.S. military aid and troop commitments in South Korea as a credible pressure against President Park's "extremely repressive" measures. While taking the position that South Korea itself was a vulnerable strategic liability to the United States, but was important only as a buffer for Japan, Reischauer contended that the political dissent provided by Park's repression was likely to build up "tremendously explosive pressures" and thus to turn South Korea into a Vietnam-type political quagmire where "American military aid and 38,000 men — or a vastly larger American military effort — would be of no avail."[150]

It is difficult to ascertain whether these widely publicized criticisms and Congressional hearings influenced Washington's approaches toward South Korea or restrained Park's domestic policies, but Presidents Nixon and Ford, along with Secretary of State Henry Kissinger, were less than assertive in exerting moralistic influence upon the South Korean government. Irrelevance of moral persuasiveness was indeed characteristic of Kissinger, who was predominantly concerned with the balance of power, and his attitude toward South Korea was no exception. Typically, he stated that since South Korea's security and stability were crucial to the security of East Asia, the United States should continue military and economic assistance even when the U.S. government would not have recommended many of the actions that were taken by the Government of South Korea. He even questioned out loud whether the goal of morality would be enhanced by subjecting South Korea to the more repressive North Korea. This position was supported by some influential congressmen whom the South Korean government diligently wooed; for example, in their study report for the House Foreign Affairs Committee, Representatives Clement J. Zablocki (Dem., Wisconsin) and William S. Broomfield (Rep., Michigan) recommended that South Korea "deserves our fullest possible support" in military and economic areas.[151]

The South Korean government strongly opposed tendencies of the U.S. Congress to link issues of military aid and human rights. In 1974 Seoul overreacted when Fraser held a Foreign Affairs Subcommittee hearing on the status of human rights in South Korea. Highly anxious over the visibility and probable testimony of the outspoken critics of its policies, Seoul called for cancellation of the hearings. In order to mollify the Park government, Congressman Richard Hanna and Park Tong-son promptly took a number of concrete steps to reduce the potential for serious damage. First, they obtained a promise of fair play from the chairman of the House Foreign Affairs Committee, Thomas E. Morgan. There would be an opportunity to counter negative testimony. Second, they contacted the "good friends of Korea" in the House leadership — Majority Leader O'Neill, Majority Whip John McFall, Deputy Majority Whip John Brademas, Minority Floor Leader John Rhodes, and Deputy Minority Floor Leader Albert Johnson. Concurring with Morgan's promise, these "friends" agreed that the hearing should not be permitted to jeopardize U.S. military assistance to South Korea. Third, Park asked Senator Humphrey to sound out Representative Fraser, a fellow Minnesotan, regarding the latter's intentions. Fourth, Hanna and Park selected six congressmen to argue the affirmative case before the subcommittee. In a letter to President Park, Hanna reported:

> While the critics of the Korean Government brought outsiders to testify before the hearings with only two Congressmen joining them, we decided to provide our speakers entirely from House membership. This in itself, we felt, would give more prestige and credibility to the pro-Korean presentations made. Consequently, the friends who made statements in Korea's favor before the Subcommittee were personally selected by us on the basis of bi-partisanship, diverse geography, committee assignments, and knowledge and experience on Korea.[152]

The letter referred to Walter Flowers, Melvin Price, G. V. Montgomery, Edward Patten, Albert Johnson, and William Minshall, but Hanna himself may have replaced Minshall. They all defended the status of human rights in South Korea and passionately argued that "South Korea needs our help to deter a Communist take-over."[153]

More significant than this "truth squad's" pro-Seoul activities was President Ford's two-day state visit to South Korea on his way to Vladivostok in November 1974. Although many U.S. and Korean human rights advocates opposed his visit, Ford joined President Park in declaring:

> The two Presidents agreed that the Republic of Korea forces and American forces stationed in Korea must maintain a high degree of strength and readiness in order to deter aggression. President Ford reaffirmed the determination of the United States to render prompt and effective assistance to repel armed attack against the Republic of Korea in accordance with the Mutual Defense Treaty of 1954 between the Republic of Korea and the United States. In this connection, President Ford assured President Park that the United States has no plan to reduce the present level of United States forces in Korea.[154]

Ford may have explained his Congressional difficulty caused by the South Korean government's domestic measures, but Ford's visit helped solidify Park's leadership and in effect condoned his continuous violations of human rights in South Korea.

The Ford-Park summitry did not dampen a serious Congressional concern with human rights violations in South Korea. In an unusual expression of this concern, Congress decided in December 1974 to reduce U.S. military assistance from $165 million to $145 million until President Ford could report that the South Korean government was making substantial progress in the observance of internationally recognized standards of human rights. The decision was consistent with the Foreign Assistance Act of 1973, which prohibited U.S. aid to countries holding political prisoners, and it was obviously a psychological blow to the South Korean government and its U.S. supporters.

Unlike his predecessors — Nixon and Ford — President Carter attached a top policy priority to the human rights issue and presented an additional challenge to South Korea's foreign policy. Already, in June 1976, Carter, as a presidential candidate, had stated that "it should be made clear to the South Korean government that its internal oppression is repugnant to our people and undermines the support for our commitment there."[155] At the televised presidential debate in October 1976, Carter had specifically pointed out the failure of Ford's human rights policy in South Korea.[156]

The acceleration of President Carter's determined public criticism of South Korea's violation of universal human rights made President Park fiercely defensive.

The forceful argument that the continued violation of human rights would erode U.S. military protection of South Korea led to President Park's grudging promise to effect a gradual release of political prisoners, but he presented all kinds of excuses not to implement his promise to a satisfactory extent. At times the Carter Administration used the instruments of indirect economic sanctions (such as abstention in the international financial institutions' decisions for South Korea's loan applications), but they were less than effective in influencing Park's domestic policies. More significantly, the Carter Administration, which cut its foreign aid to Argentina, Uruguay, and Ethiopia due to the issue of human rights, did not request a similar action toward South Korea. The threat to withhold military assistance or to weaken the mutual security treaty might have been the most tangible way to influence Seoul's human rights situation, but President Carter chose not to take this extreme step, because it contained a risk of undermining political stability in South Korea and upsetting the military balance in the Korean peninsula as well as Northeast Asia.

When President Carter visited Seoul at the end of June 1979, he made a special personal effort to meet with South Korean political dissidents and insisted on including the human rights issue in the agenda for his summit talks with President Park. In the joint communiqué, despite Park's earlier objections, Carter emphasized the importance of universal human rights.[157] Moreover, Secretary of State Cyrus Vance gave to Foreign Minister Park two lists of political prisoners in South Korea with the hope that they would be released; one list was compiled by Amnesty International, while a shorter one was prepared by the State Department. Yet the Carter-Park summitry did not improve the conditions of human rights in South Korea.

The assassination of President Park in October 1979 prompted the euphoria of a new U.S. optimism for South Korea's democratization, but the rapid political ascendancy of a military strongman, General Chon Du-hwan, dashed this premature optimism. He was successful in staging a coup d'etat in December 1979, suppressing the Kwangju uprising and arresting a large number of democratic leaders, including Kim Dae-jung, in May 1980, and taking over the presidency himself in August. The record of the Carter Administration's human rights policy toward Chon's harsh actions was replete with confusion, inconsistency, and ineffectiveness, and it reflected the weakness of the link between political conditions in South Korea and the U.S. security commitment there. In reviewing the relationship between U.S. military aid and human rights in South Korea, Patricia M. Derian, assistant secretary of state for human rights and humanitarian affairs, observed:

> The dilemma is that if we continue to supply this [military] aid in spite of warning signals, we risk perhaps equally drastic and damaging consequences in the long run. If we so support a military government that has jailed its opposition, imposed full martial law, and heavily censored its nation's press, we appear not just to condone but to reward

these violations of basic human rights. If some of South Korea's generals are determined to establish a dictatorship, economic and moral
pressure may not be sufficient to dissuade them from this goal. They
have presumably appraised the situation and may have decided that we
are exclusively concerned with national security. If we do not remain
true to our ideals, we risk a strong anti-American backlash.[158]

Her prescient assessment was distinctly a minority view, which was buried or
ignored in the dynamics of the Washington bureaucracy. In spite of the apparent
persistence of intrabureaucratic cleavages and debates, Carter's overall policy
tended to attach a higher priority to regional security and political stability
than human rights and democratic principles and to eventually accommodate
whatever political reality emerged in South Korea. The United States seemed to
have forgotten the lessons from its painful experiences in Chiang Kai-shek's
China, Nguyen Van Thieu's South Vietnam, the Shah's Iran, and Somoza's
Nicaragua. Needless to say, the U.S. security policy in these countries was
destroyed not by the lack of U.S. military aid, but by the acceptance of a government that provided a semblance of political stability but betrayed human rights
and democratic aspirations and lacked genuine and legitimate popular support.

The immediate human rights issue faced by the outgoing Carter Administration and the new Reagan Administration was Kim Dae-jung's death sentence, which was based on his alleged incitation of the Kwangju incident. As
the United States joined Japan in exerting political and economic pressure on
behalf of Kim's survival, the Chon government decided to commute his sentence
to life imprisonment. Once this nagging issue was at least temporarily disposed
of, President Reagan promptly embraced President Chon's rule and invited him
to Washington toward the end of January 1981. The issue of human rights was
conspicuously absent in the Reagan-Chon summit discussions and in their joint
communiqué. In fact, unlike Carter, Reagan strongly believed that the United
States should refrain from criticizing the violations of human rights in its
"authoritarian" allies and should direct its moralistic campaign against the
"totalitarian" communist regimes. Hence the Reagan Administration, preoccupied with the anticommunist crusade, effectively removed human rights from
the diplomatic agenda between Washington and Seoul.

NOTES

1. See *Public Papers of the President of the United States, Richard Nixon, 1969*
(Washington, D.C.: USGPO, 1971), pp. 1-4 (hereafter cited as *PPPUS, Richard Nixon*).

2. *PPPUS, Richard Nixon, 1972* (Washington, D.C.: USGPO, 1974), p. 221.

3. See Richard M. Nixon, *RN: The Memoirs of Richard Nixon* (New York: Grosset
and Dunlap, 1978), p. 545.

4. See *PPPUS, Richard Nixon, 1972*, pp. 214-17.

5. *PPPUS, Richard Nixon, 1973* (Washington, D.C.: USGPO, 1975), p. 358. This
report was prepared by Kissinger and issued by Nixon.

6. *PPPUS, Richard Nixon, 1972*, p. 233.

7. For Nixon's hope that he, as well as his daughters, can someday visit China, etc., see his memoir, pp. 546 and 549.

8. See the Chou-Kim joint statement in *Peking Review*, April 10, 1970, pp. 3-5.

9. For a detailed discussion of his Peking visit, see Henry A. Kissinger, *White House Years* (Boston: Little, Brown, 1979), pp. 163-94, 684-787.

10. For this account, see Chae-Jin Lee, *Japan Faces China: Political and Economic Relations in the Postwar Era* (Baltimore: Johns Hopkins University Press, 1967), pp. 98-99.

11. See Nagano Nobutoshi, *Gaimusho kenkyu* [A Study of the Foreign Ministry] (Tokyo: Simul Press, 1975), pp. 4-5.

12. Armin H. Meyer, *Assignment: Tokyo — An Ambassador's Journal* (Indianapolis: Bobbs-Merrill, 1974), p. 111.

13. See the press release after the Nixon-Sato meeting in *Waga gaiko no kinkyo* [Recent State of Our Diplomacy] (Tokyo: Gaimusho, 1971), pp. 410-12; and Meyer, *Ambassador's Journal*, p. 123.

14. *PPPUS, Richard Nixon, 1972*, pp. 218-19.

15. Ibid., p. 217.

16. For the text, see *Waga gaiko no kinkyo* (1972), pp. 410-13.

17. Kissinger, *White House Years*, p. 762.

18. Ibid., p. 324.

19. See House Committee on Foreign Affairs, *New China Policy: Its Impact on the U.S. and Asia: Hearings before the Subcommittee on Asian and Pacific Affairs* (Washington, D.C.: USGPO, 1972), pp. 148-52 (Ball's views) and pp. 3-18 (Reischauer's views).

20. See Nagano, *Foreign Ministry*, p. 6; and Meyer, *Ambassador's Journal*, pp. 169-71.

21. For Kissinger's views and maneuvers, see his *White House Years*, pp. 719-20, 770-74, 784-86.

22. Nixon gingerly discusses this issue in his memoir, pp. 556-57.

23. See Nagano, *Foreign Ministry*, pp. 9-19.

24. See Lee, *Japan Faces China*, pp. 101-4.

25. Meyer, *Ambassador's Journal*, p. 309.

26. *Asahi Shimbun*, January 8, 1972.

27. See the text in *Department of State Bulletin*, January 31, 1972, pp. 118-19.

28. *Asahi Shimbun*, January 8, 1972.

29. *PPPUS, Richard Nixon, 1972*, p. 232.

30. Kissinger, *White House Years*, p. 1072.

31. Nixon, *Memoirs*, p. 567.

32. See the text in Department of State, *U.S. Policy Toward China* (Washington, D.C.: Selected Documents no. 9, n.d.), pp. 6-8.

33. Kissinger, *White House Years*, pp. 1061-89.

34. *Asahi Shimbun*, February 28, 1972.

35. *Asahi Shimbun*, February 29, 1972.

36. For the negotiations for Sino-Japanese diplomatic normalization, see Lee, *Japan Faces China*, pp. 111-25; and Haruhiro Fukui, "Tanaka goes to Peking," in T. J. Pempel, ed., *Policy-making in Contemporary Japan* (Ithaca, N.Y.: Cornell University Press, 1977), pp. 60-102.

37. *Mainichi Shimbun*, September 5, 1972.

38. For the text of their joint communique, see *Department of State Bulletin*, September 25, 1972, pp. 331-32.

39. *Peking Review*, October 6, 1972, pp. 12-13.

40. Interviews with Kuriyama Yoshikazu (director of the Treaties Division as of 1972), January 13, 1977, Washington; and with Hashimoto Hiroshi (director of the China Division as of 1972), July 27, 1977, Tokyo.

41. See Chong-Sik Lee, "The Impact of the Sino-American Detente on Korea," in Gene T. Hsiao, ed., *Sino-American Detente: And Its Policy Implications* (New York: Praeger, 1974), pp. 189-206.

42. See Robert R. Simmons, "North Korea: Year of the Thaw," *Asian Survey*, January 1972, pp. 25-31; and Chae-Jin Lee, "South Korea: Political Competiton and Government Adaptation," ibid., pp. 38-45.

43. See the testimony by William J. Porter (former ambassador to Seoul) in House Committee on International Relations, *Investigation of Korean-American Relations: Hearings before the Subcommittee on International Organizations*, pt. 4 (Washington, D.C.: USGPO, 1978), p. 66; and the testimony by Marshall Green, ibid., p. 24 (hereafter cited as *IKAR*).

44. For the following discussions, see Chae-Jin Lee, "South Korea: The Politics of Domestic-Foreign Linkage," *Asian Survey*, January 1973, pp. 94-101; and B. C. Koh, "North Korea: A Breakthrough in the Quest for Unity," *Asian Survey*, January 1973, pp. 83-93.

45. See Chae-Jin Lee, "The Direction of South Korea's Foreign Policy," *Korean Studies*, vol. 2 (1978), pp. 95-138.

46. Interview with an official of the South Korean Mission to the U.N., November 9, 1979, New York.

47. For a discussion of the frozen assets issue, See Richard T. Devane, "The United States and China: Claims and Assets," *Asian Survey*, December 1978, pp. 1267-79; and Stanley B. Lubman, "Trade and Sino-American Relations," in Michel Oksenberg and Robert B. Oxnam, eds., *Dragon and Eagle: United States-China Relations: Past and Future* (New York: Basic Books, 1978), pp. 187-210.

48. See the statements regarding Ford's China visit in *U.S. Policy Toward China*, pp. 22-25.

49. See his address made at South Bend on May 22, 1977, ibid., p. 32.

50. Meeting with Holbrooke, June 17, 1977, Washington.

51. See Mondale's news conference on February 1, 1977, in *Department of State Bulletin*, March 7, 1977, pp. 190-91.

52. Interview with Stephen Eaton, Office of Japanese Affairs, Department of State, June 15, 1977, Washington.

53. See Stanley Karnow, "East Asia in 1978: The Great Transformation," *Foreign Affairs: America and the World 1978* (1979), p. 598.

54. For the documents on Vance's trip to China and Japan, see *Department of State Bulletin*, September 19, 1977, pp. 365-74.

55. See Chae-Jin Lee, "The Making of the Sino-Japanese Peace and Friendship Treaty," *Pacific Affairs*, Fall 1979, pp. 430-31.

56. *Asahi Shimbun*, May 4, 1978.

57. See *U.S. Policy Toward China*, pp. 38-39.

58. Karnow, "East Asia in 1978," p. 599.

59. See Lee, "Sino-Japanese Peace and Friendship Treaty," pp. 438-39.

60. *Newsweek*, November 6, 1978, p. 73. The same point was repeated in interview with Mansfield, July 10, 1979, Tokyo; Japan's diplomatic maturity was emphasized.

61. For the documents on diplomatic normalization, see *U.S. Policy Toward China*, pp. 45-51.

62. See Senate Committee on Foreign Relations, *Taiwan Enabling Act: Report* (Washington, D.C.: USGPO, 1979), p. 7.

63. See Christopher's testimony in Senate Committee on Foreign Relations, *Taiwan: Hearings* (Washington, D.C.: USGPO, 1979), p. 56.

64. See Robert L. Downen, *The Taiwan Pawn in the China Game: Congress to the Rescue* (Washington, D.C.: Center for Strategic and International Studies, Georgetown University, 1979), p. 37.

65. *U.S. Policy Toward China*, p. 48.

66. For Hua Kuo-feng's press conference, see *Peking Review*, December 22, 1978, pp. 9-11.

67. *Taiwan Enabling Act*, p. 7.

68. For Goldwater's legal position, see Barry M. Goldwater, *China and the Abrogation of Treaties* (Washington, D.C.: Heritage Foundation, 1978); and J. Terry Emerson, "The Legislative Role in Treaty Abrogation," *Journal of Legislation*, May 1978, pp. 46-80. For the government's legal defense and a history of treaty terminations, see *Taiwan: Hearings*, pp. 199-233. Subsequently, the Supreme Court refused to consider this issue.

69. *Taiwan: Hearings*, p. 11. For the government draft, see *Taiwan: Hearings*, pp. 3-10.

70. See the text in the House of Representatives, *Taiwan Relations Act: Conference Report* (96th Cong., 1st sess., Report no. 96-71, March 24, 1979), p. 2.

71. *U.S. Policy Toward China*, p. 64.

72. See Senate Committee on Armed Services, *United States-Japan Security Relationship – The Key to East Asian Security and Stability: Report of the Pacific Study Group* (Washington, D.C.: USGPO, 1979), p. 8.

73. Interview with Sunobe Ryozo (Japanese ambassador to South Korea), June 14, 1979, Seoul.

74. Interviews with Ogawa Heishiro (Japanese ambassador to China, 1973-77), June 26, 1978, Washington; Sunobe Ryozo, June 14, 1979, Seoul; Matano Kagechiko (director, Northeast Asia Division, Japanese Ministry of Foreign Affairs), July 10, 1979, Tokyo; and William Clark, Jr. (political counsellor, U.S. Embassy), June 14, 1979, Seoul. Ogawa met frequently with North Korean Ambassador Hyon Jun-gok in Peking. Charles Freeman (director, Office of PRC and Mongolian Affairs, State Department) recalled his meeting with Chinese Ambassador Chai Tse-min in Washington in 1980; Chai urged the United States to intervene in Seoul for the purpose of South Korea's "democratization" (meeting with Freeman, August 23, 1980, Kansas City).

75. See Richard C. Holbrooke, "Korea and the United States-The Era Ahead," *Department of State Bulletin*, February 1979, pp. 29-32.

76. The proposal for a tripartite meeting (United States, South Korea, and North Korea) was made in the Carter-Park joint statement. See *Department of State Bulletin*, August 1979, pp. 16-17.

77. For Secretary of State Kissinger's proposals for a four-party conference (United States, China, South Korea, and North Korea) and for an expanded six-party conference (the Soviet Union and Japan added), see Lee, "South Korea's Foreign Policy," pp. 127-37.

78. See Hanna's testimony, House Committee on Standards of Official Conduct, *Korean Influence Investigation: Hearings* (Washington, D.C.: USGPO, 1978), pp. 234-35 (hereafter cited as *Investigation*: pt. 2).

79. For Park's alleged payments, see Robert Boettcher, *Gifts of Deceit: Sun Myung Moon, Tongsun Park, and the Korean Scandal* (New York: Rinehart and Winston, 1980), pp. 77, 192.

80. As quoted in *Korea Week*, February 10, 1977.

81. See Senate Select Committee on Ethics, *Korean Influence Inquiry: Executive Session Hearings* (Washington, D.C.: USGPO, 1978), p. 1606 (hereafter cited as *Inquiry*, vol. 2).

82. From November 1967 to December 1967, 264 members of the U.S. House visited South Korea on 93 separate official delegations under the U.S. government sponsorship. Since 1970, 22 representatives and 37 Congressional staff members traveled to South Korea with private or non-U.S. government funds. See House Committee on Standards of Official Conduct, *Korean Influence Investigations: Report* (Washington, D.C.: USGPO, 1978), pp. 99-113 (hereafter cited as *Investigation: Report*). A number of visiting congressmen, including John Murphy, Lester L. Wolff, Edward Derwinski, William Broomfield,

Cornelius Gallagher, Tennyson Guyer, and Charles Wiggins, received honorary doctoral degrees in Seoul.

83. *Investigation*, pt. 2, pp. 256-57.

84. Ibid., pp. 394-96.

85. See testimony by Donald Ranard (former director, Office of Korean Affairs, State Department), *IKAR*, pt. 4, p. 79. A variety of Korean officials nervously asked Ambassador William J. Porter "100 times" as to the changing mood in Congress. See his testimony, ibid., p. 43.

86. Senate Select Committee on Ethics, *Korean Influence Inquiry: Report* (Washington, D.C.: USGPO, 1978), p. 1 (hereafter cited as *Inquiry: Report*).

87. Kim Hyong-wook, former KCIA director, said that although Park was not on the KCIA's regular payroll, "I gave him specific missions, tasks to be carried out," See *Inquiry*, vol. 2, p. 1117.

88. Kim Han-jo, a Korean-American businessman and close friend of President Park, received $600,000 from the South Korean government to influence congressmen, such as Tennyson Guyer (Rep., Ohio). See *Investigation: Report*, pp. 70-72. Upon Park Tong-son's recommendation, Rep. Cornelius E. Gallagher appointed Kim Kwang (Park's cousin and a South Korean citizen) as a staff member of the House Subcommittee on Asian and Pacific Affairs in the early 1970s. Suzi Park Thomson was a secretary for various congressmen, including House Speaker Carl Albert, Patsy Mink, Herbert Tenzer, William Hungate, and Lester Wolff. Park Bo-hi, former official of the South Korean embassy in Washington, was a principal associate of the Unification Church headed by Moon Son-myong, organized the Washington-based Korean Cultural and Freedom Foundation, the Freedom Leadership Foundation, the "Little Angels," and sponsored the Radio of Free Asia. For a detailed description of their activities, see Robert Boettcher, *Gifts of Deceit*.

89. They included Richard Hanna, John McFall, Jack Miller, Joseph Montoya, William Minshall, Edwin Edwards, Melvin Price, Robert Leggett, John Brademas, Seymour Halpern, Walter Flowers, Edward Patten, and Eligio de la Garza.

90. *Inquiry*, vol. 1, p. 576. Miller was a member of the George Town Club. In 1976 he received a Korean honorary degree and a diplomatic medal ("Order of Diplomatic Service") from President Park.

91. See President Park's letter (July 31, 1971) to Montoya, *Inquiry*, vol. 1, pp. 573-74.

92. *Donga Ilbo*, April 26, 1976.

93. Boettcher, *Gifts of Deceit*, p. 247.

94. Robert Boettcher, "Koreagate and the Survival of Interests," paper presented at the Korea Seminar, Columbia University, September 28, 1979, p. 3. See House Committee on Foreign Affairs, *American-Korean Relations: Hearings before the Subcommittee on Asian and Pacific Affairs* (Washington, D.C.: USGPO, 1979).

95. *Inquiry: Report*, pp. 1, 61.

96. *IKAR*, pt. 4, p. 81.

97. *IKAR*, pt. 4, p. 84.

98. See the texts, ibid., pp. 552-57.

99. See Mitchell's testimony, ibid., pp. 139-50; and Kissinger's testimony, ibid., pp. 237-49.

100. Ibid., p. 60.

101. See Habib's memo (August 2, 1973), *IKAR*, pt. 5 (1978), p. 157.

102. See Park's testimony, *Inquiry*, vol. 1, p. 192.

103. Ambassador Richard Sneider (1974-78 in Seoul) testified that Habib was "the one who took the initiative." *IKAR*, pt. 5, p. 49.

104. See Kissinger's testimony, *IKAR*, pt. 4, p. 247.

105. For Lee's testimony, see House Committee on International Relations, *Human Rights in South Korea and the Philippines: Implications for U.S. Policy: Hearings before*

the Subcommittee on International Organizations (Washington, D.C.: USGPO, 1975), pp. 179-83.

106. For the South Korean reactions, see *Washington Post*, October 29 and 30, 1976; and *New York Times*, November 5, 1976.

107. *Donga Ilbo*, December 29, 1976.

108. Interview with a South Korean diplomat, January 12, 1977, Washington.

109. See *Washington Star*, September 6, 1977; or *Korea Herald*, September 11, 1977.

110. See President Carter's letter (November 4, 1977) to Congressional leaders, *PPPUS, Jimmy Carter, 1977*, Book II (1978), pp. 1969-72; *Donga Ilbo*, September 17, 1977.

111. For the agreement, see *Korea Herald*, January 1, 1978. It was further elaborated in the 15-article agreement signed on January 10, 1978. See *Donga Ilbo*, January 21, 1978.

112. *Washington Post*, January 21, 1978.

113. See *New York Times*, February 1, 1978; and *Korea Herald*, February 2, 1978.

114. Boettcher, *Gifts of Deceit*, p. 287.

115. In addition to $9 million in rice commissions, Park, during this period, amassed $10 million in other fees (for example, $3 million for his settlement of the dispute between Japan Lines of Tokyo and Burma Oil Tanker Co. of Britain and $3-4 million consultant fee for Japan Lines) and $5-10 million in Korean currency. He admitted cash payments ($200,000 a year) to South Korean nationals, such as politicians who visited the United States and South Korean Embassy officials. See *Inquiry*, vol. 1, pp. 363-64.

116. The first meeting apparently took place in November 1961 when General Park visited Washington on President Kennedy's invitation. See the photo showing Park Tongson in the airport welcoming line for General Park, in *Bakuijang bangmi suhaeng kirok* [Record of Chairman Park's Visit to the U.S.] (Seoul: Supreme Council for National Reconstruction, 1962), p. 57. Also see Kim Hyong-wook's testimony, *Inquiry*, vol. 2, pp. 1106-7. Another meeting happened in 1965 during the Johnson-Park summitry at Washington. See Boettcher, *Gifts of Deceit*, p. 59.

117. *Investigation: Report*, p. 10.

118. See Nan Elder's testimony in *Investigation*, pt. 1 (1977), pp. 15-20; Lee's testimony, ibid., pp. 20-32; and the testimony by the wives of two congressmen, ibid., pp. 90-100.

119. The Vienna Convention on Diplomatic Relations was ratified by the U.S. Senate on September 4, 1965. Articles 31 and 39 are relevant to the Kim case.

120. As quoted in *Korea Week*, March 14, 1978.

121. AP report in *Korea Herald*, June 2, 1978.

122. Interview with a South Korean diplomat, June 26, 1978, Washington.

123. *Investigation: Report*, p. 92. Gleysteen did not initiate the formula, but it was one of several options that the State Department had considered for some time. Interview with Robert G. Rich, Jr. (director, Office of Korean Affairs, State Department), March 20, 1980, Washington.

124. See the texts in *Investigation: Report*, pp. 187-218.

125. Kim admitted that in May 1973 he had bought dinner party tickets valued at $2,000 for the fund-raising committee of Congressman Jerome Waldie (Dem., California), an aspirant for governor of California.

126. *Inquiry: Report*, pp. 142-47.

127. *Investigation: Report*, p. 93.

128. See his "additional views" in ibid., pp. 130-34.

129. Ibid., p. 93.

130. Ibid., pp. 162-71.

131. *Inquiry: Report*, pp. 1-2.

132. For Bayh, see ibid., pp. 64-79; and for Montoya, see ibid., pp. 108-18. It was ironic that Bayh himself chaired the Senate Judiciary Subcommittee to investigate Billy Carter's Libyan connection in 1980.

133. *Inquiry: Report*, p. 9.

134. *Korea Week*, December 20, 1977.

135. Richard C. Holbrooke, "Korea and the United States – The Era Ahead," *Department of State Bulletin*, February 1979, pp. 29-32.

136. Interviews with Clark, June 14 and July 3, 1979, in Seoul.

137. See *Asahi Shimbun*, January 29 and February 22, 1977.

138. See Representative James H. Quillen's (Rep., Tennessee) testimony in *Investigation*, pt. 1, pp. 115-16.

139. The Japanese and U.S. officials emphasized a correct and cooperative diplomatic relation between Tokyo and Washington in regard to the Koreagate investigations. Interviews with Matano Kagechiko (director, Northeast Asia Division, Japanese Ministry of Foreign Affairs, July 10, 1979, Tokyo) and Richard Kilpatrick (deputy director, Office for Japanese Affairs, State Department, March 14, 1979, Washington). For the view that Japan was less than cooperative, see *IKAR: Report*, p. 410.

140. Interview with a South Korean diplomat, December 28, 1978.

141. Interview with an official of the South Korean Embassy to Japan, July 7, 1979, Tokyo.

142. For the text, see *Department of State Bulletin*, August 1979, pp. 16-17.

143. Interview with a senior South Korean policy maker, July 5, 1979, Seoul.

144. Interview with a high South Korean diplomat, June 11, 1979, Seoul.

145. *Jungang Ilbo*, September 22, 1978.

146. Porter's CBS interview was reported in *Korea Herald*, April 14, 1978.

147. Kim Yong-sam, "Opening a New Age Where the People Become the Makers of History," address given at the Foreign Correspondents' Club, Seoul, June 11, 1979.

148. See Chong-Sik Lee, "South Korea 1979: Confrontation, Assassination, and Transition," *Asian Survey*, January 1980, pp. 63-76.

149. See House Committee on Foreign Affairs, *Human Rights in South Korea: Implications for U.S. Policy* (Washington, D.C.: USGPO, 1974), pp. 2-3.

150. Edwin O. Reischauer, "The Korean Connection," *New York Times Magazine*, September 22, 1974.

151. See House Committee on Foreign Affairs, *Report of Special Study Mission to Japan, Taiwan, and Korea* (Washington, D.C.: USGPO, 1974), p. 12.

152. See his letter (August 27, 1974), *Investigation*, pt. 1, pp. 636-42.

153. For their respective statements, see *Human Rights in South Korea*, pp. 153-69.

154. See the joint communiqué in *Department of State Bulletin*, December 23, 1974, pp. 877-78.

155. As quoted in Frank Gibney, "The Ripple Effect in Korea," *Foreign Affairs*, October 1977, p. 160.

156. See *New York Times*, October 8, 1976.

157. See the joint communiqué in *Department of State Bulletin*, August 1979, pp. 16-17.

158. See Derian's speech of June 13, 1980, "U.S. Commitment to Human Rights," Current Policy no. 198 (Department of State).

3

MILITARY AFFAIRS

As our discussions in Chapter 1 demonstrate, the United States successfully embraced both Japan and South Korea in its regional military containment system and effectively exercised a dominant influence over the security policies of these Asian allies during the 1950s and 1960s. The United States continued to preserve the basic framework of this system throughout the 1970s and sustained its established military influence relationship with Japan and South Korea as their ultimate security guarantor. However, Presidents Nixon and Carter decided to reorient the U.S. East Asian security posture in such a way that the United States could lessen its relative military and economic burden without disturbing the traditional alliance structure. More specifically, both Nixon and Carter wished to withdraw U.S. ground forces out of South Korea and to gain flexibility and maneuverability in the U.S. security policy toward Korea. At the same time, the U.S. government urged Japan to assume a greater share of its defense responsibilities commensurate with its growing economic power. Yet the United States found it difficult to influence the specific direction of Japan's and South Korea's security preferences and to implement its shifting policy priorities vis-à-vis the two Asian allies. Hence the U.S. security policy toward Japan and South Korea during the 1970s and early 1980s focused on the way in which the United States attempted to readjust its military presence in South Korea and to manage the strains that emerged in the Washington-Tokyo alliance as a result of their increasing policy dissonance.

U.S. MILITARY PRESENCE IN SOUTH KOREA

Nixon's Security Policy

Although the United States-South Korean defense treaty did not obligate the United States to station its combat troops on South Korean soil, the successive U.S. administrations continued to maintain the same level of military strengths in the Korean peninsula throughout the 1960s.[1] The principal rationale for the U.S. military presence in South Korea was linked to its effective deterrence of North Korea's possible aggression. The U.S. government spokesmen also cited other purposes of U.S. military policy in South Korea: (1) to avoid "hegemony" by any major power in the Korean peninsula; (2) to exert a "restraint" on South Korea's unilateral military actions; (3) to provide an "umbrella" for its continued economic expansion; (4) to give "tangible assurance" of U.S. support for South Korea's peaceful initiatives toward North Korea; and (5) to serve as a "symbol of America's continuing interest in the overall stability" of the region, especially with regard to Japan.[2]

Guided by the Guam Doctrine as well as domestic political considerations, the Nixon Administration refrained from repeating Humphrey's type of flat statement for South Korea's defense but rather sought to use big-power diplomacy for relaxation of international tensions over the Korean peninsula.[3] While encouraging North-South negotiations,[4] it also wished to lower the U.S. military posture in South Korea and to stress the latter's self-reliant defense capabilities. On March 20, 1970, Nixon issued National Security Decision Memorandum 48, which called for withdrawal of one of the two U.S. infantry divisions from South Korea.[5] He decided to redeploy the remaining U.S. forces away from the DMZ and to provide a five-year military modernization program and additional PL 480 commitments for South Korea.

President Nixon's unilateral security decision greatly upset President Park, who thought that he had secured "special relations" with the United States by South Korea's military participation in the Vietnam War. The timing of this decision was particularly disturbing to Park because he expected to face a tough reelection campaign in 1971 and because the People's Republic of China and North Korea reaffirmed their "militant solidarity." President Park told Ambassador William Porter that the United States had no right to remove its troops from South Korea.[6] The South Korean protest went to an extraordinary degree. While Prime Minister Chung Il-kwon threatened to leave a portion of the DMZ unmanned and Ambassador Kim Dong-jo hinted at South Korea's disengagement from Vietnam, Defense Minister Jung Nae-hyok bought an advertisement against U.S. troop withdrawal in the *Washington Post* (September 25, 1970). The South Koreans requested a compensation package of $4 billion but obtained a five-year promise of only $1.5 billion.[7] The United States quickly withdrew its Seventh Infantry Division (20,000 men) out of South Korea by the end of March 1971, but it took seven years for the United States to deliver its $1.5 billion military aid for South Korea. Meanwile, Defense Secretary Melvin Laird issued in August 1971 a Program Decision Memorandum to reduce the Second Infantry Division to one brigade by the end of fiscal year 1974; a year later, the target date was extended to the end of 1975.[8] However, Laird's plan was thwarted by the opposition of Assistant to the President for National Security Affairs Henry Kissinger and pro-Seoul congressmen.

In an attempt to dispel South Korea's fear of a further application of the Guam Doctrine, President Gerald Ford paid a two-day state visit to Seoul on his way to Vladivostok in November 1974. He stressed that "the United States, as a Pacific power, is vitally interested in Asia and the Pacific and will continue its best efforts to ensure the peace and security of the region." Specifically, Ford reaffirmed the "determination of the United States to render prompt and effective assistance to repel armed attack against the Republic of Korea in accordance with the Mutual Defense Treaty of 1954 between the Republic of Korea and the United States" and assured President Park that the United States had "no plan to reduce the present level of United States forces in Korea."[9] Further, Ford promised to assist South Korea in its military modernization program and the development of its defense industries. The South Korean government was particularly pleased with the renewed U.S. pledge of "prompt and effective assistance." This had been incorporated into the Johnson-Park joint communiqués of 1966 and 1968, but the Nixon-Park joint communiqué of 1969 had failed to reaffirm this commitment under the shadow of the Guam Doctrine.

In the immediate context of the Indochinese collapse in early 1975, United States government leaders offered prolific public statements guaranteeing South Korea's national security. When asked about the post-Indochina U.S. policy in South Korea, Secretary of State Kissinger answered in May 1975:

> In South Korea there can be no ambiguity about our commitment because we have a defense treaty ratified by the Congress. If we abandon this treaty, it would have drastic consequences in Japan and all over Asia because that would be interpreted as our final withdrawal from Asia and our final withdrawal from our whole postwar foreign policy.[10]

A week later (in the middle of the Mayaguez incident), Kissinger warned North Korea not to make a mistake in questioning the validity of U.S. security commitment to South Korea.[11] Further, in June, Secretary of Defense James R. Schlesinger threatened to repel North Korea's armed aggression with massive retaliation, including probable use of tactical nuclear weapons deployed in South Korea.[12] In his "Pacific Doctrine" proclaimed in December 1975, President Ford reiterated that "world stability and our own security depend upon our Asian commitments."[13] The nervous South Koreans were gratified by the profusion of these U.S. commitments, which were designed to have a deterrent effect upon North Korea's possible military provocations.

Yet it did not take long for the U.S. military commitments to be tested at Panmunjom. On August 18, 1976, when a United Nations Command work crew attempted to prune a poplar tree in the neutral Joint Security Area because the tree obstructed the observation of North Korean personnel, a group of North Korean Army guards opposed the tree-pruning operation and killed two U.S. officers in the ensuing brawl.[14] The United States immediately issued a strong protest to North Korea, demanding "explanations and reparations," and sent another work crew to cut down the tree in a show of force. The United States, along with South Korea, placed its forces on full alert, deployed to Korea F-4 aircraft from Okinawa and F-111s from Idaho, conducted daily B-52 flights from Guam to Korea, and dispatched the Midway task force to the area. As Arthur W. Hummel, assistant secretary of state for East Asian and Pacific Affairs, explained, the swift and coordinated U.S. military moves were intended to demonstrate to Pyongyang that "we were willing and able to move decisively to counter any threat in this area."[15] The military demonstration indeed forced North Korea's President Kim Il-song to express his "regret" over the incident and to offer a conciliatory proposal for new security measures in Panmunjom. The initial U.S. response was to reject his noncommittal "regret" as unacceptable, but it decided to resolve the potentially explosive crisis by agreeing to consider his proposal. The South Koreans were relieved, but unhappy about what they regarded as the pattern of Washington's nonpunitive reaction to North Korea's repeated challenges, which had started from the Pueblo (1968) and EC-121 (1969) incidents.

Carter's Troop Pullout Policy

Even before the Panmunjom crisis was completely settled, a gathering storm hung over U.S. military presence in South Korea. On June 23, 1976, Jimmy Carter, a leading contender for the Democratic presidential nomination, delivered a major foreign policy speech in Chicago and said that "it will be possible to withdraw our ground forces from South Korea on a phased basis over a time span to be determined after consultation with both South Korea and Japan."[16] His stand was due primarily to his instinctive strategic judgment and, secondarily, to tactical political considerations. Deeply touched by the national trauma of the protracted and divisive Vietnam War, he felt that the United States should avoid any situation that might require United States' automatic, massive involvement in another Asian land war. For U.S. Asian commitments, he favored a policy emphasizing strategic flexibility and mobility, that is, one giving emphasis to the navy, air force, and the marines. Carter would assign strategic priority to Europe, where the United States faced the most serious threat from the Soviet Union. In effect, he was in basic agreement with the Nixon Doctrine. Moreover, he shrewdly attempted to appeal to the prevailing neo-isolationist mood against foreign military engagement and to court those Democrats who had supported George McGovern. Intuitively, he was attracted to the military pullout as a money-saving measure consistent with his campaign theme of fiscal austerity and balanced budget.

Even if Carter's intentions were sincere and defensible, the main thrust of his proposals for military disengagement from South Korea suggested a naivete regarding strategic and geopolitical calculations. He appeared to be unaware of the complexities of the Korean situation, which was not exactly analogous to the Vietnamese case. Most important, he failed to recognize the close strategic linkage between Korea and the rest of East Asia, particularly Japan, and to understand the symbolic and psychological importance that South Korea and Japan attached to U.S. military presence in Asia. U.S. military leaders, at home and abroad, were seriously alarmed by Carter's statements on Korea. In the Pentagon, there existed a consensus that the continued U.S. presence in South Korea was essential not only to South Korea's security but also to peace in Northeast Asia. Although the Pentagon wished that Carter's statements would prove mere campaign rhetoric, a group of senior officers completed a detailed report on Carter's Korean position and submitted it to the Joint Chiefs of Staff in November 1976.[17] In Seoul, General John W. Vessey, Jr., commander of the United Nations Command and the U.S. Forces in Korea, openly warned that withdrawal of U.S. ground combat forces would "increase considerably" the risk of another Korean war and said that he would be "very reluctant" to see the Second Infantry Division pulled out.[18] It was intended as a clear signal to Carter that the U.S. forces should be left in South Korea.

As a consequence of misperceptions, the South Koreans did not take Carter's policy pronouncements seriously, including his speech in Chicago. Drawing on the Korean experience that presidential incumbents are usually reelected and influenced by preference for Ford's Korean policy, they concluded confidently that Carter could not defeat the powerful incumbent. Conscious that electoral promises were rarely fulfilled in South Korea, they dismissed Carter's campaign promise as meaningless rhetoric. Asked about Carter's Korean policy in the National Assembly, Defense Minister Suh Jong-chul answered in October 1976 that one individual could not drastically change U.S. defense policy and that the U.S. forces in South Korea served security interests of Asian and Pacific nations as well as those of South Korea.[19] Throughout 1976, Suh and other Korean leaders received frequent signals and assurances from their U.S. counterparts that U.S. forces would remain in South Korea irrespective of the outcome of the presidential contest.

Even after Carter's electoral victory surprised and dismayed the South Koreans, they refused to give immediate substantive policy attention to Carter's campaign pledge on South Korea. Foreign Minister Park Tong-jin was typical. Testifying before the National Assembly, Park stated that there would be no significant change in U.S. defense commitments to South Korea under Carter's presidency because campaign promises are not always the same as presidential policy.[20] He anticipated a change of style rather than a change of policy and predicted that if any military withdrawal was to occur, the South Korean government would enter into "prudent and sufficient consultation" with Washington. However, in a face-saving gambit, a week before Carter's inauguration, the South Korean government stated that it would not be opposed to the withdrawal of U.S. forces provided North Korea agreed to conclude a nonaggression treaty with South Korea.[21] It was highly unlikely that this proviso would be satisfied. At the same time, President Park emphasized the urgent need for accelerating key defense industries and mobilizing the nation under his continued leadership. In an attempt to discourage military provocations from North Korea and to alleviate domestic anxieties about Carter's Korean policy pronouncement, Park declared that "in terms of combat capabilities, the Republic of Korea is almost on level with North Korea." He added, "If we are invaded by the North Korean Communists, the U.S. will automatically support us in view of the presence in Korea of the American troops and the ROK-U.S. Mutual Defense Treaty."[22]

Confident that President Ford would be reelected, Japanese leaders tended to ignore Carter's campaign speeches on Korea as their South Korean colleagues had done.[23] In contrast to South Korea's cautious self-restraint after Carter's victory, the Japanese frankly expressed serious reservations about Carter's pledged military disengagement from South Korea. Tokyo was fearful that any precipitous U.S. troop pullout might easily upset the precarious military balance in the Korean peninsula and therefore have a highly destabilizing effect upon Japan's security and economy. In the Japanese scenario, the sudden pullout of U.S. forces might encourage a North Korean armed invasion followed by a probable communist victory over South Korea. The unification of Korea under Pyongyang would generate division within Japan over the most appropriate national defense strategy: full-scale rearmament or neutrality. Prime Minister Miki Takeo and Foreign Minister Kosaka Zentaro publicly expressed their apprehension about the future defense of South Korea and indirectly cautioned Carter against a drastic policy shift on Korea. Vice Minister of Defense Maruyama Takashi predicted continuity in U.S. security commitments to Japan and South Korea but declared that if Carter withdrew U.S. forces from South Korea, the move would destroy the cornerstone of Japan's defense program, thus necessitating the complete rethinking of Japan's security policy.[24] He observed that in the event of another Korean war Japan would face enormous problems with the influx of South Korean refugees. Furthermore, Kubo Takuya, former vice minister of Defense, urged that the United States postpone withdrawal until a changed international situation in East Asia provided assurances that a war would not result from North Korean miscalculations or South Korean ambitions.[25] And the Japanese ambassador to the United States, Togo Fumihiko, who emphasized the importance of a U.S. military presence in South Korea at various public forums, was the most enthusiastic spokesman for South Korea's security interests in the United States.[26]

When Fukuda Takeo, a close personal friend of President Park, replaced Miki as Japan's prime minister toward the end of 1976, the South Koreans had high hopes that as their own influence in Washington waned as a result of the Koreagate scandals, the Fukuda Administration could effectively represent South Korea's interests and persuade Carter to change his position on the troop withdrawal issue. For example, in congratulating Fukuda on his new post, the *Korea Herald* (December 26, 1976), a government-subsidized English-language daily, commented editorially that South Korea expected him to reaffirm the inseparability of the security relations of South Korea and Japan and to give "fresh, dynamic momentum" to the establishment of closer trilateral cooperation between South Korea, the United States, and Japan. In his *Newsweek* (January 10, 1977) interview, Fukuda stated that under the present circumstances it would not be "particularly wise" for the United States to withdraw its troops from South Korea. He reiterated Japan's official view that the security issue in the Korean peninsula had a "close bearing" on Japan and the rest of Asia.

Fukuda's public position and utterances on the troop withdrawal issue underwent an appreciable change about the time of Vice President Walter F. Mondale's Tokyo visit at the end of January 1977. Although Mondale told Fukuda that as an Asian and Pacific power the United States would "preserve a balanced and flexible military strength in the Pacific" and maintain "a stable situation on the Korean peninsula," the vice president explained Carter's determination to withdraw U.S. ground forces from South Korea, while keeping U.S. air power in the area.[27] Fukuda expressed Japan's apprehensions regarding the possible regional repercussion of Carter's intended move and suggested that the United States provide substantial compensatory military assistance to South Korea to prevent destabilizing military imbalance in the peninsula.[28] Mondale also received an antipullout petition signed by many LDP Dietmen, including two members of the Fukuda cabinet.[29] Soon thereafter, Fukuda moderated his public opposition to the withdrawal of U.S. troops from South Korea. Insisting that the issue was basically a bilateral matter between the United States and South Korea, the prime minister declared, "the Japanese government does not intend to intervene or mediate between the two."[30]

Understandably, the South Koreans were puzzled by Fukuda's reversal. A combination of considerations prompted Fukuda to alter his public stand. The prime minister recognized that since it was unlikely that Carter would back off from a policy that had already been decided, prolonged public opposition would be fruitless and, worse still, might damage Japan's prestige and credibility. More importantly, Fukuda was afraid that if he persisted, the United States might demand that Japan shoulder a portion of the cost of defending South Korea or share in the military responsibility.[31] Yet Fukuda informally continued his attempts to influence U.S. security policy toward South Korea, providing his assistance in the interest of better mutual understanding between Seoul and Washington. To the United States, the prime minister discreetly expressed South Korea's interests and aspirations, and with South Korea, he shared his assessment of U.S. policy intentions.

If the South Koreans were initially puzzled by Fukuda's shift, they were clearly irritated by the way in which Mondale's visit to Tokyo was conducted. They viewed Mondale's failure to include Seoul in his itinerary as a diplomatic insult.[32] The South Korean pique was intensified when the vice president summoned to Tokyo the ambassador to Malaysia, Frank Underhill, a reputed proponent of U.S. military disengagement from South Korea, but not the ambassador to South Korea, Richard Sneider. The South Koreans did not publicly display any sign of their displeasure with Mondale's mission in order to avoid complicating relations with the new Carter Administration. As we will see later, the White House's insensitivity to South Korean feelings was manifested repeatedly in the following months.

Even before Mondale's arrival in Tokyo, the newly inaugurated Carter Administration outlined a preliminary plan for military withdrawal in the Presidential Review Memorandum (PRM) No. 13 prepared by the National Security Council. The PRM indicated that Carter's campaign commitment to military pullout must not be questioned and asked the Joint Chiefs of Staff (JCS), the Central Intelligence Agency, the State Department, and the Defense Department to look at the possible courses of action that might be appropriate to reduce the ground force level in South Korea.[33] In short, having set a firm policy, Carter instructed the interagency review process to identify a range of specific methods for policy implementation.

Secretary of State Cyrus Vance and Secretary of Defense Harold Brown supported Carter's premise that with adequate U.S. air cover the South Koreans were capable of defending themselves against North Korea. However, some top career bureaucrats, such as Edward Hurwitz (director, Office of Korean Affairs, Department of State), suggested that disengagement be delayed until the South Korean forces became capable of dealing with the North Korean military threat.[34] Based on intelligence assessments of President Kim's aggressive intentions and the North's military capabilities, the CIA expressed some reservations about Carter's plan. Yet the strongest resistance came from the JCS. In their annual military posture report, submitted to Congress in January 1977, the JCS clearly stated:

> In Korea, American military presence is the tangible manifestation of our commitment to the security of the Republic of Korea. Our presence helps deter North Korean agression [sic] toward the South, thus making a vital contribution to the stability of the Northeast Asian region in general. . . . Our security relationship with Japan requires

a continued U.S. Force presence and access to bases and facilities. These bases, along with the U.S. forces deployed in Korea, visibly reflect U.S. intent, will, and readiness to live up to our commitments. . . . While South Korea continues to improve its armed forces through a qualitative modernization program, U.S. forces, and logistic support will continue to be required to maintain the relative military balance on the peninsula as the ROK progresses toward self-sufficiency.[35]

Mindful of strategic considerations, the JCS was reluctant to withdraw all U.S. ground forces from South Korea over a period of four or five years. On March 7, 1977, in response to PRM No. 13, the JCS, with General Vessey's concurrence, recommended to Secretary Brown a phased, partial reduction of 7,000 Army personnel through September 30, 1982, conditioned upon an ongoing review of the Korean situation.[36]

On the same day Foreign Minister Park Tong-jin said in New York:

In view of the fact that U.S. military presence in South Korea has been playing a deterrent role against a possible conflict on the Korean peninsula and that the North Korean Communists have not renounced their ambition to reunify the peninsula by force, the proposed withdrawal or reduction of U.S. forces in South Korea appears to be premature and unrealistic.[37]

He observed that the United States had no concrete plan for phasing out its military presence in South Korea. A couple of days later, and a few hours before his scheduled meeting with President Carter, Park was shocked by Carter's nationally broadcast press conference. In obvious disregard for the JCS recommendation and without prior consultation with South Korea or Japan, Carter stated that he would stand by his campaign pledge to withdraw U.S. ground troops from South Korea over a period of four to five years, would leave behind a residual unit of U.S. troops under South Korean control, and would provide air cover for South Korea "over a long period of time."[38] He also said that his administration would lift the ban on the travel of U.S. citizens to North Korea, Vietnam, Cambodia, and Cuba. During picture-taking ceremonies with Park at the White House, Carter casually asked his guest's reaction to the press conference, and Park replied that he had not had an opportunity to examine the full text. Then Carter strongly pressed Park to end the violation of human rights in South Korea.

The entire episode proved humiliating for Park, who never regained his respect for the president. A high-ranking South Korean diplomat frankly admitted that Park's astonishment partially resulted from the obsession of the South Korean Embassy in Washington with the bribery scandals and from its inattention to indications of active policy deliberation and rapid progress in the interagency review process.[39] In a different assessment, a prominent general in the South Korean Joint Chiefs of Staff bitterly attributed Carter's "unilateral decision and unilateral announcement" of a troop withdrawal to the president's "ignorance" and "inexperience" in international politics.[40] Another top foreign policy specialist in the Blue House characterized Carter's behavior as "insensitive," "discourteous," and "arrogant."[41] Foreign Minister Park's report on his meeting with Carter bolstered President Park's defiant approach toward the United States. President Park later stated that "even now, the nation is well-prepared to overwhelm North Korea in any confrontation."[42] In an apparent attempt to relieve public anxieties, the defense minister boasted in the National Assembly that South Korea's "military power surpasses that of North Korea at present."[43]

Japanese government leaders were also disillusioned by Carter's policy announcement on Korea. In spite of Mondale's earlier pledge to undertake full consultations with Japan, the Japanese were not consulted, nor did they receive prior notification regarding Carter's unexpected announcement. Since Fukuda, as foreign minister in 1971-72, had directly suffered from the Nixon "shocks," he was especially conscious of any indication that Carter shared Nixon's insensitivity. With the approach of the prime minister's visit to Washington, Fukuda experienced increasing pressure from influential pro-Seoul members of the LDP. The Japan-South Korea Parliamentarians' Union (which included 243 Japanese Dietmen) warned Fukuda as well as Carter that any reduction of U.S. ground forces in South Korea would produce instability not only in the Korean peninsula but also throughout the Northeast Asian region.[44] The LDP's Security Affairs Research Council, headed by former Minister of Defense Sakata Michita, urged Fukuda to inform Carter of its opposition to the military pullout from South Korea.[45] The council stressed that the U.S. ground troops in South Korea symbolized the U.S. security commitment abroad and that their withdrawal would have an undesirable social and psychological impact on Asian nations.

In the joint communiqué issued after the Carter-Fukuda summit meeting in late March 1977, Carter reiterated his commitment to a "balanced and flexible military presence in the Western Pacific," while Fukuda promised to contribute to the stability and development of that region in economic and other fields. They noted "the continuing importance of the maintenance of peace and stability on the Korean peninsula for the security of Japan and East Asia as a whole." The communiqué added:

> In connection with the intended withdrawal of United States ground forces in the Republic of Korea, the President states that the United States, after consultation with the Republic of Korea and also with Japan, would proceed in ways which would not endanger the peace on the Peninsula. He affirmed that the United States remains committed to the defense of the Republic of Korea.[46]

Carter stubbornly refused to accept Fukuda's proposal for using the term "reduction" instead of "withdrawal" in the joint communiqué. While Carter exhibited no change in his basic withdrawal policy, he responded sympathetically to Fukuda's suggestion of significant compensatory measures for South Korea.

On April 21, 1977, the Interagency Policy Review Committee chaired by Secretary Vance examined the diverse responses to the PRM No. 13, and it was followed by the National Security Council meeting chaired by President Carter on April 27. On May 5, Carter issued the Presidential Directive (PD/NSC-12) on troop withdrawal plans.[47] Although Carter's military withdrawal policy had drawn sporadic criticisms and skeptical warnings from top Republican leaders (for example, former President Ford and Senator Charles Percy), conservative Democratic senators (for example, Senator John Sparkman, chairman of the Senate Foreign Relations Committee), and retired generals (General Richard Stilwell, former commander of the U.S. Forces in Korea and Admiral Thomas Moorer, former JCS chairman), the most dramatic and devastating challenge was launched by Major General John K. Singlaub, chief of staff, U.S. Forces in Korea. In an interview with a *Washington Post* correspondent in mid-May, Singlaub bluntly stated that "if we withdraw our ground forces on the schedule suggested, it will lead to war."[48] He charged that Carter's decision was based upon outdated intelligence reports on North Korea's military capabilities. Angered by Singlaub's apparently deliberate insubordination, Carter recalled him immediately to the White House, reprimanded him, and relieved him of his Korean post. The President's swift action was taken to discourage open challenges from active-duty commanders and to reassert civilian supremacy over sensitive military affairs. Seeking to avert a smaller version of the controversy with MacArthur, Carter reassigned Singlaub to be chief of staff of the U.S. Army Forces Command (Fort McPherson, Georgia).

The Singlaub incident restrained the professional military from public anti-Carter utterances on Korea, the B-1 bomber, and other military issues. More importantly, the Singlaub uproar alerted the administration that its management of the highly controversial and politically explosive Korean issue required caution. The president's vociferous domestic critics challenged him to demonstrate that his withdrawal policy would be carried out carefully and responsibly, and in close consultation with South Korea and Japan.

In the first opportunity to answer these critics, the president dispatched to Seoul and Tokyo his top two envoys — General George S. Brown, JCS chairman and Under Secretary of State for Political Affairs Philip C. Habib, who was the former ambassador to South Korea and had years of experience in Korean affairs. Equipped with PD/NSC-12, Habib and Brown presented a preliminary withdrawal plan to President Park and apparently stated that it was Washington's nonnegotiable intention to withdraw U.S. ground forces within five years. He accepted Carter's withdrawal decision as a *fait accompli* and proposed that the United States: (1) reaffirm its treaty commitments for South Korea's security;

(2) provide a relatively modest compensatory package to South Korea *in advance* of the initial troop pullout; (3) keep the headquarters of the Second Infantry Division in South Korea until the final stage of the troop withdrawal; and (4) leave behind tactical nuclear weapons as a significant war deterrent. Park and the U.S. envoys discussed other issues, such as operational command structure, diplomatic initiatives, and human rights. A few officials in the Ministry of Foreign Affairs believed that South Korea should exploit Carter's domestic political vulnerability following the Singlaub case and press Washington for as much as $10 billion in compensatory aid. On the advice of the Ministry of Defense, President Park decided "not to beg" from the U.S.[49] Park was proud of South Korea's well-prepared, self-reliant defense posture and had confidence in his country's ability to purchase necessary arms abroad. Further, Park may have learned an unpleasant lesson from the 1970 experience, when the United States drastically slashed his $4 billion request for military assistance to $1.5 billion and then failed to fulfill that pledge on time.

Generally satisfied with Park's reaction, Habib and Brown reassured him on the U.S. treaty commitment and agreed to consider his request for compensatory measures. However, the envoys expressed their preference that delivery of compensatory measures parallel the troop withdrawal.[50] On the issue of tactical nuclear weapons, Habib and Brown were noncommittal, citing the need for further review by the United States. On their way home, they briefed Prime Minister Fukuda and other Japanese leaders on the Seoul discussions. The U.S. envoys felt that the Japanese leaders accepted the U.S. policy for troop withdrawal as a "very reasonable plan," but they were disappointed by the fact that Japanese Defense Minister Mihara Asao revealed to the press Washington's carefully guarded plan to withdraw 6,000 men from South Korea by 1978.[51]

After making a detailed report to President Carter, Habib and Brown explained their East Asian mission to the House International Relations Committee and the Senate Foreign Relations Committee. General Brown emphatically dissociated himself from Singlaub's view, stating that while there was some risk involved in U.S. troop withdrawal from South Korea, it was of an acceptable degree.[52] Habib defended Carter's decision on the following grounds: (1) South Korea had achieved impressive economic growth over the past decade and had strengthened its own defensive capabilities; (2) neither the Soviet Union nor China would encourage or support a North Korean armed invasion; (3) the United States would accommodate Seoul's and Tokyo's request to supply equipment to South Korea "to offset the fighting power of the ground forces withdrawn"; and (4) the U.S. would leave air squadrons and key support and naval units in South Korea. "These forces, coupled with the major U.S. forces remaining in the Western Pacific," he asserted, "provide a clear, visible U.S. deterrent to any possible North Korean miscalculation." Habib added that the ground troops withdrawn from South Korea would be redeployed in the United States and in consequence would "provide greater and much-needed flexibility in meeting U.S. world-wide contingency requirements."[53]

Habib's remarks graphically reflected a basic conceptual cleavage between the strategic perspective of South Korea (and Japan) and that of the United States. Whereas South Korea and Japan were preoccupied with the possible adverse effects of the announced troop withdrawal upon their narrow national or regional interests, the United States, as a superpower, needed military flexibility to deal with strategic contingencies, especially in Europe.[54] The envoy's testimony indeed confirmed the fear of both South Korea and Japan that, under President Carter, Washington was shifting its military priority from East Asia to Europe and that it became a less than dependable ally in the nuclear age. This fear prompted a Japanese Cabinet member (probably Watanabe Michio) to state that Carter's strategic orientation was antiyellow.[55] It was ironic that Habib, who only a year before had told the Congress that the U.S. troop presence in South Korea was essential in the peninsula, was now given the difficult task of defending Carter's withdrawal policy, which he had personal reservations with.

TABLE 3.1
Military Force Balance: South Korea and North Korea
(1977)

Type of Force	South Korea	North Korea
Personnel:		
Active Forces	600,000	520,000
Reserve Forces	2,800,000	1,800,000
Maneuver Divisions	19	25
Ground Balance:		
Tanks	1,100	1,950
Armored Personnel Carriers	400	750
Assault Guns	0	105
Antitank	—*	24,000
Shelling Capability:		
Artillery/Multiple Rocket Launchers	2,000	4,335
Surface-to-Surface Missiles (Battalions)	1	2-3
Mortars	—*	9,000
Air Balance:		
Jet Combat Aircraft	320	655
Other Military Aircraft	200	320
Antiaircraft Artillery Guns	1,000	5,500
Surface-to-Air Missiles (Battalions/Sites)	2	38-40
Navy Combat Vessels	80-90	425-50

*Data deleted by Senate Committee on Foreign Relations.

Source: Senate Committee on Foreign Relations, *U.S. Troop Withdrawal from the Republic of Korea: A Report by Senators Hubert H. Humphrey and John Glenn* (Washington, D.C.: USGPO, 1978), p. 27.

Shortly after the Habib-Brown mission, the Tenth Annual Security Consultative Meeting was convened at Seoul in July 1977. As suggested by President Park, Defense Secretary Brown carried a personal letter from President Carter, in which Carter declared that the U.S. decision to withdraw its ground forces from South Korea over a four- or five-year period did not signify any "change whatsoever in our commitment to the security of the Republic of Korea" and that U.S. determination to provide prompt support for South Korea against armed attack remained "firm and undiminished."[56] After a series of negotiating sessions, Brown and his South Korean counterpart, Suh Jong-chol, stated:

> The North Korean threat remains serious . . . it is essential to maintain and strengthen the defense capabilities of the Republic of Korea, at a state of readiness sufficient to deter a renewal of hostilities on the Korean peninsula.[57]

The United States' side clarified its decisions to withdraw 6,000 soldiers by the end of 1978, to phase out the remaining ground forces by 1981 or 1982, to maintain the headquarters of the Second Infantry Division until the final phase of the withdrawal, and to strengthen its air force, navy, intelligence units, and logistic support personnel in South Korea for the indefinite future. In return, the United States agreed to seek Congressional approval for transferring the Second Division's military hardware (worth $500 million) to South Korea, providing one-time credit support ($300 million) for South Korea's five-year force improvement plan (1976-81), and increasing foreign military sales (FMS) credits ($1.1 billion for five years at 8 percent annual interest rate). In a compromise the United States promised to implement the aforementioned $1.9 billion compensatory measures "in advance of or in parallel with the withdrawals."[58] The measures answered, with one or two exceptions, everything that the South Koreans requested. The two sides also agreed to expand joint military exercises and to establish a combined command structure to improve operational efficiency for South Korea's defense. There was no public reference to the pullout of U.S. tactical nuclear weapons from South Korea, but Brown committed the United States to retain its nuclear umbrella over South Korea.

Returning from Seoul, Secretary Brown consulted with Japanese Prime Minister Fukuda and Defense Minister Mihara and urged Japan to increase its economic cooperation with South Korea and to share the cost of maintaining the U.S. military presence in Japan.[59] Upon his return to San Francisco, Brown explained the role of Japan in America's troop withdrawal policy:

> Question: Is Japan prepared to contribute to the defense of South Korea?
>
> Secretary Brown: . . . Japan, while an economic superpower and a politically important power, is not a major military power. Nevertheless, Korea and the territorial integrity of South Korea, independence of South Korea, are indeed important to Japan because

of geographical proximity and economic interaction. I think that the best way for Japan to contribute to Korean defense — and it's a very important way — is the economic terms, by continuing their substantial rate of investment in Korea and by assuring liberalized trade relations. By doing that, Japan can have a very important positive effect on Korean economic capabilities, and given sufficient economic strength, I am confident that Korean efforts in their own defense — to assure their own defense — will be adequate.[60]

Meanwhile, the U.S. Congress, disturbed by the Singlaub affair and concerned about Carter's Korean policy, adopted an increasingly assertive and critical stance toward the executive branch. The new mood was particularly pronounced in the Senate. The reponse of the House was constrained by the ongoing, politically sensitive investigations of the South Korean influence-buying scandals. Republican senators spearheaded a frontal assault against the president's Korean withdrawal policy. Sharing Singlaub's view, Barry Goldwater (Rep., Arizona) called Carter's policy "ridiculous" and "dangerous." Strom Thurmond (Rep., South Carolina) accused Carter of committing a "serious mistake," based upon a politically motivated campaign promise. Two powerful pro-Carter southern Democratic senators — John Sparkman (Dem., Alabama), chairman of the Foreign Relations Committee, and John Stennis (Dem., Mississippi), chairman of the Armed Services Committee — called upon the administration to display extreme caution and to undertake a policy reassessment in regard to Korea.

On the other hand, liberal Democratic senators, notably George McGovern (Dem., South Dakota) and John C. Culver (Dem., Iowa), defended Carter's decision and worked for the Senate's formal endorsement of it. Culver argued that after maintaining a U.S. military presence in South Korea for about 25 years, it was necessary to remove the "security blanket."[61] Like Habib, Culver stressed South Korea's "enormous" economic strength and "formidable" military power, surpassing that of North Korea's numerically smaller army. In Culver's opinion, the phased troop pullout would blunt the international criticism that South Korea was a "vassal state" of the United States and could improve the atmosphere for serious negotiations between South and North Korea. He dismissed the likelihood of a North Korean invasion, contending that neither the Soviet Union nor China would support it. Characterizing Carter's policy as "responsible and prudent," Senator McGovern introduced an amendment expressing Senate support for the administration's troop withdrawal plan.

In May 1977, a few days before the Singlaub uproar, the Senate Foreign Relations Committee adopted the McGovern amendment. Less than one month later, the amendment was defeated by a vote of the full Senate. The Senate also killed the Dole amendment, which repudiated Carter's Korean policy. In an effort to find a compromise position between the two extreme amendments, while expressing the prevailing mood of the Senate, the senators accepted an amendment by Majority Leader Robert C. Byrd (Dem., West Virginia), which declared that "U.S. policy toward Korea should continue to be arrived at by joint decision of the President and the Congress." This amendment, which was incorporated into the FY 78 Foreign Relations Authorization Act, stipulated that the United States should implement the "gradual and phased reduction" of U.S. ground forces in South Korea, but not their "withdrawal."[62] This should be done, according to the amendment, in stages consistent with the security interests of South Korea and U.S. interests in Asia, notably Japan. The president was required to submit to Congress a written annual report treating implementation of this policy in Korea.

When President Carter signed the FY 78 Foreign Relations Authorization Act in August 1977, he accommodated Congressional reservations about his Korean policy. Undoubtedly, the act was a symbolic insult to the president's wisdom and integrity, but it was not a fatal blow to his Korean policy. Beyond an immediate concern with the Korean issue, the Byrd amendment represented a larger constitutional and political issue, which had emerged during the 1970s, especially in the context of the Vietnam War and the Watergate scandals. It allowed the Congress to oversee and restrain unilateral presidential decisions on sensitive international matters. The tension was exacerbated by Carter's amateurish handling of legislative liaison, especially his failure to undertake policy consultations with Congress. Regarding Carter's Korean policy, this episode was another learning experience, sensitizing him to Congressional prerogatives and the consequences of Congressional recalcitrance toward his presidential leadership. In addition, it had an unmistakably sobering effect on the administration's approach to Korea.

The Carter Administration used various diplomatic channels to explain its Korean policy to Moscow, Peking, and Pyongyang. During his visit to Peking in August 1977, Secretary Vance evidently asked the Chinese leaders to exercise their moderating influence over their North Korean allies. President Carter reported to the Congress that "we have made it clear to both the People's Republic of China and the Soviet Union that the withdrawal decision signals no weakening of our commitment." He added, "The North Korean Government should be in no doubt about our position."[63] The North Koreans cautiously welcomed Carter's withdrawal decision but remained skeptical about his ability to carry it out.[64]

The debate over Carter's Korean policy was not confined to Congress but spilled into other sectors of the attentive public, particularly academia, the media, and the strategic community. The issues examined ranged from substantive policy matters (assumptions, conditions, and consequences of withdrawal) to technical procedures (timing, phases, and methods of withdrawal). Carter's critics embraced a variety of political views and emphasized a few themes, which were reiterated in prominent national publications. But most of his defenders came from a narrowly based alliance of liberal political forces, especially radical ideologues, who were not ideologically comfortable with Carter and whose policy recommendations were more extreme than Carter could afford to accommodate. The arguments against his policy were based on the assumption that the presence of U.S. ground forces in South Korea symbolized the seriousness of the U.S. defense commitment, effectively deterred a North Korean invasion, and constituted "a key element of the American military umbrella over our principal ally in Asia — Japan."[65]

The rapid escalation of polemics that Carter's Korean policy spurred in the United States during 1977 and 1978 was matched by a similar tendency in Japan. While that sector of elite and mass opinion outspokenly opposed to a U.S. military presence in Korea and Japan remained strong, an increasing number of Japanese strategic analysts, political and economic leaders, and government officials publicly expressed their reservations about Carter's military policy toward Korea. Noting the importance of Carter's repeated security commitments and promised compensatory measures for South Korea, the Japanese Defense White Paper (1978) carefully voiced Japan's apprehension that the planned withdrawal might upset the existing military balance on the peninsula and, more importantly, might have an adverse psychological impact on South Korea's political stability and North Korea's calculations.[66] Yet it concluded that another major armed conflict in Korea was highly unlikely, which was partially due to the restraining influence of the United States-Soviet-Chinese tripolar strategic system in Northeast Asia.

In South Korea, public discussions were uniformly in opposition to Carter's policy. Even President Park's critics — opposition political parties, student activists, dissident intellectuals, and religious leaders — did not favor the withdrawal of U.S. ground troops. This section of South Korean opinion was convinced that in the absence of a strong U.S. military presence in South Korea, Park's repression would become more severe.

Processes of Carter's Policy Retreat

As the combined pressure against Carter's Korean policy mounted in the other principal centers of the U.S. power structure (that is, Congressional, military, business, and bureaucratic), it easily overwhelmed the diffuse voice of the president's supporters. It also effectively undermined his authority vis-à-vis the Congress and the military establishment. His agenda for the Panama Canal treaties and SALT II negotiations were adversely affected. Consequently, despite his tenacious personality and self-righteous conviction, the president needed to reassess the domestic political costs of his military decision on Korea and to consider an expedient, tactical retreat. In contrast to the president's ill-considered and instinctive decision on military withdrawal, the strategy of retreat was deliberate, careful, and well coordinated. Undeniably, Japan's expressed dissatisfaction with Carter's Korean policy contributed to his policy reappraisal. However, South Korea's ability to influence Carter was substantially limited by the embarrassing bribery scandals and human rights controversies. In an effort to exert indirect influence in Washington, the South Koreans relied upon the assistance of the pro-Seoul forces in Japan, publicized North Korea's aggressive designs and military buildup, and wooed United States' influential retired generals, prominent academics, and other opinion leaders.

The first public hint of Carter's policy reassessment appeared in his January 1978 State of the Union message. He said, "We are seeking to readjust our military presence in Korea by reducing our ground forces on the Peninsula and undertaking compensatory measures to ensure that an adequate balance of forces remains."[67] It seemed significant that instead of "withdrawing," he used "reducing," a term that he had steadfastly refused to incorporate in his 1977 joint communiqué with Prime Minister Fukuda. The new phrase "adequate balance of forces" was intended to reassure critics who feared that the troop pullout would create a drastic and destabilizing imbalance. It also implied that if the "compensatory measures" were not implemented and/or if the "adequate balance" were not ensured, his Korean policy might change. The theme of implicit policy change was repeated by top U.S. officials at home and in Seoul. In regard to the U.S. policy of troop pullout, Ambassador Richard L. Sneider observed that "nothing is so inflexible that it cannot be changed."[68] Similarly, in testimony given before the House International Relations Committee in February, Defense Secretary Brown hinted that the plan for military withdrawal might be modified, if, unexpectedly, North Korea's military capabilities grew faster than South Korea's or if North Korea exhibited a pattern of aggressive behavior.[69] In March Assistant Secretary of State Richard C. Holbrooke promised the House Subcommittee on Asian and Pacific Affairs a "continuing assessment of the security situation in Korea."[70] And Assistant to the President for National Security Affairs Zbigniew Brzezinski admitted his shortcomings (and by implication Carter's) in having paid insufficient attention to Asian problems, especially the issue of troop pullout from South Korea, over the past year.[71] This public self-criticism suggested a perceived need for reappraisal of the Korean policy. Taken together, these statements and suggestive language appeared to have been designed as the foundation of the first stage of Carter's policy retreat on Korea.

In early April 1978, the Investigations Subcommittee of the House Armed Services Committee prepared the most devastating report on Carter's Korean policy. It concluded that Carter had arrived at his withdrawal decision well before his inauguration and had not sought "advice, assistance, recommendations or estimates of probable impact of his withdrawal decision on U.S. security considerations or stability in the Far East from the Joint Chiefs of Staff." The report stated that North Korea was superior to South Korea in every key index of military capabilities except manpower (see Table 3.1) and that President Kim was "aggressive" and "irrational." As a regional consequence of the loss of South Korea, it contended:

With no remaining western buffer against communism, Japan would be faced with the choice of embracing Marxism or embarking on a crash rearmament program, both actions bound to create major instability in Northeast Asia. Moreover, if South Korea were to fall under Communist control as a direct result of U.S. withdrawal, this would provide conclusive proof to Asian nations of the inability and unwillingness of the United States to prevent further Communist expansion in Asia. Thus, America's influence in the Western Pacific would largely come to an end.[72]

Shortly after this report was completed, President Carter announced the adjustment in the scheduled troop pullout: the withdrawal of only one battalion (800 persons) of the Second Division in December 1978; postponement until 1979 of the withdrawal of the other two battalions of the brigade originally slated for withdrawal in 1978; and removal of 2,600 noncombat personnel by the end of 1978.[73] In justifying this decision, administration spokesmen made much of the possibility that the crowded legislative calendar and the bribery investigations would delay Congressional action on the president's requests for an $800 million equipment transfer bill and $275 million in foreign military assistance credits. Since the United States agreed in the 1977 Brown-Suh communiqué to implement compensatory measures "in advance of or in parallel with" the troop withdrawals, it became prudent for Carter to change the withdrawal schedule. Administration officials emphasized that this adjustment did not signify any substantive change in Carter's campaign promise. However, it is conceivable that Congressional inaction was used as a convenient excuse for a revision of Carter's military policy in Korea. The Carter Administration may have known the forthcoming development in Congress; in less than three weeks after Carter's announcement, the $800 million equipment transfer bill was unanimously passed by both the House International Relations Committee and the Senate Foreign Relations Committee.

South Korea was very pleased with Carter's announcement. Immediately, Foreign Minister Park praised it as a "reasonable action."[74] Many South Koreans became optimistic that Carter might give up his withdrawal plan altogether. This hope was well expressed in the *Korea Herald* editorial (April 15, 1978), which observed that Carter "may change his mind now or in years to come and consider it [troop pullout] no longer relevant or realistic in view of new developments and requirements that arise in the meantime."

The Fukuda government in Japan voiced a similar hope. In May 1978, Prime Minister Fukuda evidently urged President Carter not to pull out a single battalion of U.S. troops from South Korea before the transfer of compensatory equipment and arms. Fukuda's strong advocacy of the South Korean position conspicuously differed from his earlier public posture of announced noninterference in the bilateral affairs between Washington and Seoul. Like Fukuda's active approaches to China and Southeast Asia, this shift was a manifestation of the prime minister's newly assertive foreign policy and a reflection of his political self-confidence. Moreover, he felt freed from his earlier misperceptions that had constrained his public statements on the U.S. military presence in South Korea. In Japan, the holding of open debates on security issues sparked a pro-Seoul movement among political leaders and allowed Fukuda to express his own sympathetic positive feeling toward South Korea.[75]

Although Carter's domestic critics applauded his adjustment of the troop adjustment schedule, the very fact of his tactical retreat encouraged them to demand substantive concessions on the administration's Korean policy. The hawkish House Armed Services Committee adopted Representative Samuel Stratton's amendment that asked the President to postpone any troop pullout until Congress approved the compensatory aid legislation and to keep at least 26,000 troops in South Korea until South and North Korea sign a peace agreement.[76] A Senate Armed Services Committee report expressed concern over the anticipated destabilizing effects of Carter's policy on Korea and East Asia and asked the secretary of defense to provide the committee with a six-point analysis prior to any withdrawal of combat troops from South Korea.[77] The report was clearly designed to question the wisdom of the Carter Administration's security policy and to establish a legal basis for Congressional oversight of the administration's compliance with the terms of the Byrd amendment (1977). Predictably, Carter's Korean policy became a convenient target for partisan Republican attacks. Amidst the heightened Congressional controversy over his Korean policy, President Carter promised to House Speaker Thomas P. O'Neill and Senate Majority Leader Robert C. Byrd that "should circumstances affecting the balance change significantly, we will assess these changes in close consultation with the Congress, the Republic of Korea, and our other Asian allies. Our plans will be adjusted if developments so warrant."[78]

The full Senate adopted the Senate Armed Services Committee report by an overwhelming vote. It also approved Carter's Korean security assistance bills but declared that Carter's troop pullout plan might upset the military balance in Northeast Asia. This nonbinding declaration was a toned-down version of Senator Percy's original amendment, which characterized Carter's troop withdrawal policy as contrary to the U.S. security interests and to the interests of peace in Asia. Similarly, the House rejected the extreme amendments of Representative Stratton, which would have directed the president to maintain 26,000 troops in Korea until the conclusion of a North-South peace pact.

By signing the International Security Assistance Act in September 1978, President Carter acquiesced in all the Congressional restrictions and reservations that challenged the soundness of his Korean policy.[79] Substantively, the act authorized $1,167 million in aid for South Korea: $800 million for military equipment transfers through 1982; $275 million in foreign military sales credits; $2 million in grants for military training assistance; and $90 million in stockpiles of ammunition, spare parts, and other war reserves. Final Congressional approval of compensatory military assistance measures removed a legislative, though not political, stumbling block to the implementation of troop withdrawal in South Korea.

The specific implementation of U.S. compensatory measures for South Korea was the subject of serious negotiations between Washington and Seoul. At the Eleventh Security Consultative Meeting at San Diego in July 1978, both sides agreed on a military hardware package that the United States would either sell to South Korea or transfer at no cost. After Carter's initial military policy announcement concerning Korea, South Korea had begun urgent preparations for defense self-reliance. Seoul accelerated its ambitious $7.6 billion plan to improve its forces between 1976 and 1981 and increased military expenditures from $2 billion in 1977 to $2.8 billion in 1978. Frantically, it developed and implemented programs to purchase sophisticated arms abroad, predominantly from the United States, and to expand domestic defense industries.

Even if the U.S. government discouraged South Korea's development of sophisticated defense industries, Washington was rather enthusiastic, for security and economic reasons, about selling South Korea expensive weapons systems. During fiscal years 1977 and 1978 (that is, from October 1976 to September 1978), South Korea agreed to buy more than $1 billion in arms from the United States, and South Korea's arms purchase agreements were expected to sharply increase ($1.2 billion) in fiscal year 1981. The trend ran counter to Carter's campaign pledge to reduce foreign arms sales. At San Diego in 1978, Defense Secretary Brown agreed in principle to sell 60 F-16 aircraft to South Korea, despite objections by the Arms Control and Disarmament Agency. The sale of these highly maneuverable, superior, lightweight combat fighters would violate Carter's own rule against introducing "newly-developed, advanced weapons systems" into regional disputes.[80]

In addition to the massive arms sales, Washington enhanced deterrence capabilities and, thus, South Korean security in other ways. The Carter Administration reiterated its pledge to maintain a nuclear umbrella over South Korea, augmented the U.S. Air Force by 20 percent, and conducted impressive joint military exercises with South Korea. The United States deployed and trained its Air Force combat forces in Japan for the primary purpose of defending South Korea; Okinawa served as a staging base for United States-South Korean exercises and as a supply base for U.S. munitions designated to South Korea.[81] In November 1978, the United States and South Korea inaugurated the Republic of Korea-United States Combined Forces Command (CFC). The CFC assumed operational control over South Korean forces but was also expected to do so over U.S. forces in Korea in the event of hostilities. Even though the CFC did not completely satisfy the South Koreans' hope for a NATO-type command structure where both sides could enjoy equal and integrated operational status, it provided them with a sense of sharing operational responsibilities with their U.S. counterparts and with a further experience of coordinating both forces in the case of renewed hostilities. The CFC also permitted the United States to continue its operational influence over South Korean forces even after withdrawal of its own ground combat forces. As General Vessey suggested, the CFC was a psychological move to show that the United States was not deserting South Korea after all.[82]

By the end of 1978, the legal (Congressional approval), financial (military aid and sales), and organizational (CFC) frameworks necessary for implementation of Carter's withdrawal policy were in place. In accordance with the revised timetable, the president had completed the pullout of one battalion in April and withdrawn 2,600 noncombat personnel from South Korea in December 1978. However, at the end of the year, he was ambivalent about his withdrawal policy and uncertain about its immediate prospects. Carter faced a political dilemma. He had won the necessary conditions for policy implementation at considerable cost. He could persist in his intended course at the risk of certain, strong, domestic political opposition and damage to his ability to manage foreign and national security policy. The president's ambivalence increased with his awareness that the public aversion to U.S. foreign military commitments (especially in Asia), which prevailed in the immediate post-Vietnam years, had moderated. This shift in public mood had undercut one rationale of Jimmy Carter's initial decision regarding Korea. Most importantly, the president received new intelligence data that sharply altered his risk structure and made follow-through on his initial decision even less defensible.

The new data, as leaked to *Army Times* (January 8, 1979) and other newspapers, indicated that North Korea had 40 army divisions (not 29 as previously estimated) and 2,600 tanks (not 2,000) and that North Korea enjoyed "clear ground superiority" over South Korea. Although the administration insisted that there would be no change in policy because the new estimates reflected only an improvement in intelligence capabilities and did not demonstrate a recent North Korean buildup, the news leak generated irresistible, and ultimately decisive, domestic political pressure against implementation of the president's policy. In January 1979, Representatives Samuel Stratton (Dem., New York) and Robin L. Beard (Rep., Tennessee), members of the House Committee on Armed Services, asked the president to defer any further withdrawal of U.S. troops from South Korea until the full significance of the new intelligence data could be evaluated.[83] A group of influential bipartisan members of the Senate Committees on Armed Services and Foreign Relations issued a study report, in which they concluded that new intelligence information on the North Korean threat "argues strongly for both the retention of the 2nd Division in Korea now and an accelerated modernization and improvement of the ROK army."[84] They further elaborated on this conclusion in their meeting with President Carter. In retrospect, it is important to note that upon Carter's election General Vessey, an unmistakable opponent of Carter's withdrawal policy, had initiated the army's extensive analysis of North Korean military capabilities.[85]

Under these circumstances, President Carter did not have a viable option but to make a further tactical retreat in his Korean policy. On February 9, 1979, Carter announced:

Over a period of time, I think the troops ought to be brought back from Korea. We have had our troops there for 30 years, and I have made a basic decision that the troops should be brought back. The rate of returning them to the United States is constantly being assessed. We have already brought back a few. Right now we are holding in abeyance any further reduction in American troop levels until we can assess the new intelligence data on the build-up of North Korean force levels, the impact of the normalization with China and the new peace proposal or discussions for peace that have been put forward by both the North Korean and the South Korean Governments.[86]

The timing of this announcement was probably intended to mollify the growing Congressional criticism against Carter's Asian policy, particularly in the immediate aftermath of Washington-Peking diplomatic normalization.

Many observers in Washington, Seoul, and Tokyo expected that a complete reversal in Carter's Korean policy was only a matter of time. The U.S. intelligence agencies carefully examined the new data on North Korean military capabilities and reached the consensus that North Korea had dramatically surpassed South Korea in every major category of military might. In accordance with this consensus, the JCS, in April 1979, recommended that the United States should suspend any further troop withdrawal from South Korea at that time and reassess the issue of Korean military balance in 1981.[87]

The South Korean leaders hoped that during Carter's state visit to Seoul at the end of June 1979, he would announce the end or, at least, the indefinite postponement of U.S. troop withdrawal. However, the president's advisors considered it politically unwise for Carter to make such an announcement while in Seoul because it might convey the impression of a hasty, ill-considered decision, made under South Korean pressure. Indeed, they were prepared to reiterate in the joint communiqué President Carter's belief that U.S. ground troops should be withdrawn from South Korea. In a compromise of these opposing views, the joint communiqué stated that Carter assured Park that "the United States will continue to maintain an American military presence in the Republic of Korea to ensure peace and security."[88] By the request of the Defense Ministry and with the lukewarm support of the Foreign Ministry, which preferred not to refer to sensitive nuclear issues, the joint communiqué included a U.S. pledge to maintain its nuclear umbrella for South Korea's security.[89] The United States apparently urged South Korea to increase defense spending to 6 percent of the GNP.[90]

Privately, Carter assured Park that the administration's policy review, undertaken in the light of the new intelligence estimates, would be completed soon and strongly hinted that the decision would be favorable to South Korea's interest. On July 20, 1979, Zbigniew Brzezinski announced the president's decision to suspend withdrawals of U.S. ground combat units until 1981; at that time, the pace and timing of further withdrawals would be decided by evaluating progress made in the development of a satisfactory North-South military balance and the reduction of tensions in the peninsula. In explaining the president's decision, Brzezinski cited the new intelligence reports of North Korea's numerical military superiority, new diplomatic overtures toward North Korea, and changing regional conditions, such as the growth of Soviet military power in East Asia. "These modifications in our withdrawal plans," he said, "will best assure the maintenance of our security commitment, preserve an adequate deterrent, nurture the resumption of a serious North-South dialogue, and stabilize a favorable U.S. strategic position in East Asia."[91] Brzezinski made no reference to human rights or tactical nuclear weapons in South Korea. In contrast to Carter's initial withdrawal decision, it was emphasized that the present decision had been discussed with South Korea and Japan, the principal defense and foreign policy advisors, and leaders of Congress.

Hence, in two and a half years, Carter's controversial military policy toward South Korea was completely reversed. The completion of his gradual and deliberate retreat effectively betrayed his original campaign promise. His critics, especially those in Congress, welcomed his new decision. In Seoul, Foreign Minister Park applauded the decision as "very reasonable and timely" and pointed out its importance to the prevention of another Korean conflict and to the maintenance of peace and security in Northeast Asia. A high Foreign Ministry official interpreted Carter's decision as representing the indefinite postponement or perhaps the recision of his troop withdrawal policy.[92]

The evolution of decisions, adjustments, retreat, and reversals comprising President Carter's troop withdrawal policy reveals not only the domestic political and bureaucratic constraints impinging on the president's ability to redirect foreign security policy along a desired course but also illuminates the changing nature of U.S. security relations with two East Asian allies: South Korea and Japan. It further suggests that even an indisputable superpower, the United States, may find it extremely difficult to revise abruptly a long-established military policy and to influence directly the configuration of regional strategic order in Asia.

President Carter's initial conceptualization of United States-Korean security relations was shaped by his instinct for a political campaign issue and by broad strategic preferences that emphasized Europe. If Carter's foreign policy decisions were made in terms of the United States' variable global and regional interests, the South Koreans perceived their own security ties with the United States almost exclusively in the context of intra-Korean competition. They deeply regretted that neither the United States nor Japan fully understood their position. Predictably, the Japanese viewed South Korea's security in terms of its relevance to their own national defense and political stability. The observable dissonance of mutual perceptions among these three countries was attributable to the asymmetric character of their respective security interests and priorities. Consequently, the South Koreans failed to sufficiently appreciate Carter's rationale for the troop pullout decision, and the United States attempted to impose its own shifting policy criteria upon its smaller ally. Caught in the cross-currents of mutual misperception between Washington and Seoul, the Japanese first took an ambivalent public posture and then tried to buttress South Korea's arguments.

These problems of substantive triangular policy cleavage were further compounded by Carter's unilateral decision-making style. As a proud, sensitive, and fiercely nationalistic group, the South Koreans were ill disposed to tolerate procedural discourtesy or diplomatic insult on so fundamental a question as their own national security. Numerous unhappy experiences with the United States undermined Seoul's sense that the alliance system was based on mutual trust and reduced Washington's ability to influence South Korea's domestic and foreign policies. Although the Japanese were equally unhappy with the lack of prior consultation by the Carter Administration, eventually they were reassured that the United States attached particular importance to the routinized channels of policy consultation and coordination linking Tokyo and Washington. In particular, the United States-Japan Security Consultative Council and other bilateral forums were used for "very thorough" exchanges regarding Carter's military pullout policy.[93]

Clearly, the president underestimated the South Koreans' efforts to penetrate and influence the U.S. open, competitive, and pluralistic political system and to help mobilize domestic opposition to Carter's Korean policy. Although Seoul's direct lobbying operations in the United States were substantially restricted in the aftermath of the Koreagate scandals, the South Koreans were nonetheless diligent and innovative in conducting massive and expensive public relations campaigns by soliciting assistance from U.S. businessmen and pro-Seoul congressmen and carrying out imaginative "invitation diplomacy." A large number of prominent Asian scholars, political scientists, foreign policy specialists, retired generals and diplomats, and other U.S. opinion leaders were invited to various conferences and occasions in Seoul. It is difficult to estimate the extent to which "invitation diplomacy" affected the mobilization of opposition to Carter's Korean policy, but, most probably, it left some articulate members of the attentive public with a better understanding and favorable disposition toward South Korea's interests and needs.

Carter's withdrawal policy induced Tokyo and Seoul to explore ways of strengthening their bilateral diplomatic and economic cooperation, impelling them to cautiously expand the incipient, informal networks of their security policy ties. The Annual Ministerial Conference between Japan and South Korea paid increasing attention to their respective security policies and repeatedly urged caution in implementing Carter's withdrawal policy. In addition to the active and influential Japan-(South) Korea Parliamentarians' Union, the two neighbors organized a Parliamentary Security Consultative Council in 1978 for exchanging information and coordinating views regarding their security policies. The union and the council decided to include the U.S. Congress in their organizations and activities. More importantly, there was a rapid increase in reciprocal exchange of top-level Japanese and South Korean defense officials during the late 1970s. Many South Korean generals, including General Kim Jong-whan, the JCS chairman, visited Japanese defense agencies and observed military facilities, while their Japanese counterparts, including General Nagano Shigeto, chief of staff of the Ground Self-Defense Force, inspected South Korea's forward military installations and industrial complexes.[94] The Japanese ambassador to South Korea, Sunobe Ryozo, characterized these exchanges as "goodwill visits" aimed at sharing experience and information and visiting military installations and factories.[95] When Sunobe was asked whether Japan would assist South Korea's defense industries or join with South Korea in military alliance, he replied that such moves were "premature," citing Japan's constitutional constraint, negative public opinion in both countries, and adverse regional repercussions. Japan and South Korea vehemently denied the charge made by Japanese leftists and the North Korean media that both countries had embarked upon a road to bilateral military alliance or a trilateral security system under U.S. leadership. However, it was probable that Tokyo and Seoul were exchanging military intelligence and some military technology.

In regard to Korean military matters, the Carter Administration was more willing to heed Japan's policy assessment and recommendations than those of South Korea, mainly because the United States generally regarded its security relations with Japan as more important than those with South Korea. The United States was often skeptical of South Korea's policy analysis and intelligence reports on North Korea because they were presumed to be self-serving. As a result, Japan was influential in assuring U.S. compensatory measures for South Korea.

Ultimately, however, the subtle and complex Washington game of bureaucratic politics proved to be the key determinant in President Carter's policy reversal. A loose coalition of military establishments, Congressional leaders, top career bureaucrats, intelligence specialists, and pro-Seoul opinion makers effectively mobilized every conceivable argument, with supporting evidence. They maneuvered skillfully, first challenging, then destroying the strategic and political premises of Carter's Korean policy. As an inexperienced outsider in Washington's dynamic power game, Carter was overconfident about his formal presidential authority. He attempted to translate his own instinct and conviction into public policy, but lacking bureaucratic support, he was unable to carry out his pronouncements. The president failed to persuade his top military, diplomatic, and other career lieutenants, who shared a vested interest in, and a parochial bureaucratic perspective on, the continuation of the U.S. military presence in South Korea. From the beginning, General Brown, JCS chairman, General Rogers, Army chief of staff, and General Vessey were intensely dissatisfied with what they regarded as the unilateral, nonconsultative origin and inherent risks of Carter's Korean policy. Under Secretary of State Habib, a key foreign policy spokesman on Korea, had serious personal reservations about the general direction of Carter's policy. None of them publicly challenged the president's constitutional authority in foreign and security policy, but they offered only lukewarm, transparently qualified support for the implementation of Carter's policy. After Carter disciplined the insubordination of General Singlaub, skeptics and opponents in the administration entered into collusion with those in Congress, especially, members of the Armed Services Committees of both Houses, who were ready and able to speak out for the professional military and bureaucratic interests as much as for themselves. Eager to reassert lapsed constitutional prerogatives vis-à-vis the executive branch, Congress took advantage of the fragility of Carter's support base and launched a frontal legislative and political offensive against his Korean policy. The Korean withdrawal case became a convenient *cause célèbre*, which rallied the Congress to exercise its oversight function relative to the president's foreign policy. In the end, a loose coalition of anti-Carter forces won over the president's earlier supporters and created among the key policy-relevant bureaucracies in Washington a virtually unanimous opposition to the White House's Korean policy. The new intelligence report on North Korea's military buildup, a bureaucratic outcome in itself, ended any doubt about the president's capitulation. This episode demonstrates that in the context of intricate bureaucratic politics, a stubborn president who ignores the rules will find out that the power of the presidency can be severely limited.

Once President Ronald W. Reagan was inaugurated in January 1981, he quickly moved to demonstrate the United States' strong military commitment for South Korea's anticommunist stand. The joint communiqué issued by Presidents Reagan and Chon Du-hwan declared:

> President Reagan affirmed that the United States, as a Pacific power, will seek to ensure the peace and security of the region . . . [and] assured President Chon that the United States has no plans to withdraw U.S. ground combat forces from the Korean peninsula.[96]

Hence the Reagan Administration not only formalized the death of Carter's troop pullout policy but also agreed to bolster South Korea's defense capabilities as well as U.S. military strength in the peninsula.

STRAINS IN UNITED STATES-JAPAN SECURITY RELATIONS

In current United States-Japanese relations, there are two major sources of tension: persisting, unresolved economic strains, especially in the area of bilateral trade, and differing perceptions of Japan's security needs and alliance obligations, which are symbolized in the issue of Japan's defense posture and an appropriate level of military spending. If mishandled, these economic and defense issues could seriously undermine what Ambassador Mike Mansfield described as "the most important relationship in the world." The controversy over Japanese defense spending has ominous implications for bilateral relations since it is likely that Washington, in its growing concern with the Soviet military buildup and erosions of the U.S. position vis-à-vis the Soviet Union, will intensify its demands that Tokyo do more for regional defense. However, Japan will be unable to respond in a completely satisfactory way for political and economic reasons of its own.

In recent years, the United States has issued repeated bipartisan calls for increased defense commitments by its major allies. In January 1981, outgoing Defense Secretary Harold Brown declared, "No American government, and still less the American people or the American Congress, are going to accept a situation in which some other country feels that it's our job to defend them and they needn't bother to defend themselves."[97] Later, the new Republican administration put the issue more forcefully. At a military policy conference held in Munich in February 1981, President Reagan's new deputy secretary of defense, Frank C. Carlucci, pointedly asked the European allies to increase their own contributions to the combined defense effort.[98] The U.S. policy makers have become increasingly concerned about the steady growth of Soviet military outlays over the past decade and a half and a roughly parallel decrease in U.S. and Western European military expenditures, measured in real terms. Georgia Senator Sam Nunn notes: "Since 1970, the Soviet Union has invested a total of $104 billion more than the United States in military equipment and facilities and $40 billion more in research and development."[99]

If the United States is displeased with the defense commitments of its European allies, it is even more unhappy about the level of the Japanese commitment. As shown in Chapter 1, U.S. dissatisfaction with Japan's limited defense role has had a long, postwar history. Particularly after the mid-1960s, Washington has often criticized Japan as a "free rider," which failed to assume international responsibilities commensurate with its newly acquired economic power while depending heavily on the United States for its own defense. Although such criticism did not always lead to an explicit call for increased Japanese defense expenditure, it was usually associated with a demand that Japan speed up liberalization of its trade and capital investment practices or restrain its exports to the U.S. market. In recent years, the "free ride" criticism has become closely and directly linked to what many people in the United States see as an insufficient Japanese defense effort.[100] U.S. critics point out that while the United States has been spending over 5 percent of its GNP annually for defense and the European allies between 3 and 5 percent, Japan allocates less than 1 percent, despite that country's enormous economic success and large trade surplus with the United States. However, as Table 3.2 indicates, the Japanese failure to increase defense spending beyond 1 percent of the GNP does not necessarily mean that Tokyo's defense budget has not been growing at

TABLE 3.2
Defense-related Expenditures of Japan: 1960-80

Fiscal Year	Defense Expenditures[1] (original budget) unit: 100 million yen[2]	Defense Expenditures[1] (original budget) unit: million dollar	Growth from Previous Year (%)	Ratio of Defense Budget to GNP (%)[3]	Ratio of Defense Budget to General Accounts (%)
1960	1,569	436	0.6	1.23	9.99
1961	1,803	501	14.9	1.15	9.23
1962	2,085	579	15.6	1.18	8.59
1963	2,412	670	15.7	1.18	8.46
1964	2,751	764	14.1	1.14	8.45
1965	3,014	837	9.6	1.07	8.24
1966	3,407	946	11.8	1.10	7.90
1967	3,809	1,058	11.8	0.93	7.69
1968	4,221	1,173	10.8	0.88	7.25
1969	4,838	1,344	14.6	0.84	7.18
1970	5,695	1,582	17.7	0.79	7.16
1971	6,709	1,864	17.8	0.80	7.13
1972	8,002	2,598	19.3	0.88	6.98
1973	9,355	3,037	16.9	0.85	6.55
1974	10,930	3,549	16.8	0.83	6.39
1975	13,273	4,309	21.4	0.84	6.23
1976	15,124	4,910	13.9	0.90	6.22

(continued)

Table 3.2, continued

| Fiscal Year | Defense Expenditures[1] (original budget) | | Growth from Previous Year (%) | Ratio of Defense Budget to GNP (%)[3] | Ratio of Defense Budget to General Accounts (%) |
	unit: 100 million yen[2]	unit: million dollar			
1977	16,906	5,489	11.8	0.88	5.93
1978	19,010	7,256	12.4	0.90	5.54
1979	20,945	10,473	10.2	0.90	5.43
1980[4]	22,302	9,912	6.5	0.90	5.24

[1] Defense expenditures represent the total amount of expenditures of Defense Agency, Defense Facilities Administration Agency, and National Defense Council plus part of Finance Ministry's national property special consolidation fund.

[2] The exchange rate of $1 is equivalent to 360 yen (1960-71), 308 yen (1972-77), 262 yen in 1978, 200 yen in 1979, and 225 yen in 1980.

[3] To calculate the ratio of defense budget to GNP, the estimated GNP at the beginning of each fiscal year is used.

[4] Government draft budget.

Sources: Boei Hakusho 1980 [Defense of Japan 1980] and the Ministry of Foreign Affairs, 1980.

a fairly high annual rate. Nor does it mean that the Japanese have not become relatively more conscious of defense during the past decade.

The Changing Japanese Attitude toward Defense

For many years, the memory of prewar militarism and of the national experience with the scourge of war has sustained a dominant, antimilitary (or pacifist) mood in Japan. This mood has often been expressed in popular and political opposition to the United States-Japan mutual security treaty and Japan's Self-Defense Forces (SDF), as well as to increased defense spending. However, over the last several years, emotionalism has given way gradually to a greater realism in security discussions within Japan, and public support for the treaty and the SDF has increased. According to a 1978 *Asahi Shimbun* public opinion poll, 49 percent of the respondents said the treaty was beneficial for Japan, as compared with 34 percent in a 1974 poll.[101] Public opinion surveys conducted by the prime minister's office showed that support for the SDF had increased from 58 percent in 1956 to 86 percent in 1979, as shown in Table 3.3. Traditionally, opposition political parties (particularly the Japan Communist Party, the Japan Socialist Party [JSP], and the *Komeito*) have parroted the slogan of "demilitarized neutrality" for Japan. However, they now appear more pragmatic about the realities of Japan's security. Thus, the JSP and *Komeito* "coalition government" plan (January 1980) incorporated important qualifying statements, which the parties had staunchly opposed, regarding the security treaty and the SDF. The treaty would be abrogated "without damaging friendly relations between the U.S. and Japan," and "for

TABLE 3.3
Public Opinion: Is a Self-Defense Force Necessary to Japan?

Year	Better to Have	Don't Know	Better Not to Have
1956	58%	24%	18%
1959	65	24	11
1963	76	18	6
1965	82	13	5
1967	77	17	6
1969	75	15	10
1972	73	15	12
1975	79	13	8
1977	83	10	10
1979	86	9	5

Source: Prime Minister's Office, Japan.

the time being" the two parties would concentrate on the creation of a new international environment that would render the treaty unnecessary. In accordance with Japanese public opinion and the principles of an independent and peaceful diplomacy, the JSP and *Komeito* pledged to reduce and restructure the SDF and, "for the time being, strengthen civilian control over the forces."[102] Moreover, according to a poll cited by Okazaki Hisahiko, a ranking Defense Agency official, 61.3 percent of those who voted for the Communist Party answered that defense forces are necessary even though the party still refuses to recognize the existence of the Self-Defense Forces.[103]

Until the mid-1960s, it was taboo for Japanese public figures to talk about the need for improving the country's defense or security. Now, defense-related discussions occur routinely in the National Diet, and in April 1980 a "Special Committee on Japan-U.S. Security Treaty and Defense Matters" was established in the House of Representatives. Former Foreign Minister Okita Saburo called the creation of the committee a product of "the popular consensus to deal with the issue of our security."[104]

What factors account for the changing Japanese attitude toward defense? First, Japan is increasingly aware of the growing Soviet military presence in Northeast Asia. The Soviet Union has permanently deployed supersonic Backfire bombers along the coastal zones of its Maritime Province. Strategic analysts believe that more than half of the 2,060 fighters and fighter-bombers in the Soviet Union's Far Eastern air force are of the most advanced types.[105] Furthermore, the Soviets have added at least one new, major surface ship and one submarine to their Pacific Fleet every year for the last decade. At the beginning of the 1980s, there were approximately 785 ships, 75 submarines (3 nuclear-powered), and more than 350 naval aircraft. Soviet warships and aircraft operate in the outer seas including the area around Japan. Approximately 195 Soviet aircraft approaches to Japan have been reported each year, and an estimated 360 Soviet warships pass through the Tsushima, Tsugaru, and Soya Straits annually.[106]

In addition, the Soviet Union has begun a significant military buildup a few miles off Hokkaido — in the "northern territories" (Kunashiri, Etorofu, and Shikotan islands and the Habomai group) claimed by Japan since 1945. Currently, more than a division of Soviet troops along with a large contingent of MIG-17s and ground-to-air missiles are deployed in the area.[107] Finally, the Soviet invasion of Afghanistan increased Japanese nervousness about the Kremlin's intentions.

Changing attitudes of Japan's Asian neighbors also may be a factor underlying Tokyo's growing defense consciousness. Most importantly, after the Sino-Japanese diplomatic normalization in 1972, China ended its harsh attacks on "new Japanese militarism" and today encourages greater Japanese defense efforts within the framework of the United States-Japan security system. Undoubtedly related to Peking's perception of an increasing Soviet military threat, this Chinese policy shift apparently influenced the attitudes of the opposition parties and their supporters who had been parroting the Chinese criticism of the "new Japanese militarism." In addition to the regional Soviet military buildup, the "diminishing" U.S. presence is a source of apprehension among Japan's Asian neighbors. In a January 1981 interview with the *Asahi Shimbun*, Prime Minister Lee Kuan Yew of Singapore asserted: "In East Asia, the reduction of U.S. forces since the Vietnam War contrasts disconcertingly against the buildup of Soviet power around the Indian and Pacific oceans . . . Japan should complement U.S. effort to match this growing challenge."[108]

With the U.S. withdrawal from Indochina and U.S. efforts to reduce its regional military presence (for example, the 1976-77 Carter policy on troop levels in South Korea), the Japanese themselves are becoming more apprehensive about a possible "security vacuum" in Asia. Thus, while increasingly conscious about the need for assuring the security of their country (as reflected in higher levels of expressed public support for the SDF and the security treaty), the Japanese have become less confident about the U.S. security commitment to Japan. As 1968 and 1979 *Asahi* polls suggest, there has been a decline in the credibility of U.S. pledges to protect Japan.

Question: In case of emergency, do you think the United States will come and defend Japan?

	Oct. 1969	Nov. 1978
Yes	31%	20%
No	47	56
Others (including "Don't Know")	22	24

Source: "The Trend of Public Opinion in Japan Concerning Japan-U.S. Security Treaty and Defense Issues," Ministry of Foreign Affairs, June 1979.

Momoi Makoto, a staff member of Japan's Defense Research Institute, goes so far as to say: "The American commitment to Japan is now a limited commitment. It is no longer the unlimited commitment Japan once thought it was."[109]

The foregoing attitudinal and perceptual changes notwithstanding, there remain significant differences between the defense consciousness of the public in Japan and the United States. According to opinion polls conducted in March 1980 in Japan and the United States by the *Yomiuri Shimbun* and the Gallup organization respectively, U.S. citizens are much more willing to fight for their country and to pay more taxes for increased defense spending.

Question: Which statement best describes what you personally would do if our country were invaded by a foreign power?

	Japan	U.S.
Take up arms to fight	20.6%	72.8%
Resist without taking up arms	33.7	10.9
Escape to a place of safety	23.9	8.7
Give in to the invaders	6.7	0.6
Don't know	15.1	7.1

Question: Would you approve or disapprove of increasing personal
income taxes for the purposes of national defense?

	Japan	U.S.
Approve	21.0%	42.7%
Disapprove	68.1	47.3
Don't know	10.9	10.0

Source: The Daily Yomiuri, May 13, 1980.

Suzuki and the Fiscal Year 1981 Defense Budget

In response to mounting U.S. pressure for a greater Japanese defense commitment following the Iranian takeover of the U.S. Embassy in Teheran, Prime
Minister Ohira Masayoshi assured President Carter in their May 1980 Washington
meeting that Tokyo would make a serious effort to improve Japan's self-defense
capabilities. In one of his first official statements, the new Japanese Prime
Minister Suzuki Zenko said that he supported Ohira's earlier pledge to the
United States. Suzuki advised the new defense minister, Omura Joji, to undertake the qualitative improvement of the SDF.[110]

Encouraged by the prime minister's public posture, prodefense groups
in and outside the Japanese government lobbied for a major defense budget
increase in Japan. Calling attention to recent international developments and the
U.S. pressure for more Japanese defense spending, the Defense Agency and the
defense-related committees of the Liberal Democratic Party demanded a 15
percent increase for fiscal year 1981. They argued that anything less than 15
percent would not placate U.S. Congressional critics or meet Washington's
request for accelerating the implementation of Japan's five-year defense plan.[111]
Major opposition to a substantial increase in the defense budget came from the
leftist parties as well as the Finance Ministry, which was eager to limit increases
in government spending in order to reduce Japan's bulging deficit.[112] The
ministry had set an across-the-board 7.5 percent ceiling on budget increases for
fiscal year 1981. Defense Agency officials and their supporters requested an
exemption for the defense budget, which, it was agreed, would not exceed 1.0
percent of the GNP. Arguing that in view of the high rate of deficit financing,
the defense budget should not go over 0.9 percent of the GNP, and that budgets
for education, welfare, and official development assistance were equally important, the Finance Ministry refused to accede to the Defense Agency's request.[113]
The issue was finally resolved through direct negotiations between Defense Minister Omura and Finance Minister Watanabe Michio. Watanabe agreed in principle
that his ministry would allow defense a de facto budget increase of up to 9.7
percent without formally exempting the defense budget from the across-the-board
ceiling. This would be done by excluding from the defense budget the expenses
for U.S. military aircraft that Japan had contracted to buy.[114]

On the basis of this agreement, the Defense Agency thought that it had approval for at least a 9.7 percent increase in defense spending for fiscal year 1981. This interpretation quickly reached U.S. officials, who felt that the 9.7 percent increase was not enough. On August 1, 1980, the U.S. State Department issued a statement asking Japan to increase the defense budget. In a speech at the Commonwealth Club in San Francisco on August 8, Secretary of State Edmund Muskie called for more Japanese defense spending. On September 16, Ambassador Mike Mansfield called on Foreign Minister Ito Masayoshi to ask for more defense spending.[115]

In subsequent intragovernmental budget negotiations, opposition grew to a budget increase much beyond the 7.5 percent ceiling. Focusing on the dangers of runaway deficit financing, this group gradually gained the upper hand in the bureaucratic "tug-of-war." Also, many people rejected the notion that Japan had to increase its defense spending simply because the United States was pressuring Japan. By November 1980 it had become less certain that the Defense Agency would get a budget increase close to 9.7 percent. Against this background, Ambassador Mansfield advised Foreign Minister Ito that many U.S. officials regarded the 9.7 percent increase as "the touchstone of our bilateral relations."[116] In Washington, U.S. officials told three visiting former Japanese defense ministers, Sakata Michita, Kanemaru Shin, and Mihara Asao, that Japan should secure at least the 9.7 percent increase.[117]

On the eve of Defense Secretary Harold Brown's scheduled visit to Japan from December 11 to 12, Prime Minister Suzuki was not confident that the 9.7 percent increase could be attained for the Defense Agency. Critics insist that Suzuki did not push the Finance Ministry hard enough. Unlike most of his predecessors (for example, Ikeda Hayato, Sato Eisaku, Fukuda Takeo, and Ohira Masayoshi), Suzuki was not a Finance Ministry bureaucrat who had become a politician and may have lacked expertise and influence on the budgetary process. Also, he may have underestimated the power of the Finance Ministry bureaucracy.[118] Facing mounting domestic pressure to control the country's deficit financing, the prime minister stated on the eve of Secretary Brown's visit that "it would be wrong to assume that the trustworthiness of the U.S.-Japan relationship will be [damaged] unless [we achieve] certain levels of defense spending."[119] Upon learning of the Japanese government's apparent difficulty in getting the 9.7 percent increase in defense spending, the U.S. defense secretary expressed his deep concern and warned that "this [problem area] could spill over into other areas of the U.S.-Japan relationship." Brown indicated that the United States was not satisfied with the size of the proposed increase and called for additional increases. He made it clear that the incoming Reagan Administration agreed with the Carter Administration that Japan's failure to strengthen its military stance would affect the bilateral relationship. Suzuki's reply was that the 9.7 percent increase would be the maximum Japan could afford in the deficit-ridden 1981 budget.[120]

Despite repeated U.S. warnings, the defense budget underwent a substantial downward revision in the final stages of the Finance Ministry's budget compilation process. On December 29, the Suzuki Cabinet adopted its final defense budget for fiscal year 1981, which allowed a 7.6 percent increase over the previous budget. This decision reportedly "dumbfounded" some U.S. officials. Secretary Brown was quoted as saying the 7.6 percent increase "falls seriously short . . . [and] is so modest that it conveys a sense of complacency" on Japan's part. Responding to domestic and U.S. criticisms, Prime Minister Suzuki said that his government did its best under the circumstances. He stated that there simply "does not exist a national consensus for giving 'special treatment' to the defense budget, especially at a time when the government is in deep deficit and may have to boost taxes."[121] Although the Foreign Ministry officials advocated a larger increase for Japan's defense budget, they took the responsibility to explain to their U.S. counterparts that in both fiscal years 1980 and 1981 the percentage increase for the defense budget far exceeded the percentage increase for general government expenditures and that in 1981 the increase for general expenditures was held down to a 4.3 percent level, while the defense budget increase edged out that of social welfare (7.61 percent vs. 7.60 percent).[122] Japan's total defense spending for 1981 would be about $11.5 billion. When calculated by NATO methods (which include pensions and other extra items not in the Japanese defense budget), it would amount to $18 billion, thus making Japan the sixth largest defense spender in the world.[123]

Given the existing gap in defense consciousness between the two countries and the continuing pressures of heavy deficit financing on the Japanese government, the bilateral dispute over Japanese defense spending is likely to be repeated unless the United States can take a long-term view and refrain from pressuring Tokyo for a specific budget increase. As noted earlier, some of the intragovernment opposition to a high defense budget increase came from those people who resented the U.S. pressure tactics. In a spring 1980 *Nihon Keizai* poll of members of Japan's House of Representatives, almost 50 percent (including LDP members) responded negatively to the question of whether they should accept the U.S. request for increasing Japan's defense budget, while only 29 percent answered in the affirmative. Among those giving a negative reply, there were quite a few who favored improving Japan's defense capabilities.[124] Apparently, they wanted to determine Japan's defense policy on the basis of its own national interest and not simply in response to U.S. pressure.

Now that the Japanese people have regained their self-confidence and national pride, excessive U.S. pressures in defense (and other) matters may prove counterproductive. The Japanese are becoming more conscious of defense at their own pace and in their own way. U.S. pressures to rapidly accelerate this trend may reverse it or, more likely, provoke an anti-United States nationalistic backlash among the people, thereby encouraging Japanese rearmament efforts divorced from the U.S.-Japan security system. This is not to say that the United States should not try to influence Japanese defense policy. Rather U.S.

policy makers would be well advised to act with greater sensitivity to the pressures on Japanese policy makers and quietly encourage the ongoing trend in Japan.

Japan's Comprehensive Security Policy

In the Japanese view, the U.S. concept of security is often too narrowly construed in military-strategic terms. A recent study of Japan's national security requirements (commissioned by former Prime Minister Ohira) conducted by a group of Japanese government officials and academics concludes that Japan's defense policy should be based on a mixture of military and nonmilitary measures ranging from diplomacy and alliance building to maintaining and augmenting, if necessary, its self-defense forces. Thus, the study suggests that despite the recent deterioration of Japan's relations with the Soviet Union as a result of closer Sino-Japanese relations, Tokyo should cultivate relations with the Soviets in a manner that appears "self-confident, [yet] unhostile."[125] In fact, the Japanese seem to be inclined toward an equidistant policy toward Moscow and Peking.

Although it is difficult to ascertain the extent to which the Japanese government has decided to incorporate these and other study recommendations, the Suzuki government has begun to emphasize what it calls a policy of "comprehensive security," which appears similar in substance. In a policy speech at the ninety-fourth session of the National Diet in January 1981, Prime Minister Suzuki defined his government's security policy as follows:

There has been heightened popular understanding and concern for defense questions in recent years. National concern for defense is fundamental to the state's survival, and I hope that this will be widely and constructively debated as an issue for all of the people and a national consensus formed.

Under our peace constitution, Japanese defense is dedicated to purely defensive capabilities, we will not become a military power threatening neighboring countries, and we have as our basic policy a firm commitment to the three non-nuclear principles [not to manufacture, not to use, and not to possess nuclear weapons]. I am resolved to continue to firmly uphold this position and to ensure Japan's security in the spirit of defending our country ourselves with the cornerstone of the Japan-U.S. Security arrangements while seeking to build up a moderate yet sophisticated defense capability.

At the same time, in considering recent international developments and Japan's position in the world, it is clear that it is difficult to ensure Japan's peace and security through enhancing the defense capability alone. In order to protect Japan's peace and security, it is crucial that we promote the various foreign and domestic policy measures comprehensively and integratedly.

Accordingly, the first imperative is that we persist in our diplomacy for peace. It is especially important that we participate actively in the North-South Summit scheduled to be held this year and that we vigorously promote economic and technical cooperation in order to contribute to solving the problems of developing countries. Although Japan faces a period of difficult fiscal restructuring, I will make efforts to expand our official development assistance and increase the rate of ODA to gross national product. For this purpose, I will take measures which include, among others, aiming at more than doubling in the coming five years the aggregate ODA-related budget in the past five years.

Also it is essential that the security of stable and smooth supplies of foodstuffs and resources such as energy be promoted while seeking harmony with all countries.

It was with these thoughts in mind that I established the ministerial conference on comprehensive security within the Cabinet last December. For the future, I am resolved to promote a comprehensive Japanese security policy while maintaining consistency among the various measures in this conference.[126]

While the Suzuki government is not necessarily undertaking a major shift from traditional postwar Japanese policy, it appears to have reinterpreted the basic premises in a more comprehensive way, which foreshadows a more activist posture. This may not please the Reagan Administration, which will expect more visible military support from the United States' main ally in Asia. Yet even within the U.S. policy community, there are those who approve of Japan's low military posture. For instance, a study on Japanese security policy conducted by the U.S. Arms Control and Disarmament Agency in June 1980 underscores the stabilizing role of the low level of Japanese military efforts in postwar Northeast Asia:

Japan's role as an economically powerful, but lightly armed nation is an important influence [in the maintenance of stability in the region]. Japan's deliberate policy of foregoing the development of offensive military capabilities has demonstrated to traditional adversaries that Japan's economic and technological strength need not foreshadow military ambitions, nor otherwise threaten the security of other nations. The acceptance of this perspective has encouraged the development of mutually advantageous economic and political relations between Japan and other near-by nations, heightening a common stake in the stability of the status quo. This is particularly evident with respect to China's progressive opening to the West, including its recent dramatic steps to normalize relations with both Japan and the United States. Although Soviet-Japanese relations remain less friendly [a result mainly of continuing territorial dispute], although correct, the limited character of Japanese rearmament, coupled with Japan's firm alliance with the United States, has made possible the avoidance of significant political conflict and, to some extent, permitted at least the prospect of mutually beneficial economic ties.

While it is unclear to what extent Japan's salutary influence on regional stability would have been less had it pursued rapid rearmament at some point during the past 25 years, at a minimum, a significant Japanese military buildup would have made Japan's reconciliation with former adversaries more difficult, delayed Japan's reentry into the international community, potentially threatened Japan's economic growth, and hurt Japan's attempts to sustain a viable, if fragile domestic consensus on defense and foreign policy issues.[127]

Senator John H. Glenn, who (as chairman of the Senate Subcommittee on East Asian and Pacific Affairs) commissioned the study, concurred with its findings, saying, "I would certainly agree that it would be neither in the Japanese interest, nor in our interest, for Japan to embark on a sudden, massive build-up of its military forces."[128] Although the climate of opinion among Japan's Asian neighbors is changing slowly in favor of a more active regional role for Japan, thus compensating for the "diminishing" U.S. military presence, most leaders of Southeast Asian countries would agree with Senator Glenn. "Japan is a successful economic empire," President Ferdinand L. Marcos of the Philippines recently told Japanese reporters in Manila. "She would find it in her interest to see that she limits her defense expenditure to purely defensive equipment."[129]

Suzuki signaled the high priority that Tokyo attaches to relations with Southeast Asia when he made his first overseas trip as prime minister to the Association of Southeast Asian Nations (ASEAN) — the Philippines, Indonesia, Singapore, Malaysia, and Thailand — in January 1981. On this trip, he pledged greater Japanese economic assistance to the ASEAN countries, not a greater Japanese military role in the region. In the past five years, Japan has spent about $10.7 billion on Official Development Assistance (ODA), and, as Suzuki said in his National Diet speech, its ODA is to be doubled to $21.4 billion. A Japanese Foreign Ministry spokesman commented: "The speed with which Japan is increasing aid is not surpassed by any other country. In 1980 Japan overtook France and is now very close to West Germany in absolute volume. We will become No. 2 [after the U.S.] very soon."[130] But in terms of the percentage of GNP, Japan dispenses more economic assistance than the United States. In a role reversal, a Japanese Foreign Ministry official walked over to the U.S. Embassy in Tokyo to deliver a message of consternation: big cuts in U.S. foreign aid under the Reagan Administration, he declared, would have "a deplorable effect on international efforts to help poor countries."[131]

Politically, it is much easier for the Japanese government to increase spending in economic assistance than on rearmament. Thus, it is conceivable that if Japan's *combined* spending for aid and defense increased visibly, while the defense budget *per se* remained below or did not grow much above 1 percent of the GNP, U.S. criticism of "insufficient" Japanese defense efforts might be defused. At the least, it seems worthwhile for Japan to move in that direction. In a published interview, former CIA Director William Colby implicitly recognizes the value of this approach for strengthening bilateral relations between the two allies.

> Let's say the [Japanese] military budget is 1% or below 1% of GNP. I think there will be continuing [U.S.] criticism. . . . I do not think you're going to eliminate that criticism by jumping from 1 to 2%. I do think you might eliminate that criticism if you increased it to 4 or 5%, putting most of it into economic progress, and thereby show that there is a comprehensive security approach. . . .
>
> . . . if Japan were way ahead of us in terms of the amount of effort that she is making [in the area of economic assistance], then I think there would be general understanding that the Japanese have made a major effort in the area appropriate for Japan to contribute. This is the way alliance should work: that we do not necessarily do the same things, but we each do the thing that is appropriate to a good relationship between us.[132]

The combined or comprehensive security approach might be appreciated even more by the United States if Japan were to increase its military cooperation with the United States in every possible way, within the framework of the incremental annual increase in defense spending. For example, Tokyo could assume an increasingly larger portion of the costs for maintaining U.S. troops in Japan. With the relative decline of the U.S. economic position, this financial burden is strongly felt by the United States and may sharpen Washington's perception of the security treaty as an asymmetrical and increasingly onerous obligation. Article 5 of the treaty gives the United States the responsibility for defending Japan, although Japan has no reciprocal obligation to defend the United States. However, Article 6 of the treaty permits the United States to use military bases in Japan for the maintenance of peace and security in the Far East as a whole. Presently, the United States spends about $1.4 billion each year to maintain 45,000 military personnel in Japan. In the future, the United States may be tempted to reduce substantially the size of these forces to cut expenses. In fiscal year 1979, Japan contributed about $1 billion (about 10 percent of the defense budget) to help offset the costs of the U.S. military deployment in Japan. This Japanese financial contribution could be increased further, at least in the same proportion as the defense budget increase. Although the Status of Forces Agreement stipulates that the Japanese will shoulder the expenses in providing bases (acquiring land, etc.) and the United States will assume all other expenses, this provision can be interpreted liberally. Formal revision of this agreement, which requires National Diet approval, may create an unnecessary political controversy in Japan.

In addition to such financial support, it will be important for Japan to increase cooperation with the United States in the area of joint defense planning and coordinated military exercises. In this sense, the adoption of the Guidelines for Japan-U.S. Defense Cooperation in November 1978 was a step for mutual benefits.[133] Insofar as Japan's security is vitally dependent on a stable supply of energy and other natural resources from foreign sources (for example, the Middle East in the case of oil), simply defending the country against direct foreign aggression would not be sufficient to assure security for the country. In this regard, Wohlstetter writes: "Our major allies in Western Europe and in Northeast Asia vary in their dependence on oil from the [Persian] Gulf, but their dependency is very great. It is so great that it makes little sense to ask whether an attack on the gulf is less important than an attack on [their own territory]."[134]

In light of this interpretation of national security, it might be logical for Japan's SDF (and NATO forces) to participate in joint allied efforts to maintain peace and security in the Persian Gulf and to keep the oil-shipping lanes open. After all, "Washington has shouldered the burden of defending Western and Japanese interests in the Middle East, which provides 70 percent of Japan's oil but only 10 percent of United States consumption."[135] While such undertakings are logical, Japanese laws do not permit the dispatching of the SDF outside Japan for military operations. The alternative may be the creation of an allied deterrence force not requiring Japanese combat participation. This was recommended in late 1980 by a United States-Japan binational security study group (headed by U. Alexis Johnson, former U.S. ambassador to Japan and under secretary of state for political affairs). Among other things, this study urges that nations not now involved in joint military operations provide merchant shipping and civil aviation support to strengthen the U.S. Rapid Deployment Force, which has not yet established itself as a credible deterrent.[136] Another recent study (jointly conducted by the Council on Foreign Relations in New York City, the Royal Institute of International Affairs in London, the French Institute for International Relations in Paris, and the Research Institute of the German Foreign Policy Association in Bonn) recommends that the United States, Britain, France, West Germany, and Japan establish a watch committee to monitor developments in Southwest Asia and that European ground and sea forces be prepared for active participation or intervention in the Middle East.[137] There is nothing in Japanese laws that would preclude Japanese civilian officials from sitting on such a watch committee.

Energy and the Credibility of the Security Relationship

Lack of cooperation in nonmilitary areas can undermine the viability of the security alliance between the United States and Japan. In the area of energy, the United States-Japanese relationship has not been without serious problems. With Japan highly dependent on external sources of energy, the issues of energy and security have long been linked in Japanese perceptions. Japan imports 85 percent of the primary energy it consumes, while imports cover only about 20 percent of total U.S. energy needs. Japan's foreign energy dependency is intensified insofar as oil constitutes 75 percent of the country's primary energy supply and as much as 99.7 percent of Japan's oil must be purchased abroad.[138] Frequently, Japanese officials have found their U.S. counterparts, preoccupied as they were with their global security concerns, not sufficiently attentive to the Japanese energy situation. On the other hand, the United States sometimes thought that the Japanese were overly preoccupied with their "narrow" economic concerns and not sufficiently supportive of the U.S. global strategic initiatives. As a result, serious strains arose in bilateral relations from time to time, such as those over Japan's nuclear energy policy and over economic sanctions against Iran.

Since the mid-1950s, Japan has been involved in a major program of nuclear energy development in order to generate electricity for commercial use. In its haste to rapidly secure more energy for economic growth, Japan entered a series of licensing arrangements with General Electric and Westinghouse companies and became heavily dependent on the importation of "proven" nuclear reactor technology. Consistent with the U.S. policy of providing technical and economic assistance for the recovery and development of its allies, the U.S. government encouraged such technology transfer and guaranteed the supply of enriched uranium (and enrichment services), while strictly prohibiting the transfer of enrichment technology. For Japan and other countries choosing U.S. reactors, this created reliance on U.S. enriched uranium supply. The U.S. government retained approval authority over where and how reprocessing of United States-supplied nuclear fuel would be done.[139]

There were no major problems in this arrangement until 1973, when the United States began to impose arbitrary conditions for enrichment services. The 1974 Indian nuclear explosion made U.S. policy makers particularly wary of the risk of further nuclear weapons proliferation and eventually culminated in President Ford's nonproliferation policy statement of October 1976, which called for a temporary deferral of commercial reprocessing and plutonium utilization. In April 1977 President Carter announced an "indefinite" moratorium on commercial reprocessing and plutonium recycling as well as on the commercialization of fast breeder reactors (FBRs).[140] Carter's policy was a serious blow to the Japanese nuclear energy program, which became a priority after the OPEC oil embargo and the energy crisis of 1973-74. Japan had planned to undertake its own reprocessing and to develop advanced fuel-efficient reactors, including the FBRs. Washington's opposition to the operation of Japan's first nuclear reprocessing plant at Tokai Mura was particularly annoying to Tokyo. Japanese leaders interpreted this opposition as an expression of the United States' completely unjustified distrust of its major Asian ally, which was unequivocally committed to the nonmilitary use of nuclear energy after its horrifying experience with the atomic bomb. The U.S. position demonstrated a high degree of insensitivity to Japan's difficult energy situation. Only after several months of arduous bilateral negotiations did the United States finally agree to allow the two-year trial operation of the Tokai Mura plant.[141]

On November 4, 1979, the U.S. Embassy in Teheran was occupied and U.S. diplomatic personnel were taken hostage by Iranian "students." President Carter immediately condemned the Iranian action as an outright violation of international law and began a series of punitive steps against Iran. The U.S. government was disappointed by the failure of the Japanese government to issue immediately a formal statement condemning the Iranian action or expressing support and sympathy for the United States. The hesitation of the Japanese government (which was subsequently criticized by some Japanese) was related to Tokyo's fears regarding Japanese-Iranian trade, particularly Teheran's continued willingness to serve Japan's oil needs. Japan was then buying from Iran more than 500,000 barrels of oil a day — that is, about 10-11 percent of Japanese daily oil consumption. Japanese officials were concerned also about the fate of the Mitsui Group's $3.5 billion petrochemical project at Bandar Khomeni on the Persian Gulf. The Japanese inaction prompted Secretary of State Cyrus Vance to tell Japanese Foreign Minister Okita Saburo in December 1979 that Japan was being "insensitive" to the U.S. anguish over Iran.[142]

The United States stopped buying Iranian oil, and U.S. oil companies that had been supplying Iranian oil to Japan cut off their supply. In urging Japan (and Western Europe) to impose economic sanctions against Iran, the Carter Administration did not mention the possibility of sharing the U.S. oil supply to compensate for the possible loss of Iranian oil. Under these circumstances, Japanese companies began to purchase a large quantity of Iranian oil on the spot market at considerably higher prices. "Washington bristled," wrote a U.S. analyst, "as the Japanese bought up at least 20 million of the 30 million barrels of Iranian oil once destined for the United States." According to the analyst, "To add further salt to the wounds — infuriating both President Carter and Secretary Vance — Japanese banks were advising Iranian financiers on how best to skirt the U.S. freeze of Iranian assets, both in American banks and in their European branches."[143] The Japanese "felt somewhat betrayed as the Department of Energy conveyed approval for Japan's purchasing of Iranian oil, given Japan's enormous reliance upon Persian Gulf crude, while the State Department publicly castigated Japan's actions."[144] Bilateral tensions did not subside until April 1980, when Prime Minister Ohira began to emphasize Japan's alliance with the U.S. in his public speeches and Japanese companies refused to pay Iran's new price of $35 per barrel for oil.[145]

What factors contributed to escalation of the conflict? The analysis of Destler and Sato singles out poor communication, especially "U.S. failure to communicate in advance, in any consistent manner, what it expected of its allies in the situation; Japanese inability, in the absence of a clear signal, to read the American scene and make reasonable adjustment to it. The latter in turn was the product, in part of decentralized Japanese decisionmaking on oil purchases."[146] On another level, as Ushiba Nobuhiko (former ambassador to the

United States) said, "Japan mistook the hostage incident's significance and acted, not from the viewpoint of violation of international law, but from the Japanese-Iranian bilateral economic relationship."[147] The United States, preoccupied with its own immediate problem with Iran, failed to appreciate the dire energy needs of Japan. Kenneth L. Adelman concludes, "The United States can and should, in such a crisis, help Tokyo find alternative means of gaining its requirements rather than leaving it out in the cold."[148]

In the years ahead, the issue of energy will continue to be crucially important in relations between Japan and the United States, the largest consumers and importers in the noncommunist world. Whether the United States can be sufficiently responsive to the energy needs of its main Asian ally will significantly affect U.S. credibility in Japan. Would the United States be willing to ship oil from Alaska to Japan instead of to the U.S. West Coast and divert imports of Indonesian oil to Japan in the event of the total interruption of oil from the Persian Gulf? This question is as important as the other fundamental question pertaining to the alliance: Would the United States come to the defense of Japan with military force if it is attacked by the Soviet Union or any other country?

The Troubled "Alliance" under Reagan and Suzuki

Ten months after he came to power in July 1980, Prime Minister Suzuki visited Washington for his first summit talks with President Reagan. But prior to this visit, there occurred two events that tended to erode further the credibility of the United States in Japan.

On April 9, 1981, a U.S. nuclear submarine named George Washington collided with a Japanese freighter, the Nissho Maru, in the East China Sea. The freighter sank and two of its crew members died as a result. The Japanese public was outraged over the fact that the U.S. submarine did not even make an attempt to rescue the Japanese crew and did not report the accident to the Japanese authorities until a day later. All major Japanese newspapers assailed this "hit-and-run" behavior of the U.S. submarine and cast doubt on the trustworthiness of the United States as an ally. The incident raised an inevitable question: Could the United States, which would not even bother to rescue the crew of a sinking Japanese freighter, be trusted to come to the defense of Japan in case of an enemy attack? A United States Navy report of the accident, which was issued almost a month later, stated that the submarine surfaced after striking the vessel but did not note any signs of damage or distress. This was unconvincing to the 13 surviving Japanese crewmen, who said the submarine surfaced 30 to 100 meters from the sinking Nissho Maru as it was hoisting a distress flag.[149]

Another unfortunate event in United States-Japan relations took place only a week before the Suzuki-Reagan summit of May 8-9. President Reagan decided to lift the grain embargo against the Soviet Union — apparently to placate the domestic farm lobby — without consulting the Japanese government "suffi-ciently in advance." Secretary of State Alexander Haig did notify Japanese officials of the upcoming U.S. policy change, but to the Japanese it appeared more like "an announcement rather than consultation." The United States had asked Japan and Western Europe in early 1980 to follow the U.S. example in imposing economic sanctions against the Soviet Union in the wake of the USSR invasion of Afghanistan. Japan went further with the sanctions than the West European countries did; it restricted the supply of new credit by Japan's Export-Import Bank, prohibited the export of high-technology products, and reduced the exchange of senior officials.[150] And even before the U.S. policy shift on the grain embargo, Japanese officials and businessmen had been annoyed by the fact that the United States did little to discourage several Western European firms from taking over Japan's plant export contracts with the Soviet Union.

During his talks with Suzuki, Reagan referred to the ship's collision as "tragic" and promised to consult Japan fully on future matters of mutual concern. But one wonders if this "promise" was sufficient to restore U.S. credi-bility in the minds of many Japanese. Reagan did express his sympathy for Japan's request to go ahead with plans for nuclear reprocessing at Tokai Mura — in contrast to his predecessor who had discouraged such Japanese efforts out of his preoccupation with nuclear nonproliferation.

While the summit itself was considered fruitful by both leaders, Suzuki immediately faced two defense-related controversies upon his return to Tokyo, which created further strains in the Tokyo-Washington relationship. The first controversy arose over the use of the word "alliance" (rather than "partners") in the Reagan-Suzuki joint communiqué.[151] The Japanese press interpreted this to mean that the bilateral relationship had entered a new period characterized by a strong military posture. The opposition parties quickly charged that Suzuki had pushed Japan into a dangerous military commitment. Although Suzuki later explained that the word "alliance" had no special military significance, this semantic controversy resulted in the resignation of Ito Masayoshi as foreign minister. This episode clearly demonstrates that the defense issue is still extremely delicate in Japanese politics, and therefore overt U.S. efforts to influ-ence Japanese policy in this area may backfire to the detriment of the best bilateral relationship.

The second controversy originated from a statement made by former Ambassador Edwin O. Reischauer during an interview with a *Mainichi Shimbun* reporter. Reischauer related that U.S. vessels had been making regular calls at Japanese ports *with nuclear weapons on board* and that the Japanese govern-ment had tacitly agreed to overlook such practices — despite Japan's "Three Non-Nuclear Principles" (not to possess, produce, or introduce nuclear weapons into the country). Reischauer's statement precipitated a major political storm in Japan, which threatened to undermine the authority of the Suzuki government and the party in power.

The United States continues to provide the nuclear umbrella over Japan, but the Japanese hypersensitivity to nuclear weapons places obvious constraints on the maneuverability of U.S. weapons systems. But if the U.S. policy is to encourage Japan to expand conventional defense capabilities while discouraging Japan's own nuclear armament, such policy may be better served by respecting the aversion to nuclear weapons among Japan's assertive domestic populace.

In the final analysis, despite the growing Japanese defense consciousness, there is a wide disparity in security perception between the two allies, and this disparity sets a clear limit on the U.S. ability to influence Japanese security policy.

NOTES

1. In 1966 Secretary of Defense Robert McNamara proposed a U.S. troop reduction in South Korea, but President Johnson overruled it. See House Committee on International Relations, *Investigation of Korean-American Relations: Report of the Subcommittee on International Organizations* (Washington, D.C.: USGPO, 1978), p. 61 (hereafter cited as *IKAR: Report*).

2. For this discussion, see Chae-Jin Lee, "The Direction of South Korea's Foreign Policy," *Korean Studies*, vol. 2 (1978), pp. 107-8.

3. As early as August 1969, Nixon told Ambassador William Porter prior to the Nixon-Park summit meeting in San Francisco that he would have to remove U.S. troops from South Korea because he was under great pressure from Representative Wilbur Mills (chairman of the powerful House Ways and Means Committee). (Nixon also made a campaign pledge to reduce troops in Asia.) See Porter's testimony in House Committee on International Relations, *Investigation of Korean-American Relations: Hearings before the Subcommittee on International Organizations*, pt. 4 (Washington, D.C.: USGPO, 1978), p. 38 (hereafter cited as *IKAR*).

4. Ambassador Porter stated in February 1970 that he had repeatedly urged the South Korean leaders to initiate a dialogue with their Northern counterparts. See Senate Committee on Foreign Relations, *United States Security Agreements and Commitments Abroad: Republic of Korea* (Washington, D.C.: USGPO, 1970), pp. 1680-81.

5. For NSDM48, see *IKAR: Report*, pp. 62-63; and *IKAR*, pt. 4, p. 41. The memorandum originally designated the Second Division to be withdrawn, but the Seventh Division was actually withdrawn.

6. *IKAR*, pt. 4, p. 41.

7. See House Committee on International Relations, *Human Rights in Korea and the Philippines: Implications for U.S. Policy: Hearings* (Washington, D.C.: USGPO, 1975), p. 41.

8. For Laird's plan, see House Committee on Armed Services, *Hearings on Review of the Policy Decision to Withdraw United States Ground Forces from Korea* (Washington, D.C.: USGPO, 1978), p. 89.

9. For the joint communiqué, see *Department of State Bulletin*, December 23, 1974, pp. 877-78.

10. Ibid., May 26, 1975, p. 669.

11. Ibid., June 2, 1975, p. 734.

12. *New York Times*, June 21, 1975.

13. *Department of State Bulletin*, December 29, 1975, pp. 913-16.

14. For conflicting interpretations, see *Axe-Murders at Panmunjom* (Seoul: Korea Herald, 1976); and *The Truth of the Panmunjom Incident* (Pyongyang: Foreign Languages Publishing House, 1976).

15. See House Committee on International Relations, *Deaths of American Military Personnel in the Korean Demilitarized Zone* (Washington, D.C.: USGPO, 1976), p. 6.

16. As quoted in Frank Gibney, "The Ripple Effect in Korea," *Foreign Affairs*, October 1977, p. 160.

17. Interview with Major Stephen Delp, May 3, 1979, Fort Leavenworth, Kansas.

18. *Washington Post*, January 9, 1977.

19. *Korea Herald*, October 19, 1976.

20. Ibid., November 5, 1976.

21. See President Park's New Year's press conference (January 12, 1977), *New York Times*, January 13, 1977.

22. *Korea Herald*, January 29, 1977.

23. Interview with Kubo Takuya (former vice minister of defense and former secretary general of the National Defense Council), July 6, 1979, Tokyo; and interview with Japanese Ambassador Sunobe Ryozo, June 14, 1979, Seoul.

24. *Asahi Shimbun*, November 9 and 12, 1976.

25. Ibid., November 11, 1976.

26. *Wall Street Journal*, November 26, 1976.

27. See *Department of State Bulletin*, May 7, 1977, pp. 190-91.

28. Interview with David Blakemore (deputy director, Office of Korean Affairs, Department of State), March 14, 1979, Washington. He gives credit to Prime Minister Fukuda for the United States' subsequent compensatory measures for South Korea. "On a number of occasions," Ambassador Sunobe Ryozo recalls, "Japan, on its own initiative, expressed a deep concern to the U.S. and presented its suggestions on compensatory military measures." Interview, June 14, 1979, Seoul.

29. They are Ishihara Shintaro (minister of the Environmental Agency) and Watanabe Michio (minister of Health and Welfare); both belong to the ultra-right wing Seirankai faction in the LDP and the Japan-South Korea Parliamentarians' Union.

30. Reuter report quoted in *Korea Herald*, February 3, 1977.

31. Interview with Kubo Takuya.

32. Interview with a foreign policy specialist in the Blue House, June 21, 1979, Seoul.

33. See the testimony of General Bernard W. Rogers (Army chief of staff) before the House Committee on Armed Services on July 13, 1977, in *Hearings on Review of the Policy Decision*, p. 78. Contents of the PRM No. 13 were leaked to *Boston Globe*, March 6, 1977.

34. *Korea Herald*, January 20, 1977.

35. See George S. Brown, "Current JCS Theater Appraisals," *Commanders Digest*, March 17, 1977, pp. 16-17.

36. Rogers' testimony, *Hearings on Review of the Policy Decision*, p. 79.

37. *Korea Herald*, March 9, 1977.

38. *Public Papers of the Presidents of the United States, Jimmy Carter, 1977*, Book I (Washington, D.C.: USGPO, 1977), p. 343.

39. Interview, June 11, 1979, Seoul.

40. Interview, June 27, 1979, Seoul.

41. Interview, June 21, 1979, Seoul.

42. *Korea Herald*, April 16, 1977.

43. Ibid., April 29, 1977.

44. See the Union's messages (February 16, 1977) sent to Carter and Fukuda, *Nikkan giren tokuho* [Special News of the Japan-South Korea Parliamentarians' Union] (Tokyo: Nikkan giinrenmei, March 1977), pp. 44-48.

45. *Asahi Shimbun*, March 15, 1977.

46. For the text, see *Department of State Bulletin*, April 18, 1977, pp. 375-77.
47. See House Committee on Armed Services, *Review of the Policy Decision to With-draw United States Ground Forces from Korea: Report of the Investigations Subcommittee* (Washington, D.C.: USGPO, 1978), p. 8. Carter announced this decision at his press conference on May 26, 1977, and promised to undertake "a very careful, very orderly withdrawal." See *Public Papers of the Presidents of the United States, Jimmy Carter, 1977*, Book I (Washington, D.C.: USGPO, 1977), p. 1018.
48. *Washington Post*, May 19, 1977.
49. Interviews with South Korean diplomats and generals, June 11 and 27, 1979, Seoul.
50. For the Habib-Brown missions, see *Juhan migun samsipnyon* [Thirty Years of U.S. Military Presence in South Korea] (Seoul: Seoul Shimmunsa, 1979), pp. 393-94. *New York Times*, May 24 and 26, 1977.
51. See *Hearings on Review of the Policy Decision*, pp. 150-56.
52. For his testimony, see *New York Times*, June 11, 1977. The same points were reiterated in his appearance before the Singlaub investigation panel on July 14, 1977. See *Hearings on Review of the Policy Decision*, pp. 111-60.
53. *Department of State Bulletin*, July 11, 1977, pp. 48-50.
54. Just as Habib argued, General Bernard W. Rogers, Army chief of staff, bluntly stated in July 1977 that "the greatest threat still . . . lies in the European scene with the Soviets and Warsaw Pact forces that have enhanced their capabilities – size, sophistication – over the past 10 or 12 years, while we were engaged in war in Southeast Asia." See *Hearings on Review of the Policy Decision*, p. 98.
55. See Professor Morton A. Kaplan's testimony in *Hearings on Review of the Policy Decision*, p. 176.
56. *Korea Herald*, July 26, 1977.
57. Ibid., July 27, 1977.
58. See General Vessey's testimony in *Hearings on Review of the Policy Decision*, p. 237.
59. For Brown's five-point requests, including Japan's increased aid to South Korea and Japan's cost sharing for U.S. military presence in Japan, see *Nihon Keizai Shimbun*, August 5, 1977.
60. *Department of State Bulletin*, September 5, 1977, p. 303.
61. For Senator Culver's view, see *U.S. News and World Report*, June 20, 1977, pp. 27-28.
62. See *New York Times*, June 17, 1977. For the White House's pledge to continue Carter's withdrawal plan despite the Senate action, see ibid., June 18, 1977.
63. See Carter's Congressional message (October 1, 1977), in *Department of State Bulletin*, December 12, 1977, pp. 852-54.
64. Interviews with North Korean diplomats, June 30, 1977.
65. Richard Stilwell, *U.S. News and World Report*, June 20, 1977. Also see his statement in House Committee on International Relations, *IKAR*, pt. 6, pp. 2-7.
66. *Boei Hakusho* [Defense White Paper] (Tokyo: Okurasho, July 1978), pp. 51-52.
67. *Public Papers of the Presidents of the United States, Jimmy Carter, 1978* (Washington, D.C.: USGPO, 1979), p. 122.
68. *Korea Herald*, January 24, 1978.
69. As quoted in *Korea Herald*, February 24, 1978.
70. *Department of State Bulletin*, April 1978, p. 32.
71. *New York Times*, March 21, 1978.
72. *Review of the Policy Decision*, pp. 1-7. The subcommittee was headed by Samuel S. Stratton (Dem., New York), one of Carter's outspoken critics.
73. See *Department of State Bulletin*, June 1978, p. 36.
74. *Korea Herald*, April 26, 1978.

75. For example, the Japan-South Korea Parliamentarians' Union, in its message sent to President Carter in January 1978, transcended its earlier public position of mild reservation and forcibly expressed its opposition to Carter's troop pullout policy. See *Asahi Shimbun*, January 14, 1978.

76. See *New York Times*, April 27, 1978.

77. The Senate Committee on Armed Services attached this amendment to the FY79 Defense Authorization Bill in 1978. See Senate Committee on Armed Services, *Korea: The U.S. Troop Withdrawal Program: Report of the Pacific Study Group* (Washington, D.C.: USGPO, 1979), p. 2.

78. See Carter's letter of June 20, 1978, in ibid., p. 7.

79. For the final bill signed by Carter in September, see *New York Times*, September 12, 1978.

80. House Committee on International Relations, *United States Arms Transfer and Security Assistance Programs* (Washington, D.C.: USGPO, 1978), p. 73. Also see *Washington Post*, November 23, 1978. For Senator Glenn's opposition to F-16 sales, see Senate Committee on Foreign Relations, *U.S. Troop Withdrawal from the Republic of Korea: An Update, 1979* (Washington, D.C.: USGPO, 1979), pp. 3-4.

81. See General Loving's testimony in *Hearings on Review of the Policy Decision*, pp. 299-302.

82. House Committee on Armed Services, *Impact of Intelligence Reassessment on Withdrawal of U.S. Troops from Korea: Hearings Before the Investigations Subcommittee* (Washington, D.C.: USGPO, 1979), pp. 72-73.

83. House Committee on Armed Services, *Report on Impact of Intelligence Reassessment on Withdrawal of U.S. Troops from Korea by the Investigations Subcommittee* (Washington, D.C.: USGPO, 1979), p. 1.

84. See *Korea: The U.S. Troop Withdrawal Program*, p. 7.

85. Interview with Major Stephen Delp (a participant in the Army's intelligence analysis), May 3, 1979, Fort Leavenworth, Kansas. For Vessey's profound concern about Carter's policy, see Robert Shaplen, "Letter from South Korea," *New Yorker*, November 13, 1978, p. 198. In July 1979, Vessey testified that it was in January 1977 that he "recommended a number of specific actions to improve our warning posture and correct basic intelligence deficiencies." See *Impact of Intelligence Reassessment*, p. 64.

86. *Public Papers of the Presidents of the United States, Jimmy Carter, 1979* (Washington, D.C.: USGPO, 1980), pp. 247-48.

87. For JCS Chairman David C. Jones' testimony, see *Impact of Intelligence Reassessment*, pp. 45-59.

88. See the Carter-Park joint communiqué, in *Department of State Bulletin*, August 1979, pp. 16-17.

89. Interview with a South Korean diplomat, July 3, 1979, Seoul.

90. *Donga Ilbo*, July 16, 1979.

91. *Department of State Bulletin*, September 1979, p. 37.

92. *Donga Ilbo*, July 23, 1979.

93. Interview with Richard Kilpatrick (deputy director, Office of Japanese Affairs, Department of State), March 14, 1979, Washington.

94. *Korea Herald*, April 7 and May 1, 1979.

95. Interview with Sunobe Ryozo, June 14, 1979, Seoul.

96. See *Department of State Bulletin*, March 1981, pp. 14-15.

97. *New York Times*, January 11, 1981.

98. Ibid., February 22, 1981.

99. Sam Nunn, "Defense Budget and Defense Capabilities," in W. Scott Thompson, ed., *From Weakness to Strength* (San Francisco: Institute for Contemporary Studies, 1980), p. 376.

100. Defense Agency of Japan, *Boei Hakusho 1980* (Tokyo: Okurasho, 1980), pp. 158-59.

101. *Asahi Evening News*, November 1, 1978.

102. *Boei Hakusho*, pp. 206-7.

103. *Look Japan*, November 10, 1980, p. 2.

104. Speech before the Special Committee on Japan-U.S. Security Treaty and Defense Matters, House of Representatives, April 26, 1980.

105. *New York Times*, December 13, 1980; *Boei Hakusho*, p. 47.

106. *Boei Hakusho*, pp. 46-47, 56; Elmor R. Zumwalt, Jr., "Heritage of Weakness: An Assessment of the 1970s," in Thompson, ed., *From Weakness to Strength*, p. 33.

107. *Boei Hakusho*, pp. 52-53. The Soviets are reportedly planning to replace MIG-17s with more advanced MIG-23s. *New York Times*, December 13, 1980.

108. *New York Times*, January 11, 1981.

109. Quoted in Zumwalt, "Heritage of Weakness," p. 38.

110. *Asahi Shimbun*, July 18 and 25, 1980.

111. *Japan Insight*, no. 47 (December 19, 1980), pp. 9-10. Published by the United States-Japan Trade Council, Washington, D.C.

112. Japan's dependence on government bonds to finance the fiscal 1979 general account budget was as high as 40 percent. The amount of bonds issued was comparable to the combined total amount issued by the governments of the United States, West Germany, the United Kingdom, and France. United States-Japan Trade Council, *Yearbook of U.S.- Japan Economic Relations 1979*, p. 36.

113. *Asahi Shimbun*, July 25-26, 1980.

114. Ibid., July 29, 1980.

115. Ibid., August 2, August 9, and September 17, 1980.

116. *New York Times*, November 14, 1980.

117. *Asahi Shimbun*, November 27, 1980.

118. *Washington Post*, February 6, 1981.

119. *Japan Insight*, no. 47 (December 19, 1980), pp. 9-10.

120. Ibid.; *New York Times*, December 13, 1980.

121. *Japan Insight*, no. 1 (January 9, 1981), p. 2.; *Asahi Shimbun*, January 1 and 4, 1981.

122. *Japan Insight*, no. 1 (January 9, 1981), pp. 2-3.

123. *New York Times*, February 20, 1981.

124. *Japan Insight*, no. 18 (May 9, 1980), p. 9.

125. *Japan Insight*, no. 28 (July 25, 1980), pp. 5-6.

126. Speech delivered at the 94th session of the Japanese National Diet, January 26, 1981.

127. U.S. Arms Control and Disarmament Agency, *Japan's Contribution to Military Stability in Northeast Asia*. Prepared for the Subcommittee on East Asian and Pacific Affairs of the Committee on Foreign Relations, United States Senate. (Washington, D.C.: USGPO, 1980), p. 60.

128. Ibid., p. III.

129. *New York Times*, January 11, 1981.

130. Ibid., January 30, 1981.

131. *Washington Post*, February 7, 1981.

132. *Look Japan*, November 10, 1980, p. 11.

133. The guidelines consist of the following three sections: (1) posture for deterring aggression; (2) action in response to an armed attack against Japan; and (3) Japan-U.S. cooperation in the case of situations in the Far East outside of Japan that would have an important influence on the security of Japan. *Look Japan*, November 10, 1980, p. 5.

134. Albert Wohlstetter, "Half-Wars and Half-Policies in the Persian Gulf," in Thompson, ed., *From Weakness to Strength*, p. 124.

135. *New York Times*, December 28, 1980.

136. Ibid., December 1, 1980.

137. Ibid., February 26, 1981.

138. Keiichi Oshima and Mason Willrich, eds., *Future U.S.-Japanese Nuclear Energy Relations* (Tokyo and New York: National Institute of Research Advancement and Rockefeller Foundation, 1979), pp. 41-42.

139. For details of the history of Japan's nuclear technology importation, see Hideo Sato, "The Politics of Technology Importation in Japan: The Case of Nuclear Reactors," in Gary Saxonhouse, ed., *Innovations and Diffusion of Technology in Japan* (forthcoming).

140. *Future U.S.-Japanese Nuclear Energy Relations*, pp. 80-83, 98-103.

141. Hideo Sato, "Japanese-American Relations," *Current History* (November 1978), p. 145.

142. *New York Times*, April 17, 1980.

143. Kenneth L. Adelman, "Revitalizing Alliances," in Thompson, ed., *From Weakness to Strength*, p. 299.

144. Ibid., p. 300.

145. *New York Times*, April 18 and 22, 1980.

146. I. M. Destler and Hideo Sato, "Political Conflict in U.S.-Japan Economic Relations: Where It Comes From: What to Do about It," summary report prepared for the Japan-U.S. Economic Relations Group, p. 30.

147. *Japan Insight*, no. 2 (January 11, 1980), p. 4.

148. Adelman, "Revitalizing Alliances," p. 300.

149. See *Asahi Shimbun*, April 13, 1981; *Japan Times*, April 26, 1981; and *New York Times*, May 7 and 9, 1981.

150. *Japan Insight*, no. 18 (May 8, 1981), p. 5.

151. See the text in *Department of State Bulletin*, June 1981, pp. 2-4.

4

ECONOMIC INTERACTION

There have been increasing economic frictions among noncommunist industrialized and industrializing countries since the mid-1960s, which are seriously undermining the international economic order created in the early postwar years. Commodity trade has been the most salient source of such economic frictions; trade issues have now been elevated from "low politics" to "high politics" demanding time and attention of top-level policy makers. In this chapter, therefore, we will focus on trade in examining economic influence relations among the United States, Japan, and South Korea. The United States and Japan are now the world's two largest economies, each being the largest overseas trading partner for the other. South Korea, while substantially a smaller economy, provides the largest market for Japanese exports and the second largest for U.S. exports in Asia. How have these countries influenced one another's economy, how has each of them responded to such influence, and what strategies are available for each of them to maximize gains and minimize losses from this triangular economic interaction? After a brief examination of broader economic relations, we will examine the structure of trade relations among the three countries and then the two specific trade cases, one involving textiles and another involving color television sets. We have chosen textiles and color televisions because all three countries have interacted extensively on these issues in recent years; other recent issues like automobiles and telecommunication equipment have only involved the United States and Japan.

As in the diplomatic and security relationships, the United States has clearly been the most influential actor of the three in the economic arena. But the nature of influence relationship has naturally changed over time. For one thing, GNP differentials among the three economies have changed considerably since the early postwar period, due to the remarkably high economic growth of Japan (since the 1950s) and South Korea (since the 1960s) compared to a relatively slow growth of the United States. Between 1957 and 1978, Japan's GNP grew more than 35 times from $28 billion to slightly over $994 billion and South Korea's GNP increased 12 times from a little less than $4 billion to $47 billion. During the same period the United States GNP grew only 4.8 times from $443 billion to about $2,128 billion.[1] Thus, the GNP ratio among South Korea, Japan, and the United States shifted from 1:7:111 to 1:21:45. The Japanese GNP increased to almost one half the U.S. size, and the United States-South Korean differential was narrowed (though the Japan-South Korea differential grew three times).

In addition to the relative size of the three economies involved, one must bear in mind the shifting comparative advantage situation for specific sectors of trade. Over the years, the United States has been steadily losing its comparative advantage in merchandise trade.[2] In the meantime, Japan has been gaining its competitive edge over many U.S. industries, with South Korea following Japan's footsteps at some distance. As a result, the nature of economic influence among the three countries has become more complex, moving from simple dependence of Japan and South Korea on the United States to greater interdependence, particularly between Japan and the United States. But economic factors alone are not sufficient to explain this change, for the U.S. foreign economic policy and practice in the postwar period cannot be fully divorced from the context of its broader foreign and defense policies.

U.S. economic relations with Japan and the Republic of Korea after the outbreak of the Korean War in 1950 were clearly an integral part of its global politico-military strategy of containment. The economic stability of Japan and South Korea (as well as other U.S. allies) was considered essential for preventing the spread of communist influence in the world. The United States thus took an active part in the economic reconstruction and development of these countries and generally maintained liberal and benevolent trade policies, which often deflected domestic pressures for protection from imports originating in the allied countries. The United States could also afford to practice these generous policies, since it enjoyed overall export surpluses and its balance of international payments situation remained favorable (until the late 1950s).

However, as the cold war tension declined in the latter half of the 1960s, the United States began to deemphasize its patron role, gradually paying more attention to narrower domestic economic interests. The United States became less and less patient with its allies over intrabloc economic disputes. This coincided with the relative decline of the macroeconomic position of the United States in the world and the declining U.S. competitiveness in specific industries. C. Fred Bergsten wrote:

> Support for continued liberal trade policies on foreign policy grounds
> has . . . been sharply eroded. This is primarily due to the neo-nationalist
> views which counsel that we turn away from world involvement . . .
> the generally reduced fear of a threat to our security from the Commu-
> nist world — in the industrialized or lower-income countries — renders
> our society increasingly unwilling to inflict economic pain on important
> [domestic] groups to promote our overall foreign policy.[3]

Before 1965, the United States dealt with Japan and South Korea only
bilaterally, and there was no formal three-way economic interaction among the
three countries. It was during the second half of the 1960s that Japan began to
have a trade surplus with the United States and the South Korean economy
achieved a takeoff for sustained growth. Moreover, the normalization of Tokyo-
Seoul diplomatic relations, for which Washington had long worked, formally
opened an era of trilateral economic influence relationships among the United
States, Japan, and South Korea.

EMERGENCE OF THE ECONOMIC TRIANGLE

Since the mid-1960s, the United States-Japanese economic relationship has
become increasingly interdependent in the sense that both economies have
shown greater sensitivity to economic changes or developments in the other
nation.[4] In contrast, despite South Korea's rapid economic growth in the last
two decades, economic relations between United States and South Korea
continued to be characterized by Seoul's one-way sensitivity to economic
changes in Washington. "Although [South] Korea's share of world exports has
risen remarkably from 0.34 percent in 1971 to about 0.80 percent in 1976,"
says Hee-Yhon Song, "[South] Korea is likely to remain primarily as impulse
taker rather than an impulse maker in the world for some time to come."[5]

Nevertheless, South Korea's economic success altered the pattern of United
States-South Korean economic interaction significantly. South Koreans have
not only pursued their developmental objectives aggressively but have gained
self-confidence in international economic activities. With the diversification of
external economic relations, Seoul gradually reduced the constraints of its
hierarchical economic linkage with the United States, thereby ending South
Korea's exclusive dependence upon U.S. paternalistic grants and pervasive
policy tutelage. The year 1971 was a turning point in U.S. economic aid policy
toward South Korea. Acting on the assumption that Seoul was at last economically able to handle its own defense budget and meet its foreign loan
obligations, the United States terminated its security-oriented assistance
programs, which had amounted to $2.3 billion since 1954 and had constituted
96 percent of South Korea's defense budget in 1960. Also, for the first time,
loans exceeded grants in the total amount of U.S. economic assistance to South
Korea. By 1974-75, U.S. economic aid for South Korea had dwindled to only

$37 million, less than one-tenth of the total for the peak year (1956) or about one-seventh of 1961. The figure increased in subsequent years, but it was primarily earmarked for long-term low-interest loans under PL 480. Peace Corps programs were supported at the level of $2.3 million annually.

With the exception of the PL 480 programs, AID's policy role in South Korea changed from one of direct decision making to that of an advisory and mediatory partnership. While providing considerable assistance in research and training operations, AID played a peripheral role in drawing up the Third and Fourth Five-Year Plans. In an attempt to reduce economic dependence on the United States, South Korea cultivated increasingly important ties with several countries, but above all with Japan, its former colonial ruler (1910-45). As a result, the earlier United States-Japanese cooperation in strengthening the South Korean economy showed an element of competitiveness during the 1970s, especially in the areas of trade, economic assistance, capital investment, and technology transfer.

The United States and Japan were South Korea's most important trade partners. In 1978 they accounted for 31.9 and 20.6 percent of South Korea's total exports and 20.3 and 39.9 percent of its total imports respectively. The United States and Japan also were the two largest sources of economic assistance to Seoul. The total value of foreign loans committed to South Korea between 1959 and 1978 was $17.6 billion, that is, 47.2 percent from public sources and 52.8 percent from commercial sources. More than 70 percent of all loans were granted from 1974 to 1978. Between 1959 and 1978, the United States made about $5 billion in loans ($1.1 billion in 1978), divided almost evenly between public and commercial loans. With 28.5 percent of the total dollar amount, the United States was the largest foreign source of loans to South Korea, but its relative importance declined in the late 1970s. Although Japan did not make any loans to South Korea until after diplomatic normalization, its committed share through 1978 (that is, $3 billion or 17.5 percent) reflected greater emphasis on commercial loans. A large portion of about 40 foreign banks in South Korea, which competed in offering short-term loans, was owned by Japan or the United States.

In addition to these bilateral lending arrangements with South Korea, both the United States and Japan emphasized multilateral approaches. They jointly supported South Korea's loan applications to international financial institutions (including the International Bank for Reconstruction and Development, the International Financial Corporation, and the Asian Development Bank) in which they enjoyed considerable influence over decisions. Moreover, both countries have been active in the Consultative Group on Development Assistance to the Republic of Korea, a consortium of 11 countries and 5 international financial agencies involved in providing financial assistance to South Korea.

The United States and Japan were the two largest investors in South Korea. U.S. businessmen have been less than enthusiastic about undertaking direct capital investments and joint ventures in South Korea. As Table 4.1 shows,

TABLE 4.1
Foreign Investments in South Korea: 1962-78

Country	Number of Cases	Percentage	Amount (in million dollars)	Percentage
United States	116	13.5	193.9	19.2
Japan	665	77.6	583.6	57.9
Netherlands	4	0.5	72.3	7.2
All countries	857	100.0	1,008.4	100.0

Source: South Korean Ministry of Commerce and Industry.

through the end of 1978 foreign companies were able to invest slightly more than $1 billion or an amount less than 10 percent of that originating in foreign loans. Between 1962 and 1978, U.S. firms invested $194 million in 116 cases. While U.S. corporations were the dominant foreign investors in South Korea during the 1960s, Japanese companies were conspicuously more active investors during the 1970s. A similar pattern developed in the area of foreign technology transfers to South Korea. Japan's share of total foreign investments was 51.9 percent measured in value or 77.6 percent measured by the number of cases. By 1977 Japan had concluded with South Korea 564 technological-licensing agreements as compared with 209 cases in the United States (see Table 4.2). In establishing Japan's dominance in these areas, Japanese businessmen benefited from geographical proximity, cultural affinity, active government support, comparable legal systems, and an adaptiveness to local practices. They were particularly effective in penetrating South Korea's 29 specialized industrial complexes and two free trade zones. In the Masan Free Trade Zone, for example, Japan set up 76 totally owned enterprises, while the United States had only 4 such enterprises.[6] As South Korea's economic capabilities grew, some

TABLE 4.2
Foreign Technology Transfer to South Korea: 1962-77

Country	Number of Cases	Percentage	Royalty Paid (in million dollars)	Percentage
United States	209	23.0	46.9	27.3
Japan	564	62.1	89.1	51.9
West Germany	39	4.3	10.8	6.3
All countries	905	100.0	171.6	100.0

Source: South Korean Ministry of Commerce and Industry.

South Korean businesses invested in U.S. construction, trade, and other companies, so that by the end of 1978 their amount ($25 million) was one-eighth of total U.S. investments in South Korea.

Narrow economic motives alone cannot fully explain the wide-ranging United States' and Japanese economic activities in South Korea. Both Washington and Tokyo believed that the economic stability of the Republic of Korea was essential to regional stability. The United States emphasized the linkage between its security commitment to South Korea and U.S. economic policies. The U.S. government also encouraged Japan and other industrialized allies to increase their share of inputs for the South Korean economy, particularly in the 1970s, following the Indochina debacle and the intensification of economic difficulties in the United States. The primacy of these larger strategic and diplomatic considerations was illustrated by the U.S. ambassador's 1975 initiative to reduce South Korea's balance-of-payments burden. Notwithstanding Treasury Department's criticism of Seoul's "irresponsible" economic measures, U.S. ambassador to Seoul, Richard Sneider, urged AID Administrator Daniel Parker and Assistant Secretary of State Philip Habib to accommodate South Korea's urgent request for additional development loans. Sneider stated:

> Such lending would be most useful in influencing a more forthcoming attitude on the part of the Japanese and possibly other donors toward assistance for Korea. It would clearly serve broader U.S. interests by providing both tangible and symbolic evidence of our continued concern and support for Korea's economic and social growth and development, as well as their defense capabilities.[7]

After 1976, political considerations, especially the human rights policies of the Carter Administration, prompted negative responses to South Korea's aid requests. For example, in 1977 Washington withheld support for Seoul's two loan applications pending in international financial agencies. Again, in 1978, the Bureau of Humanitarian Affairs in the U.S. Department of State strongly recommended that because of President Park's poor human rights record, the United States should decrease its aid to South Korea and abstain on South Korea's loan request at the Asian Development Bank (ADB). However, this recommendation was not implemented.[8] Similarly, after President Park undertook a series of repressive measures in October 1979, the question of an appropriate U.S. response to South Korea's ADB loan application was again raised.

Politics superseded economics occasionally in Japanese-Korean relations as well. In August 1973 Kim Dae-jung, South Korea's opposition leader, was kidnapped by the KCIA while he was staying in Tokyo. Viewing the incident as an infringement of Japanese sovereignty, Tokyo "indefinitely" postponed the bilateral ministerial conference scheduled for early September 1973. The ministerial conference was convened only after South Korean Prime Minister Kim Jong-pil visited Tokyo in early November to express Seoul's regrets for the kidnapping incident and promised to restore Kim Dae-jung's full civil rights and freedom and to take appropriate actions against Kim Dong-woon, a South Korean Embassy official centrally involved in the incident. Even then the Japanese government agreed to provide only $45 million in aid to South Korea, an amount far below the $300 million requested by the Park government. Moreover, Seoul's request for a yen loan for the second stage construction of the integrated Pohang steel mill was not approved. The Tanaka government's (1972-74) policy of expanding economic, cultural, and personal exchanges between Japan and North Korea reinforced the coolness between Tokyo and Seoul arising over the Kim kidnapping case. In 1980 the possibilty of Kim's execution by the new Chon Du-hwan government produced renewed political tensions between Washington and Seoul and between Tokyo and Seoul; the Carter Administration and the Suzuki government implicitly threatened to levy economic sanctions if the Chon government went ahead with the execution.[9]

As noted above, United States-Japan economic relations are becoming more interdependent. In the past, Japanese dependence on the U.S. economy was summarized by the saying, "When the U.S. economy gets a cold, the Japanese economy gets pneumonia." Now, if the Japanese economy gets a cold, the U.S. economy is likely to catch one, too. U.S. economic policy makers demonstrated their appreciation of Japan's impact on the world economy when they pressed Japan to seek an 8 percent economic growth in 1977 in accordance with the so-called "locomotive thesis."[10] Japan's trade surplus with the United States has been growing since 1965, and by 1978 totaled nearly $12 billion. Since the late 1960s, U.S. frustration with the overall trade imbalance and with bilateral sectoral trade issues, ranging from textiles to steel, color televisions, and automobiles, has made "belaboring the Japanese" "one of the most popular American pastimes."[11]

Still, the United States remains economically more important to Japan than vice versa. While Japan's 1978 trade in goods and services with the United States constituted 26.1 percent of Japan's total volume of trade (a decline from 30.9 percent in 1955), U.S. trade with Japan amounted to 12.2 percent of U.S. total trade in the same year (an increase from 4.1 percent in 1955).[12] The Japanese economy is about half the size of the U.S. economy, although the per capita GNP in Japan and the United States is just about the same. While there remains an absolute difference in terms of various economic capabilities in the two countries, Japan is growing and moving much faster, as seen in Table 4.3. It is the high speed of Japanese economic growth that seems most alarming to U.S. officials and industrialists. As an astute U.S. economic reporter noted, "Japan has challenged — probably more seriously than at any other time in the past 50 years — an essential part of the American self-image."[13]

TABLE 4.3
Major Economic Indicators of the United States and Japan

	United States	*Japan*
GNP growth (1979)	2.3%	6.0%
Productivity growth (1979)[1]	1.8	12.1
Output per worker (1960-77)	2.6	8.8
Growth in R&D spending (1966-75)	5.6	20.1
Capital formation (1978)[2]	12.7	23.2

[1] The U.S. figure is for manufacturing and the Japanese figure is for all industry.
[2] Ratio of gross fixed capital formation to GDP.

Sources: General Accounting Office, *United States-Japan Trade: Issues and Problems*, 1979, pp. 162, 169; United States-Japan Trade Council, *Yearbook of U.S.-Japan Economic Relations 1979*, pp. 3, 46, 89; Science and Technology Agency, Japan, *White Paper on Science and Technology 1978*.

THE STRUCTURE OF TRADE RELATIONS

Having discussed the general pattern of changing economic relations among the three countries, we now focus on contemporary trade relations, particularly their structural dimensions. In Table 4.4, one sees three major trends in the triangular trade relations. First, as already noted, after 1965 a large trade imbalance developed between the United States and Japan in favor of the latter. Second, the United States had a favorable trade balance with South Korea until 1975 but then was faced with a deficit in 1976-78 (though it was subsequently reversed in 1979-80). Third, Japan consistently has earned a surplus from trade relations with South Korea and the trade imbalance has been widening.

Why has the United States accumulated such a large trade deficit with Japan? Earlier, we referred to the decline in the U.S. competitive position. For many people in the United States, it was unthinkable that the United States would lose in free competition with one of its Asian protégés. These critics insisted that Japan must be resorting to "unfair" trade practices, such as dumping and export subsidies,[14] or argued that Japan benefited from stiff import barriers, while the United States keeps its market open. While it is true that Japan has had high import (as well as investment) barriers, which the United States tolerated on largely foreign policy grounds, most of these barriers have been eliminated or lowered substantially. In 1964 the number of Japan's import quotas was reduced from 500 to 136. Currently, Japan has only 27 import quotas, while the United States has 23 quotas, including those with GATT waivers. Japan's average import tariff rate on dutiable goods is about 6.9 percent, which is slightly lower than the U.S. rate. After the Tokyo Round agreements are fully implemented, Japan's tariff levels will be under 6 percent.[15]

TABLE 4.4
Trade among the United States, Japan, and South Korea: 1961-80
(in million dollars)

Year	U.S. Imports from Japan	U.S. Exports to Japan	Japanese Imports from South Korea	Japanese Exports to South Korea	U.S. Imports from South Korea	U.S. Exports to South Korea
1961	1,055	1,837	19	69	7	143
1962	1,358	1,574	24	109	12	220
1963	1,498	1,844	25	159	24	184
1964	1,768	2,009	38	110	36	202
1965	2,414	2,080	44	167	62	182
1966	2,963	2,364	66	294	96	254
1967	2,999	2,695	85	443	137	305
1968	4,054	2,954	100	624	236	452
1969	4,888	3,990	133	754	321	530
1970	5,875	4,652	234	809	395	585
1971	7,209	4,055	262	954	532	678
1972	9,065	4,965	408	1,031	759	647
1973	9,676	8,313	1,242	1,727	1,021	1,202
1974	12,456	10,679	1,380	2,621	1,492	1,701
1975	11,425	9,563	1,293	2,434	1,536	1,881
1976	15,504	10,144	1,802	3,099	2,493	1,963
1977	18,547	10,414	2,148	3,927	3,119	2,447
1978	24,458	12,885	2,627	5,982	4,060	3,034
1979	26,243	17,579	3,353	6,657	4,374	4,603
1980	30,701	20,575	3,039	5,858	4,607	4,890

Sources: U.S. Department of Commerce; South Korean Agency of Customs Administration; and *Korea Herald*.

A recent U.S. Congressional study concedes that "Japan today is generally an open trading nation, although some very tough residual attitudes of protectionism remain."[16] Trade barriers do not explain why the United States has been losing its share of the Japanese market to other countries, especially developing countries.[17] Indeed, as a General Accounting Office study concludes, "the worst bilateral balance with Japan has occurred when Japan's tariff and the NTBs [Non-Tariff Barriers] have been at their lowest, and when the dollar/yen alignment has given the United States its greatest export price advantage in the Japanese market."[18] More importantly, the U.S. business and trade communities always have been oriented toward domestic markets (or toward imports) and have failed to aggressively promote exports (though they have been very much oriented toward investments abroad). The proportion of U.S. exports to GNP was only 9 percent in 1977 (up from 4 percent in 1970) compared with 47 percent for Belgium, 24 percent for United Kingdom, and 23 percent for West Germany. But it is also important to note that the proportion of Japanese exports to GNP is not particularly high either (12 percent in 1977).[19]

An examination of trade structure may offer some clues to structural shifts in recent trilateral economic relations. Lacking natural resources, Japan depends heavily on imports in meeting domestic demand for minerals, fuels (including oil), and important agricultural products such as wheat, soybeans, and corn. In order to earn the foreign exchange necessary to import these materials, Japan has to export manufactured products. The United States is the largest and most prosperous market for manufactured products, but, while the United States also has manufactures to export, the Japanese market is highly competitive, except for agricultural and primary goods. Consequently, major Japanese exports to the United States consist of manufactured products that are largely high technology, whereas a large portion of U.S. exports to Japan include agricultural products and raw materials. This is particularly true in recent years. For instance, the share of manufactured imports from the United States in Japan's total U.S. imports declined from 39 percent in 1972 to 29 percent in 1978.[20] The aforementioned Congressional study goes so far as to say that "we are a developing nation [aircraft excluded] supplying a more advanced nation — we are Japan's plantation: haulers of wood and growers of crops, in exchange for high technology, value-added products."[21] But in view of Japan's basic need to export manufactured products in order to import needed non-manufactured materials (especially, oil from the Middle East), any substantial change in the bilateral trade structure is unlikely in the short run. This situation makes Japan vulnerable to protectionist attacks from the United States, such as those by John B. Connally during the 1980 presidential campaign. Speaking primarily for domestic political consumption, he warned Japan that unless imports from the United States were increased, Japanese products would be shut out of the U.S. market. In a similar vein, Philip Caldwell, chairman of Ford Motor Company, asserted: "Look at the types of trade between the U.S. and Japan: what is it that Japan has that we are vitally required to have? The answer is zero."[22] While this kind of thinking revives the specter of the 1930s protectionism and denies the reality of increasing economic interdependence, it may reflect a current of U.S. political thinking that cannot be taken lightly by policy makers in both countries who want to maintain a viable alliance.

U.S. officials foresee that the kind of trade problems that the United States had had with Japan will recur with other Asian countries. The new challenge will come from the so-called "New Japans" of the Far East, including South Korea and Taiwan; the United States has already been accumulating trade deficits with these two countries in some years. At present, there remain important quantitative and qualitative differences between the U.S.-Japan and U.S.-South Korea trade relationships.

In 1978 the U.S. trade deficit with South Korea was about $1 billion in bilateral trade, which totaled $7 billion. South Korea exports to the United States a substantial amount of labor-intensive manufactured products, particularly standardized electrical equipment and such light-industrial goods as textiles, wigs, and plywood. In recent years, steel became an important export item, increasing South Korea's foreign earnings from $86 million in 1974 to $504 million in 1979. In 1978 textiles and apparel, electric appliances, steel, footwear, and plywood constituted 62.6 percent of total South Korean exports to the United States. In return, South Korea imports U.S. industrial machinery and chemicals as well as agricultural products.[23] Here the United States looks more like an advanced industrial country trading with a developing industrial country.

Nonetheless, U.S. officials were seriously concerned about South Korea's aggressive trade policy toward the U.S. market. As in the case of Japan, Washington negotiated voluntary restraint agreements with South Korea (as well as with other "New Japans") in such areas as textiles, television sets, and footwear, while urging the South Korean government to reduce restrictions on U.S. imports. Initially, Seoul resisted U.S. pressures tenaciously but eventually agreed to export restraints. In 1977-78 the South Korean government took a number of steps that lowered existing barriers to imports. For instance, in July 1978 South Korea made major revisions in its tariff structure. "Of 1,179 changes in the tariff, 983 resulted in duty reductions, while 119 caused increases."[24]

Some U.S. officials saw "the Japan connection" in U.S. trade deficits with South Korea and Taiwan. A 1979 Congressional study noted that "the estimated U.S. $2.6 billion deficit with Taiwan in 1978 is almost a mirror of Taiwan's $2.1 billion deficit with Japan." The report continued: "While our trade with [South] Korea vis-a-vis Japan is not as bad as the situation in Taiwan, it is trending the same way. The [South] Koreans in particular would like to see less dependency on Japan for imports (or at least more export sales to Japan to balance better that bilateral trade)."[25] Here, the implication is that if more South Korean exports went to Japan the size of the U.S. trade deficit with South Korea would be lessened.

Why was the United States unable to expand its exports to South Korea sufficiently to achieve balance in bilateral trade? Why did the South Koreans find it easier to penetrate the U.S. market than the Japanese market? South Korean exports to the United States have been growing faster than U.S. exports to South Korea partially because the share of South Korea's major, foreign currency earners — textiles, electrical appliances, and steel — increased sharply, possibly in response to the reduction of Japanese textile and television exports to the United States. Thus, South Korean textiles, which brought in $495 million during 1975, earned $987 million in 1978. Similarly, the value of exported electrical appliances (including color televisions) rose from $343 million in 1976 to $691 million in 1979.[26] On the other hand, one must note the "lack of an American presence in the [South] Korean market able or ready to take advantage of what must be declining Japanese competitiveness," a decline allegedly caused by the appreciation of the yen vis-à-vis the dollar.[27] Indeed, a senior member of the U.S. Embassy in Seoul admitted that Japan was still more competitive than the United States in the South Korean market because Japanese had more business personnel stationed there than did the United States.[28]

In attempting to explain why the South Koreans have succeeded in penetrating U.S. markets but have been far less successful in expanding exports to Japan, a number of Korean and United States observers argue that Japan maintains "notoriously restrictive commercial policies."[29] This contention exploits the image of the "closed Japanese market," which was a factor in the 1950s and early 1960s. However Japan is much less restrictive to South Korean imports today than either the United States or the European Economic Community (EC). On the basis of an Industrial Bank of Korea survey, a Japanese economist states that "the share of restricted commodities in the ROK's total exports by country of destination amounted to 18.9% relative to Japan, compared with 34.1% and 27.4% for the U.S. and the EC, respectively."[30] A report in the August 30, 1978 issue of *Donga Ilbo* (a South Korean daily) offers other explanations: the insufficient variety of Korean goods relative to Japanese demand; residual colonial prejudices leading the Japanese to underestimate the quality of South Korean goods; and, compared to Japanese and EC policies, the U.S. Generalized System of Preferences (GSP) for trade promotion with developing countries was more advantageous for South Korea's exports.

According to a more basic and convincing explanation focusing on industrial structure, Japan has a "self-sufficient" industrial structure in that "a nearly complete set of domestic industries have grown to be capable of sustaining the whole streams of various production cycles." On the other hand, the South Korean industrial structure is "essentially geared to generate processed-goods exports" while depending on imports of producers goods from Japan.[31] The more processed or assembled goods South Korea sells to the world, the more producers goods (which are higher value-added) it needs to buy from Japan. Thus, the South Korean trade with Japan may be more structurally "vertical" than one can tell from the bilateral trade figures. While Japan buys foodstuffs, textile products, and fiber yarns from South Korea, chemical and such heavy-industrial goods as general machinery, electrical and electronic machinery, transport equipment, and primary iron constitute a major portion of total Japanese exports to South Korea (82.7 percent in 1978).[32] This trade pattern is characteristic of the pattern often found between developed and developing countries, that is, the former providing capital-intensive products and the latter offering primary and labor-intensive commodities.

RESOLUTIONS OF TRADE CONFLICTS: CASE STUDIES

We have discussed structural characteristics underlying trade relations among the United States, Japan, and South Korea. In order to gain a better understanding of the dynamics of economic influence relationships, let us now focus on two specific areas of trade — textiles and color televisions — in which the three governments have interacted extensively over the years. Textiles and household electric appliances, including television sets, have been Japan's and South Korea's important foreign-exchange earners in the 1970s.

Exporting Textiles

In the immediate postwar period, the United States was the world's dominant textile exporter. Beginning in the mid-1950s, foreign cotton textile imports, particularly from Japan, increased steadily, although such imports remained a small portion of U.S. domestic consumption (see Table 4.5). The United States persuaded Japan to adopt a policy of "voluntary" export restraint. However, the Japanese soon saw their "restraint" rewarded by having much of the U.S. market they were forbidden to fill go to other Asian textile exporters, including Hong Kong, Taiwan, and South Korea. By 1960 U.S. imports of

TABLE 4.5
U.S. Imports of Cotton Manufactures
(in millions of dollars)

	1956	1957	1958	1959	1960	1961
Total	154.3	136.2	150.0	201.3	248.3	203.3
Japan	84.1	65.8	71.7	76.7	74.1	69.4
Hong Kong	0.7	5.8	17.4	45.8	63.5	47.0
Other Asian Countries	15.3	13.0	14.3	24.0	34.0	25.0
Spain and Portugal	0.3	0.4	0.7	2.6	12.4	5.5

Source: Warren Hunsberger, *Japan and the United States in World Trade* (New York and Evanston: Harper & Row, 1964), p. 325. Copyright 1964, Council on Foreign Relations, Inc. Reprinted by permission.

cotton cloth exceeded exports for the first time since 1878. In 1962 the Kennedy Administration concluded a multilateral, cotton textile trade accord, the "Long-Term Arrangement" (LTA), which established rules by which cotton-textile-importing countries could limit exports from any country by bilateral agreement or unilateral action.[33]

In the 1960s U.S. dominance as a synthetic textile exporter was challenged, and in 1968 U.S. imports of synthetic textiles exceeded its exports for the first time. Although Japanese imports comprised only 1 percent of U.S. domestic demand, Japan was the United States' largest supplier of synthetic textiles at that time. In the 1968 presidential election campaign, Richard Nixon, who had lost to Kennedy by a narrow margin in 1960 due in part to his insensitivity to the Southern textile interests, pledged that as president he would seek an international agreement to control imports of noncotton textiles (including woolen as well as synthetic textiles). As soon as he was elected president, his administration pressured Japan to restrain its noncotton textile exports to the United States.[34] Recalling the earlier bitter experience with export restraints, Tokyo initially refused to discuss the idea. In offering to discuss a possible export restraint arrangement in the fall of 1969, Japanese officials insisted that at least three other Asian textile-exporting countries (South Korea, Hong Kong, and Taiwan) be included in the discussion. But U.S. officials continued to deal bilaterally with Japan until the spring of 1971, when they rejected Japanese industry's unilateral export restraint plan. In announcing the plan, Japanese textile producers had made it clear that the plan would be implemented on the condition that South Korea, Taiwan, and Hong Kong submit to similar export restraints (though they later went ahead without cooperation from other Asian exporters, in part because of the Japanese government's promise to provide generous compensations).

The White House resolved to take strong action to reduce textile imports from Japan, since the administration looked upon unilateral Japanese industry restraint as both insufficiently restrictive and a product of conspiracy among the industry, Tokyo, and Nixon's political enemy, Wilbur Mills. One of the trade restrictive measures considered by the White House and Nixon's new textile negotiator, David Kennedy, was Article 204 of the 1956 Agricultural Act as amended. Under the act, the president could impose textile quotas unilaterally on a country, if a multilateral restraint agreement had been reached with other countries "accounting for a significant part of world trade." Thus, it was thought that the United States could first negotiate an export restraint agreement with South Korea, Taiwan, and Hong Kong, and then threaten Japan with mandatory import quotas unless Japan acceded to U.S. terms. However, Kennedy's effort to reach agreement with South Korea, Taiwan, and Hong Kong prior to winning Japanese concessions failed. South Korean negotiators insisted that they would not hold further negotiations until Japan, the largest textile exporter, acted first. In the end, the United States had to threaten to invoke the "Trading with the Enemy Act" and to unilaterally impose strict import quotas before Japan and other Far Eastern textile-exporting countries finally accepted U.S. proposals. The terms were clearly the toughest for Japan. For instance, the permissible annual growth rate for synthetic textile imports was 5 percent for Japan as compared to 7.5 percent (with 10 percent in the first year) for South Korea. Moreover, in return for the South Korean textile export restraint, the United States agreed to increase its development loans by $100 million and its PL 480 programs by $275 million over a five-year period.[35]

Ironically, Japan was unable to meet the export quotas allowed under the three-year agreement because the 1971 currency reevaluations and Japanese domestic inflation had eroded the comparative advantage of Japanese industry. By 1973 Japan was importing more manufactured textiles than it was exporting. Despite a decrease in Japanese textile exports to the United States, U.S. aggregate textile imports continued to increase rapidly, particularly as measured by value. Against this background, in 1974 the U.S. government concluded the Multi-Fiber Agreement (MFA) Regarding International Trade in Textiles, which contained 18 bilateral agreements governing the access of all foreign textiles and apparel to the U.S. market.

While a new United States-Japan bilateral agreement was concluded within the MFA framework for 1974-78, Japanese exports to the United States never reached the upper ceiling of the established quotas. In response to this situation, the United States gradually eased its restrictions on Japanese textile imports, culminating in 1978 in the elimination of overall import ceilings. In January 1979, acting under pressure from domestic industry, Washington concluded another somewhat more restrictive agreement, which increased the number of category ceilings from six to ten.[36]

In negotiating the 1974-77 bilateral agreement within the MFA framework, South Korea attempted to minimize U.S. import restrictions to the benefit of its rapidly expanding domestic industry. Since U.S. import restrictions involved quantities, South Korea deliberately sought greater advantage by increasing the value of its exports during the mid-1970s. Table 4.6 records the gains realized

TABLE 4.6
South Korea's Textile Exports to the United States: 1975-78
(in thousand dollars)

Year	Total Textile Exports	Textile Exports to U.S.	Percent of Total Textile Exports	Percent of Total Exports Tolls
1975	1,869,800	495,700	26.5	32.3
1976	2,740,100	754,700	27.5	30.3
1977	3,246,200	968,300	29.8	31.0
1978	3,981,886	987,178	24.8	24.3

Source: Southern Korean Ministry of Commerce and Industry.

from this tactic. In 1977 the value of South Korean exports to the United States registered a 28.3 percent jump over the previous year, even though the permissible quantitative increase was limited to 6.75 percent.[37]

In the 1977 negotiations concerning the renewal of the bilateral agreement, Washington was determined to freeze the volume of South Korean exports in 1978 at the 1977 level. Seoul insisted on a 6 percent increase for 1978 but was forced to accept the U.S. demand. South Korean negotiators, led by assistant minister of foreign affairs, Choe Ho-jung, then tried to secure the best possible growth rates for the next four years (1979-82). A basic theme of their arguments was expressed in the *Korea Herald* editorial of July 29, 1977:

> Any substantial reduction in the annual increase rate will throw many Korean workers out of work, not to mention hurting the nation's effort to increase overall exports. It would be grossly unfair if the United States attempted to solve its unemployment problem at the expense of Korean textile workers and industries. In managing import restrictions, the U.S. government has to take into account the economic and other conditions of each affected country. Any expedient or unilateral approach to the problem of textile-import restrictions would not serve the interest of the United States, and Korea is probably the very country which deserves the U.S. government's generous consideration when taking import-restrictive moves.

The editorial also argued that since the U.S. government had decided to withdraw its ground forces from the peninsula, it should support South Korea's stable economic growth as a necessary condition of a strong, ROK self-defense capability.

The South Korean side asked for the maximum rate of 7.9 percent and the minimum of 6.75 percent, but the United States side insisted on a 6 percent to 6.25 percent range. A compromise was reached with both parties agreeing to a 6.5 percent growth rate (and a 1 percent for woolen textiles). Many South Korean textile manufacturers were disappointed because the new agreement established exceptionally low growth rates (ranging from 3.14 to 3.62 percent) for a dozen items in which U.S. manufacturers are weak in competition. These items comprised a large share in South Korea's total textile exports to the United States. South Korean government negotiators comforted themselves with the thought that the terms of their hard-fought agreement were much more favorable than those that their archrival, Hong Kong, had obtained from the United States.[38]

In addition to circumventing the intent of U.S. import restriction by increasing the value of its textile exports through the tactic of upgrading textile quality, South Korea decided to increase its export earnings by launching an aggressive campaign to penetrate the prosperous and nearby Japanese market. As Japan's comparative advantage in the textile trade continued to decline, the proportion of imports in domestic demand had been growing steadily during the 1970s — from 4.3 percent in 1970 to 18.2 percent in 1978.[39] As seen in Table 4.7, the share of South Korean imports was the largest, increasing from about 21 percent of Japan's total textile imports in 1971 to 40 percent in 1976 (the share declined slightly to about 38 percent in 1980).

Nevertheless, South Korean textile exports to the United States have been somewhat greater in value than those to Japan, the geographical proximity between Seoul and Tokyo notwithstanding. This is because the Japanese market is smaller and more competitive and not because the Japanese trade policy is more "restrictive," as some people contend. In fact, the Japanese textile import

TABLE 4.7
Japan's Imports of Textile Products by Countries (in thousand dollars)

Import from:	1966	1971	1976	1980
I. Developed Countries	49,778 (72.4)	152,701 (39.9)	411,165 (24.2)	745,899 (27.3)
II. Asian ADCs	7,252 (10.6)	146,732 (38.3)	956,261 (56.3)	1,470,470 (53.8)
Korea	4,597	80,400	681,012	1,035,147
Taiwan	596	39,757	158,673	281,883
Hong Kong	2,018	26,031	108,342	144,076
Singapore	14	344	8,185	9,364
III. Other ASEAN	222 (0.3)	3,803 (1.0)	37,144 (2.2)	54,945 (2.0)
Thailand	147	2,722	22,518	29,291
Philippines	14	591	10,250	7,492
Malaysia	1	104	2,518	12,289
Indonesia	60	386	1,858	5,873
India	583	6,232	20,940	40,546
Pakistan	—	10,564	32,191	40,666
China	4,597 (6.7)	32,050 (8.4)	166,740 (9.8)	307,029 (11.2)
IV. All Countries	68,721	382,934	1,699,240	2,730,815

Note: Table includes only Standard International Tariff Code 65+84. Figures in parentheses represent percentage shares of total imports.

Source: Ministry of International Trade and Industry, *White Paper on International Trade.* Taken from Ippei Yamazawa, "Adjusting to the ADCs in the Face of Structurally Depressed Industries: Japan," paper presented to the 11th Pacific Trade and Development Conference, September 1-4, 1980, Seoul, p. 37.

policy has been more liberal than that of the United States (or of the EC). While the United States has the bilateral quota agreement with South Korea and 17 other countries for all textiles under the MFA, Japan has no quantitative textile import restrictions, except for silk and silk fabrics. In addition, Japanese textile teriff rates are much lower than the U.S. rates, as shown in Table 4.8.

As textile imports to Japan continue to increase, Tokyo may be tempted to follow the example of the United States by seeking voluntary quota agreements under the MFA. As the U.S. economist, Brian Ike, suggests: "MITI [Ministry of International Trade and Industry] has thus far resisted industry pressure for protective measures for other textile products [than silk and silk fabrics] as well in view of Japan's large balance of payments surpluses [with South Korea and other textile exporters], but as the balance is restored to equilibrium, it is not too difficult to imagine Japan abusing the MFA in the same fashion as most developed countries have done to date."[40] Yet, for reasons mentioned earlier, achievement of an overall bilateral trade equilibrium between Japan and South Korea is not likely in the foreseeable future. One must also note that textile trade between the two countries is a two-way street, although Japanese exports to the ROK are much less (Japan sold $345 million to Korea in 1979). In addition, the existing division of labor in production, which works to South Korea's disadvantage, may persist. While South Korea specializes in the exportation of silk products, cotton yards, and various types of apparel, it depends heavily on Japan for imports of textile goods that require capital-intensive or technology-intensive large-scale production systems and sophisticated textile machinery.[41] Furthermore, part of South Korean textile products exported to Japan (and other countries) has been produced by South Korean subsidiaries of Japanese textile companies. Among the 427 textile firms in South Korea, 89 are Japanese subsidiaries, and as much as 69 percent of the total production of these subsidiaries has been shipped to Japan.[42] A number of large Japanese textile manufacturers had shifted part of their operations to the neighboring Asian countries, particularly in South Korea, in response to protectionist moves against Japanese products in the United States (and Western Europe) as well as to rising labor costs in Japan.

Exporting Color Television Sets

While textiles remain a potential source of tension among the three countries, the main focus of attention shifted in the late 1970s to another trade sector, which is slightly higher on the technological ladder — color television sets. As in the case of textiles, the first major dispute arose from Japan's growing exports to the United States market. Once Japan had consented to restrain its exports to the United States, South Korea and other Asian countries took advantage of the situation and increased their own share in the U.S. market. While this basic pattern was the same as in the textile case, there were some significant differences.

TABLE 4.8
Comparison of Tariffs on Selected Textile Products: Japan, EC, and the United States
(Percent)

Textile Product	Japan				EC		United States	
	1965 pre-KR[1]	1978 basic	1978 temporary	1987 offer[2]	1978 basic	1987 offer[2]	1978 basic	1987 offer[2]
Cotton fabric 55.09 (U.S. 321)[3]	10.0	7.0	5.6	5.6	13	10	13.3	10.0
Synthetic fabric (spun) 56.07 (U.S. 338.30)	25	10.0	8.0	8.0	16	11	25.6	14.8
Synthetic fabric (filament) 51.04 (U.S. 338.30)	25	12.5	8.0	8.0	13	11	25.6	14.8
Outergarment 61.01, 61.02 (U.S. 380.84)	20	17.5	14.0	14.0	17	14	31-34	10-30
Underwear 60.04, 61.03 (U.S. 378.60)	25	14.0	11.2	11.2	17	13	39.0	15.6

[1] Pre-Kennedy Round.
[2] Offered rates, not finally concluded yet.
[3] Brussels Trade Nomenclature code for Japan and EC, U.S. tariff code in parentheses.

Source: Tariff table of each country. Taken from Ippei Yamazawa, "Adjusting to the ADCs in the Face of Structurally Depressed Industries: Japan," paper presented to the 11th Pacific Trade and Development Conference, September 1-4, 1980, Seoul, p. 38.

Owing to Japan's aggressive manufacturing and marketing efforts, Japanese color television exports to the United States increased rapidly in the 1970s. For example, in 1976 exports to the United States grew nearly 150 percent over the previous year (that is, from 1.04 million units to 2.53 million units), thus taking about 40 percent of the U.S. market.[43] Seeking import relief, U.S. domestic producers resorted to a "shotgun approach of multiple jeopardy."[44] They initiated a variety of actions directed at their Japanese counterparts, including legal proceedings against alleged Japanese dumping, price fixing, and customs fraud. More importantly, in September 1976 the Committee to Preserve American Color Television (COMPACT), a domestic industry-labor lobby, filed with the International Trade Commission an escape clause petition, which was authorized by Section 201 of the 1974 Trade Act. Charging that Japanese imports had caused serious injury to domestic industry, through the elimination of 19,000 U.S. jobs and the threatened loss of an additional 65,000 jobs, the petition asked that Japanese imports be drastically curtailed.[45] Japanese industry representatives replied that the sudden increase in Japanese color television imports was a transitory and minor cause of the difficulties suffered by the U.S. industry. The Japanese argued that far more important were the factors of "the dominant position of Zenith and RCA in the U.S. color television market, inadequate investment in plant and equipment by some producers, the impact of the 1974-75 recession on production and sales, and the effects of rapid technological advances on employment."[46]

On March 14, 1977 the International Trade Commission (ITC) ruled in favor of COMPACT. With the aim of alleviating import damages, it recommended a substantial, phased tariff increase (20 percent for the first two years, 15 percent in the third and fourth, and 5 percent in the fifth year). While Tokyo and Japanese industry representatives regarded the ITC ruling as "too severe" and the proposed unilateral U.S. tariff increases as destabilizing overall trade relations, Japanese officials were prepared to take a flexible trade policy stance in order not to repeat the experience of the 1969-71 textile issue. Thus, Tokyo signaled its willingness to negotiate an orderly marketing agreement (OMA) with the United States.[47] The Carter Administration, which also favored the OMA approach, instructed Special Trade Representative Robert Strauss to begin negotiations with the Japanese.

The United States side proposed, initially, an annual ceiling of 1.2 million units for Japanese color television exports to the United States, but Japan wanted at least 2 million units. Conscious that this issue could have a corrosive effect on overall bilateral ties, Washington and Tokyo struck a compromise on May 20, 1977. The two governments agreed that beginning July 1, 1977 the Japanese could ship 1.75 million color television sets to the U.S. market from Japan for each of the next three years.[48] Apparently, Prime Minister Fukuda Takeo's last-minute intervention during the seven-nation economic summit in London had removed the remaining obstacles to the compromise agreement.[49] At Japan's request an "equity clause" was included in the OMA, stipulating that the United States would take "appropriate remedial measures" if other foreign suppliers increased their color television exports to the United States in order to exploit the agreement to the disadvantage of Japan. While Tokyo accepted the OMA on the grounds of broader political considerations, many Japanese were troubled at the growing virulence of U.S. attacks against Japan and with what they regarded as "distorted charges of 'unfair Japanese trade practices.' "[50]

The OMA was intended to provide a necessary respite for U.S. television manufacturers so that they could improve their competitive capabilities and the domestic employment situation. Instead, in September 1977, Zenith, the United States' largest television manufacturer and the "most active champion of protecting domestic production against foreign competition," decided to shift a substantial portion of its production overseas, thereby eliminating one-quarter of its U.S. work force.[51] One disappointed U.S. trade official reacted by saying: "We tried to give Zenith what it wanted with the OMA, and then Zenith goes ahead and pulls out. Now the OMA will benefit television-production in Mexico and Taiwan more than in the United States."[52] In a similar vein, the 1978 report prepared by Developing World Industry & Technology, Inc., a Washington consulting firm, for the U.S. Department of Labor noted that "American firms have failed to take advantage of the respite from imports provided by the OMA." The report continued, "The only major change in the industry during this time has been Zenith's move to join the other manufacturers in low-wage production sites and a severe curtailment in its research and development expenditures and personnel."[53]

The OMA and other U.S. efforts to limit Japanese color television exports to the U.S. market had three important, interrelated consequences. First, they encouraged the Japanese manufacturers to increase the production of color television sets in the United States. When the OMA was signed, three Japanese manufacturers (Sony, Matsushita, and Sanyo) were producing in the United States, and the agreement induced them to expand existing production facilities. Later, three other Japanese companies (Mitsubishi, Toshiba, and Hitachi) decided to produce in America. In effect, "In 1977, virtually all export losses mandated by the negotiated OMA were offset by increased American production of color-TV sets by Japanese-owned firms."[54]

As a consequence of the increased Japanese production in the United States and the Japanese companies' additional, self-imposed export restraints (due to the continuing controversy over the assessment of dumping duties), Japanese color television shipments to the United States fell below the quota sanctioned by the OMA. U.S. imports of Japanese-made sets fell from 1,842,196 units (including 1,643,767 "complete" sets and 199,429 "incomplete" sets) during the first year of the OMA to only 1,238,689 sets (consisting of 1,014,666 "complete" sets and 224,023 "incomplete" sets) during the second year.[55] Finally, President Carter allowed the three-year OMA to expire as scheduled on June 30, 1980.

Predictably, as imports from Japan declined, shipments from Taiwan and South Korea increased rapidly. In 1976, for instance, Taiwan exported fewer than 250,000 sets to the United States, but the figure had expanded to 625,000 by 1978.[56] The change was even more dramatic in the case of South Korea. The ROK's exports to the United States increased as much as ten times from 52,000 units in 1976 to 520,000 units in 1978, as shown in Table 4.9. Under these circumstances, the United States asked both Taiwan and South Korea to follow Japan's example by accepting an orderly marketing agreement. This was in line with the "equity clause" in the OMA with Tokyo. Taiwan agreed but South Korea resisted. Subsequently the United States and South Korea conducted a series of tough negotiations from August to December 1978.

In negotiating with the South Koreans, Stephen Lande, a Strauss deputy, emphasized that despite Japan's export restraint, the administration was under great pressure from COMPACT because imports of color television sets increased in 1978, reducing the market share of U.S. manufacturers and causing a 7 percent decrease in employment in the domestic color television industry.[57] He explained that Japan had invoked the equity provision, and Taiwan agreed to restrict its exports on the condition that South Korea consent to similar restraint. The U.S. position created a dilemma for the South Korean officials because Seoul's color television exports had depended almost entirely on the U.S. market. This heavy dependence on the U.S. market had developed as a result of a South Korean government policy. As part of the expanding electronics industries, the Park government had identified color television as a leading export industry for the 1980s and encouraged the domestic television industry to form licensing agreements or joint ventures with RCA and Matsushita, even though there had been little prospect of an expanding domestic market that could possibly absorb a major part of production in the event of import restrictions abroad. South Korea's initial response to Lande was that

TABLE 4.9
South Korean Exports of Color Television to the United States: 1974-78

Year	Units (in thousands)			Amounts (in thousand dollars)		
	Total Exports	Exports to U.S.	Percent	Total Exports	Exports to U.S.	Percent
1974	39	33	84.6	5,161	4,254	82.4
1975	28	23	82.1	4,733	3,965	82.8
1976	52	52	100.0	7,822	7,822	100.0
1977	109	105	96.3	16,627	15,953	95.5
1978	576	520	90.3	93,773	84,649	90.3

Source: South Korean Association for Promotion of Electronic Industries.

"no restrictions are appropriate." Assistant Minister of Commerce and Industry Park Pil-su argued: (1) that the U.S. demand was unfair and unreasonable because South Korea, unlike Japan and Taiwan, was a relative newcomer to television exports; (2) that the U.S. problem arose from increased imports of incomplete sets from Taiwan and Mexico, whereas South Korea's exports were mostly complete sets; and (3) that the unemployment problem in the U.S. television industry was a product of technological innovations and the lack of price competitiveness.[58] In an effort to influence the U.S. position, South Korean officials solicited assistance from U.S. electronics companies with investments in South Korea and U.S. importers of South Korean color television sets. The United States threatened to apply the 1972-75 base period unilaterally to control television imports from South Korea if Seoul failed to accept an orderly marketing agreement. Having little choice, the South Korean government accepted an OMA that allowed South Korean exports at a level far below Seoul's initial offer of 482,011 sets per year.[59]

Period	Color TV Sets
December 1, 1978-January 30, 1979	122,000
February 1, 1979-October 31, 1979	153,000
November 1, 1979-June 30, 1980	136,000
Total	411,000

Even though the U.S. agreement with the ROK was more favorable than that with Taiwan, it represented a serious setback to South Korea's ambitious plan of exporting to the United States at least 700,000 units in 1979 (and 1,200,000 units in 1981).[60] The new quotas dealt a severe blow to South Korea's domestic color television industry, which had expanded its annual production capacity to 1.1 million sets. In effect, the OMA meant only a 23 percent utilization of South Korea's production capacity, resulting in the layoffs of 4,500 workers. It was clear that the South Korean Ministry of Commerce and Industry, along with the domestic industry, had grossly overestimated the television export prospect in the United States and underestimated U.S. domestic political reactions to expanded foreign imports.

Have U.S. efforts to curb the importation of Japanese and South Korean (as well as Taiwanese) color television sets affected the nature of television trade between Tokyo and Seoul? As noted, the OMA encouraged the Japanese manufacturers to produce more television sets in the United States. One might also anticipate that these companies would increase exports to countries other than the United States, including South Korea. Between 1977 and 1978, there was a slight increase in Japanese color television exports to South Korea, with sales of complete sets rising from $5.8 million to $7.4 million, while parts sales increased more dramatically from $9.7 million to $16.7 million. Possibly as a result of the implementation of the United States-South Korean OMA in

December 1978, Japanese exports to South Korea dropped during 1979 to $2.5 million in complete sets and $11.9 million in parts. One might expect that once South Korean color television exports to the United States were restricted, the South Koreans would try to sell more in Japan and elsewhere, as they had done in the case of textiles. While South Korean color television parts shipped to Japan did increase from $8.8 million in 1978 to $12.7 million in 1979, exports in complete sets, which were negligible to begin with, declined from $277,000 in 1978 to $251,000 in 1979.[61]

When compared with the level of United States-South Korean trade, the scale of bilateral color television trade between Tokyo and Seoul has been considerably smaller. For Tokyo, the increased television production by the Japanese companies in the U.S. market was clearly more important than its other export increases, which were intended to offset the decrease of Japanese exports to the United States. This factor and the problem of overcapacity in the South Korean television industry also meant that the Japanese companies had little incentive to increase investment in South Korea, unlike the case of textiles. The increase of $3.9 million on color television parts in exports to Japan in 1979, while not unimportant to Seoul, was insufficient to offset the lost exports to the United States. In view of the highly competitive nature of the Japanese color television industry (dominated by a few big, established firms) and of the Japanese market, it is unrealistic for South Korea to expect substantial increases in its television exports to Japan.

STRATEGIES FOR FUTURE ECONOMIC INTERACTION

The United States responded to increasing textile and color television imports from Japan and South Korea by resorting to a tempered protectionism in the form of voluntary restraint or orderly marketing agreements, thereby avoiding outright mandatory quotas or unilateral tariff increases. Japan's initial export restraint was exploited by South Korea and other Asian countries, which quickly increased their share in the U.S. market. Then the United States expanded the import-control arrangements to include these other Asian exporters. In the textile case, the Japanese response was to adopt a scrap-and-build policy with major firms investing heavily in South Korea and other countries with low labor costs. South Korea's response to the U.S. textile restrictions has been to diversify its export markets, increasing shipments to Japan, in particular, and to upgrade textile shipments to the United States. In the area of color television, the Japanese companies opted to increase production in the U.S. market in order to offset the decrease in exports. South Korea has had a more difficult time adjusting itself to the slowdown in its export growth in the United States. It has increased exports to Japan and elsewhere, but such increases have not been sufficient to offset the loss of sales in the U.S. market that had previously been rapidly expanding.

In addition to textiles and color television sets, the United States has had numerous disputes over foreign imports in recent years, including steel and automobiles from Japan. In the case of steel, Washington has resorted to the "Trigger Price Mechanism," a price-oriented import-control arrangement applying to all foreign suppliers.[62] With regard to imported automobiles, the Carter Administration refrained from establishing either mandatory or voluntary quotas. The lack of an ITC determination that domestic industry has been injured by imports hampered efforts to set voluntary quotas. Nevertheless, the automobile issue became a major source of tension between Japan and the United States in 1980, due to well-publicized protectionist campaigns by the UAW and Ford. Finally, despite the ITC ruling made in November 1980 against automobile import restrictions, the new Reagan Administration successfully negotiated a voluntary quota agreement with Japan in May 1981.

The United States seems increasingly aware of the problems of declining industrial productivity and competitiveness and thus, of the need for drastic improvements in research and development, business management, trade policy, etc., instead of creating new protectionist barriers against foreign competition. It is in this spirit that a recent U.S. Congressional study advises the United States to face the Japanese economic challenge:

> We believe that Japan's rate of industrial progress and stated economic goals should be as shocking to Americans as was Sputnik. And like Sputnik, we should be shocked into responding to the challenge. Nothing could serve the world economy better than good, clean competition with Japan in high-technology innovation. It is time that we respond to the Japanese economic challenge. As with Sputnik, we did not block Soviet efforts — we bettered them. The same approach should guide us in dealing with Japan; *we don't need protectionism — we need to make our own economy better.*[63]

Indeed, the Japanese challenge may very well do to the U.S. economy what Sputnik did to U.S. space technology, and trade liberalism may again become firmly rooted in the United States. However, given various economic difficulties facing the United States, there is no reason to expect that the United States will become any more accommodating to foreign imports in the near future than it has been in the recent past. Under these circumstances, what strategies are available for Japan and South Korea in order to minimize damages to their economies while maintaining a viable overall relationship with the United States *and* with each other?

Japan is destined to clash with the United States in trade in the increasingly capital-intensive and high-technology areas, such as computers, semiconductors, and telecommunication equipment. Given the structure of bilateral trade noted earlier, a bilateral imbalance in favor of Japan is likely to persist, causing strains in the relationship. One obvious strategy for Japan is to diversify its export markets. Indeed, Japan's heavy dependence on the U.S. market, while gradually decreasing, has been a major reason why Japan has often been singled out as a target of U.S. criticisms — despite the fact that Japan's share of exports in GNP is considerably smaller than that of many West European countries, as we saw earlier. For instance, West Germany depended on the U.S. market for only 6.7 percent of its exports in 1977 when the comparable figure for Japan was 24.9 percent. This is even more significant in view of the fact that West Germany's share in world exports is larger than Japan's (12.0 vs. 8.3 percent in 1978).[64] However, when one considers the increasing protectionist sentiment in Western Europe, the political instability in the Middle East, and the limited buying power in the rest of the third world, the possible effectiveness of such diversification policy will be limited. The United States is likely to remain the largest and most prosperous market for Japan for some time to come.

Another strategy for Japan is to increase imports from the United States. Since 1977 some efforts have been made by the Japanese government and industry, but the overall effectiveness of such efforts will also depend on accompanying U.S. efforts to overcome the traditional domestic market orientation and to promote exports. Now that most import quotas have been eliminated and tariffs have been lowered to the levels of the United States and the EEC, the Japanese government should take the initiative in further efforts to reduce nontariff barriers, instead of passively reacting to external pressures. Whenever the United States makes trade expansionist demands, such as its recent demands on agriculture and government procurement, Japan would do well to accommodate the U.S. position as much as domestic economic and political conditions allow. Moreover, to the extent that much of U.S. criticism of the "closed" Japanese market derives from outdated images of the past, Japanese may need to speak up more to minimize misunderstandings.[65]

Another task that can be pursued concurrently is that of increasing Japanese investment in the United States. Increased investment in the production of Japanese color television in the United States helped offset the decrease in exports and defuse friction with the United States. With regard to automobiles, U.S. government officials and labor leaders have encouraged Japanese investment in the United States as a way of ameliorating the unemployment problem in the domestic industry. West Germany avoided a potential conflict with the United States by starting Volkswagen production in the United States several years earlier.[66] The biggest advantage of investment is that local workers and politicians may come to identify their interests with those of foreign investors. Japan's investment in the United States is still small compared with that of other advanced industrialized countries. In fact, Japan ranks only sixth in order of the dollar value of investment in the United States as shown in Table 4.10. The U.S. investment in Japan might also be encouraged. Since 1978 U.S. investment in Japan was only 3 percent of its total manufacturing investment abroad.[67]

More generally, it will be essential for Japan to keep in mind the linkage of economic issues with broader diplomatic and strategic considerations. Japan has often been criticized by the United States as a "free rider" for not bearing

TABLE 4.10
1978 Foreign Direct Investment in the United States

Country	Millions of Dollars	Percent of Total
Netherlands	9,767	23.9
United Kingdom	7,370	18.1
Canada	6,166	15.1
West Germany	3,191	7.8
Switzerland	2,844	7.0
Japan	2,688	6.6
France	1,939	4.7
All countries	40,831	100.0

Source: John Oliver Wilson, "Japanese Investment in the United States: An Analysis of the Public Policy Issues," paper prepared for the Japan-United States Economic Relations Group, July 1980, p. 4.

a larger defense burden commensurate with its economic power, and the U.S. pressure on Japan to play a more active role in the security arena increased under the Reagan Administration. While Japan has had its own domestic-political (as well as international-political) reasons for maintaining a low defense posture, Japan can be relatively more accommodative of U.S. interests: for example, by further increasing its share of the cost of maintaining U.S. troops in Japan and by contributing to an "allied deterrence force" as recently recommended by a binational study group.[68] Here again, it may be equally important to achieve a better understanding of Japan's position by U.S. policy makers.

In dealing with South Korea, Tokyo's best strategy may be to keep the Japanese market as open as possible. It is important *not* to follow the example of the United States and create new trade restrictions. In order for Japan to keep its markets open for foreign competition, it will need to continue its efforts to upgrade its production lines and to develop higher-technology sectors whenever possible. This approach also may help South Korea increase its sales of more value-added products, and more Japanese investment in Seoul — preferably through joint ventures with South Korean firms — can be encouraged to upgrade South Korean production lines. To the extent that South Korea can expand its exports to Japan and thus reduce its bilateral trade imbalance, a more favorable perception of Japanese trade policy may emerge in the United States.

As in the United States case, it is essential that Japan maintain a good dialogue with South Korea on legitimate policy differences, for example, over transactions with North Korea or on human rights in South Korea. If left unattended, major policy differences may lead to a more serious, bilateral political conflict, which in turn may have a disastrous effect on economic relations. In view of the historically sensitive nature of this particular set of bilateral relations, Japan's blatant use of pressure tactics may provoke an anti-Japanese, nationalistic backlash and prove counterproductive. As Japanese Ambassador to Seoul Ryozo Sunobe emphasized, in view of the unfortunate colonial experience, Japan should always be watchful of South Korea's sensitivity and should handle economic issues with "tender care."[69]

If new, protectionist trends in the United States (and elsewhere in the industrialized world) present a serious challenge to Japan, the challenge is even graver for South Korea, which depends very heavily on exports of labor-intensive products against which most protectionist moves are directed. According to a study by the International Monetary Fund, industrialized countries have implemented over 70 import-restrictive measures against South Korea, including those on textiles, color televisions, and nonrubber footwear.[70]

Recently, David B. Yoffie and Robert O. Keohane have argued that for minimizing economic damages "the best strategy [for South Korea and other 'advanced developing countries'] is one of short-term compromise and willingness to make concessions."[71] Citing the example of Japanese resistance in the textile wrangle of 1969-71, they contend that firm resistance is counterproductive in the long run. While it is true that dogmatic resistance often induces the importing country to apply stronger restrictive measures, it does not follow that the exporting country should *always* acquiesce to protectionist pressure. Easy concessions will only help multiply protectionist demands. In fact, it was not the Japanese resistance per se that delayed the resolution of the textile issue and led to undesirable consequences for both parties. Rather, the main problem was that Prime Minister Sato Eisaku agreed to President Nixon's plan for textile concessions but later was unable to deliver on his promise. Had Sato clearly disagreed in the beginning, Nixon might have been persuaded to modify his textile demand substantially, thus helping to end the issue early. After all, many in the Nixon Administration were opposed to the textile demand, and Japanese officials were inclined to consider a loose export restraint arrangement as early as the fall of 1969.[72] Whether one should make concessions depends on the circumstances. In 1965 President Lyndon Johnson was pressured by domestic woolen textile producers to restrict Japanese imports, even though he was basically opposed to the idea. Thus, he needed a clear negative signal from Japan to dissuade domestic industry. When the Japanese did disapprove, the Johnson Administration gladly dropped the case, while pointing out that at least it had explored the possibility of restraining Japanese imports.[73] Of course, once one has agreed to negotiate export restraints, there is a compelling case for good bargaining as Yoffie and Keohane suggest.

One of the important lessons for South Korea that can be drawn from our earlier discussions is that Seoul should not develop a particular export industry that depends heavily on the U.S. market (or any other single market), and the speed with which an export industry is developed should be in line with the expected growth and the "political tolerance" level of foreign markets. The experience of the South Korean color television industry was disastrous. The diversification of export markets is an important strategy for South Korea as for Japan. Only in a gradual fashion can South Korea achieve some success in diversifying its trade partners, particularly by turning to Western Europe and the Middle East. However, as shown earlier, South Korea is still too heavily dependent on the U.S. and Japanese markets.

In view of the rising protectionism in the industrial world, it will be necessary for South Korea to export more to the third world countries. Indeed, South Korea's export dependence on the LDCs did increase from 12.8 percent in 1973 to 25.6 percent in 1978, but decreased from 34.4 percent in 1963. It is noteworthy that Japan's export dependence on LDCs has been much higher by comparison (44.3 percent in 1978).[74] LDCs will compete increasingly among themselves in the production and exportation of labor-intensive and light-industry manufactures. For this reason, too, it is essential for South Korea to continue its planned efforts to upgrade its production lines or to move on to more capital-intensive heavy and chemical industries if adequate funds are available. As in the case of Japan, South Korea needed to encourage more imports from the United States in order to reduce the likelihood of effective protectionist actions against South Korean exports. Recent South Korean efforts (for example, the dispatch of a buying mission to the United States, lowering tariffs, and liberalization of import procedures) contributed to changing the bilateral trade relations from about $1 billion deficit in 1978 to about $230 million surplus for the United States in 1979.[75]

The Korea Development Institute projects that by 1991 South Korea will join the ranks of "advanced industrial nations" (with $350 billion GNP and $7,700 per capita GNP) and will become the number-ten trading nation (with $255 billion trade volume) in the world.[76] If this projection is to become a reality, South Korea will continue to need large foreign capital (and technology) inflows, either through investment/joint ventures or direct aid and loans. According to one estimate, at least $4.5 billion in annual capital inflows will be required to finance South Korea's development plans in the early 1980s.[77] This will involve the difficult task of striking a balance between greater foreign capital and less foreign dependence. "While the Koreans have been adamant in their desire to restrict Japanese entrepreneurs and prevent them from re-establishing any sort of Japanese hegemony over Korean economic life," says David C. Cole, "the measures adopted in pursuit of these objectives have also served to restrain the activities of other foreigners."[78] At the least, South Korea can try to balance the influence of different foreign countries and companies to minimize dominance by Japanese (or United States) companies.

Can South Korea use the United States to influence its economic and political relations with Japan? Thus far, South Korea has been restrained in its ability to solicit U.S. assistance in regard to Tokyo-Seoul economic disputes. The United States and Japan regard their bilateral economic relations as much more important than their respective trade with South Korea. As a South Korean economic official explained, United States-Japanese competitiveness in South Korea was rather limited because South Korea had no common-market-type relations with the two countries and because it sought the advantages of worldwide competition.[79] Another reason cited by this official was the fact that the United States and Japan rarely engaged in a direct, intense two-way rivalry in the South Korean market. Only on a few occasions did South Korea maneuver to derive optimum economic benefits from United States-Japanese competition (for example, Westinghouse-Mitsubishi competition over electric generators). Generally, South Korea was simply unable to exploit United States-Japanese competition. In 1979, for instance, South Korea planned to import a total of more than 6 million metric tons of foreign grains at the cost of $1 billion. While the United States wished to gain a large share in supplying grains to Korea, Japan attempted to sell 620,000 tons of rice to Seoul. South Korea was inclined to buy cheaper rice from Japan, but the United States pressured Seoul not to buy rice from Tokyo. In the end, constrained by the perceived linkage between grain trade agreements with the United States (which involved PL 480) and military assistance programs, South Korea was compelled to give a higher policy priority to grain purchases from the United States than from Japan.[80] More broadly, in promoting regional policy objectives, the United States has often urged Japan to increase its economic commitments (such as loans and investment) to South Korea.

The South Korean ability to use the United States in influencing Japanese policy on sensitive political matters has been even more limited. As we noted, Japan made South Korea uneasy by opening semiofficial trade relations with North Korea. South Korea has emphasized repeatedly that any drastic increase in Japan's commercial, financial, or diplomatic ties with North Korea would jeopardize Tokyo-Seoul relations. There has been no evidence to suggest that the United States has intervened in this dispute on behalf of South Korea. Although the Carter Administration lifted bans on travel to North Korea, there has been no visible effort made to open the gate to United States-North Korean economic relations.

As we have seen, Japan has come to present a serious challenge to the U.S. economy through its highly competitive exports. South Korea has followed a similar path, though on a much reduced scale. U.S. efforts to influence Japan and South Korea into limiting their textile and color television exports were far from easy and were successful only after long, painstaking intergovernmental discussions. A basically similar pattern was subsequently repeated in the cases of Japanese steel and automobile exports to the United States. However, indecision within the U.S. political system regarding these bilateral issues was as much a problem as the lack of consensus between the two countries. As domestic interest groups in all these countries become increasingly self-assertive, management of these trade issues will naturally become even more formidable unless these countries can make appropriate anticipatory responses in a concerted effort to minimize future trade conflicts.

NOTES

1. See Japanese Ministry of Foreign Affairs, *Comparative Economic Statistics for Canada, Japan, and the United States* (April 1980), p. 1; The Bank of Korea, *Economic Statistics Yearbook* (1958 and 1979); Donald C. Hellmann, *Japan and East Asia* (New York: Praeger, 1972), p. 27. Japan's GNP for fiscal year 1980 is projected at $1.26 trillion, slightly more than half the United States' GNP. *New York Times*, December 28, 1980.

2. For a detailed analysis, see Stephen D. Krasner, "United States Commercial and Monetary Policy: Unravelling the Paradox of External Strength and Internal Weakness," in Peter J. Katzenstein, ed., *Between Power and Plenty* (Madison: University of Wisconsin Press, 1978), pp. 67-71.

3. C. Fred Bergsten, "Crisis of U.S. Trade Policy," *Foreign Affairs*, July 1971, p. 625.

4. See Richard N. Cooper, "Economic Interdependence and Foreign Policy in the Seventies," *World Politics*, 1972, pp. 159-60.

5. Hee-Yhon Song, "Economic Miracles in Korea," in Lawrence B. Krause and Sueo Sekiguchi, eds., *Economic Interaction in the Pacific Basin* (Washington, D.C.: Brookings Institution, 1980), p. 117.

6. See Boum Jong Choe, "An Economic Study of the Masan Free Trade Zone," in Wontack Hong and Anne O. Krueger, eds., *Trade and Development in Korea* (Seoul: Korea Development Institute, 1975), pp. 229-53.

7. See House Committee on International Relations, *Investigation of Korean-American Relations: Report of the Subcommittee on International Organizations* (Washington, D.C.: USGPO, 1978), p. 199.

8. See Wayne Patterson, "The State Development and Human Rights in Korea, 1978-1979," paper presented at the American Political Science Association, August 31-September 3, 1979, Washington D.C.

9. *New York Times*, September 29, November 5, and December 7, 1980. Also, see Andrew Nagorski, "East Asia in 1980," *Foreign Affairs: America and the World 1980*, 1981, pp. 667-95.

10. According to this thesis, Japan, along with West Germany and the United States, should act as a "locomotive" in stimulating demand and drawing in imports in order to help the weaker economies of the world.

11. Robert C. Christopher, "They Try Harder," *New York Times Magazine*, January 22, 1978, p. 27.

12. Hugh Patrick, "The Economic Dimensions of the United States-Japan Alliance: An Overview," unpublished paper, Yale University, 1980, p. 10.

13. Robert J. Samuelson, "U.S., Japan Find Old Relationships Have Unraveled," *National Journal*, June 30, 1979, p. 1068.

14. See Robert C. Angel, "Japan's Most Serious Economic Problem in the United States: The Image of 'Unfair Japan,'" United States-Japan Trade Council, September 1978.

15. Samuelson, "Old Relationships Have Unraveled," p. 1072.

16. Subcommittee on Trade of the House Committee on Ways and Means, *United States-Japan Trade Report* (Washington, D.C.: USGPO, January 1980), p. 1.

17. Ibid., pp. 5-7.

18. Comptroller General of the United States, *United States-Japan Trade: Issues and Problems* (Washington, D.C.: USGPO, 1979), p. 171.

19. *United States-Japan Trade Report*, p. 2.

20. *United States-Japan Trade: Issues and Problems*, p. 15.

21. *United States-Japan Trade Report*, p. 5.

22. *Washington Post*, November 2, 1980.

23. South Korean Agency of Customs Administration, *Statistical Yearbook of Foreign Trade*, various issues.

24. Subcommittee on Trade of the House Committee on Ways and Means, *Task Force Report on United States-Japan Trade* (Washington, D.C.: USGPO, 1979), p. 15.

25. Ibid., pp. 55-56.

26. South Korean Agency of Customs Administration, *Statistical Yearbook of Foreign Trade*, various issues.

27. *Task Force Report*, p. 56.

28. Interview with William Clark, Jr., counsellor, U.S. Embassy, June 14, 1979, Seoul.

29. Paul W. Kuznets, *Economic Growth and Structure in the Republic of Korea* (New Haven: Yale University Press, 1977), p. 74.

30. Toshio Watanabe, "An Analysis of Structural Dependence between the Republic of Korea and Japan: Toward a More Optimal Division of Labor," paper presented to the 11th Pacific Trade and Development Conference, September 1-4, 1980, Seoul, p. 14.

31. Ibid, p. 14.

32. Ibid, pp. 2-3.

33. For a detailed analysis of U.S. postwar trade with Japan, see Hideo Sato, "The Crises of an Alliance: The Politics of U.S.-Japan Textile Trade," Ph.D. dissertation, Department of Political Science, University of Chicago, 1976, chap. 2.

34. For a comprehensive account of this 1969-71 textile dispute, see I. M. Destler, Haruhiro Fukui, and Hideo Sato, *The Textile Wrangle: Conflict in Japanese American Relations, 1969-1971* (Ithaca, N.Y. and London: Cornell University Press, 1979).

35. See the United States-South Korean agreements, in House Committee on International Relations, *Investigations of Korean-American Relations: Appendixes to the Report* (Washington, D.C.: USGPO, 1978), vol. 1, pp. 546-51.

36. United States-Japan Trade Council, *Trade Roundup*, no. 1 (February 6, 1979), pp. 6-7.

37. Already in 1976 the value of Japanese textile exports to the United States ($597 million) was less than that of South Korean textile exports to the United States ($754 million).

38. Internal Memoranda on Textile Negotiations prepared by the Ministry of Commerce and Industry, 1977-78, South Korea; interview with Lim Dong-wung, director, Research Department, Korean Traders Association, June 27, 1979, Seoul, South Korea.

39. Ippei Yamazawa, "Adjusting to the ADCs in the Face of Structurally Depressed Industries: Japan," paper presented to the 11th Pacific Trade and Development Conference, September 1-4, 1980, Seoul, p. 35.

40. Brian Ike, "The Japanese Textile Industry: Structural Adjustment and Government Policy," *Asian Survey*, May 1980, p. 550.

41. Watanabe, "Analysis of Structural Dependence," pp. 3-4.

42. Masayuki Yoshioka, "Overseas Investment by the Japanese Textile Industry," *The Developing Economies*, March 1979, pp. 3-44.

43. Ronald I. Meltzer, "Color TV Sets and U.S.-Japanese Relations: Problems of Trade-Adjustment Policymaking," *ORBIS*, Summer 1979, p. 421; *Nihon Keizai Shimbun*, March 13, 1977.

44. This expression is in Meltzer, "Color TV Sets," p. 421.

45. *Nihon Keizai Shimbun*, January 9, 1977.

46. United States-Japan Trade Council, *Trade Roundup*, no. 32 (July 25, 1978), p. 3.

47. *Nihon Keizai Shimbun*, March 15 and 18, 1977.

48. Ibid., May 21, 1977.

49. Interview with a ranking Japanese Foreign Ministry official, December 15, 1978, Tokyo.

50. United States-Japan Trade Council, *Trade Roundup*, no. 8 (May 23, 1977), pp. 1-2.

51. Meltzer, "Color TV Sets," p. 436.

52. Quoted in ibid., p. 436.

53. Quoted in Thomas M. Bodley, "U.S. Imports of Japanese Color TVs: Case Study of a Trade Problem," unpublished paper, Yale University, 1979, p. 12.

54. Meltzer, "Color TV Sets," p. 438.

55. United States-Japan Trade Council, *Trade Roundup*, no. 26 (August 17, 1979), p. 6.

56. Meltzer, "Color TV Sets," p. 437.

57. Internal memorandum on color television negotiations, South Korean Ministry of Commerce and Industry, 1978.

58. Ibid.

59. The OMA was later extended through June 30, 1982, though the terms were significantly liberalized. See United States-Japan Trade Council, *Japan Insight*, no. 25 (July 3, 1980). Internal Report of the South Korean Ministry of Commerce and Industry, 1978.

60. *Long-Term Prospect for Economic and Social Development 1977-91* (Seoul: Korea Development Institute, 1978), p. 263.

61. South Korean Agency of Customs Administration, *Statistical Yearbook of Foreign Trade*, 1977-78 issues.

62. For details, see Hideo Sato and Michael Hodin, "The Politics of Trade: The U.S.-Japan Steel Issue of 1977," paper prepared for the Japan-United States Economic Relations Group, November 1980.

63. *United States-Japan Trade Report*, p. 39.

64. Tun-jen Cheng, "On the 'Differential Treatment' of Japan and West Germany," Occasional Papers no. 7, Department of Political Science, Carlton University (June 1980), pp. 15-16; *United States-Japan Trade*, p. 170.

65. For an elaboration of this point, see I. M. Destler and Hideo Sato, "Political Conflict in U.S.-Japan Economic Relations," summary report prepared for the Japan-United States Economic Relations Group, December 1980.

66. For a detailed account of the United States-Japan automobile issue, see Gilbert Winham and Ikuo Kabashima, "The Politics of U.S.-Japan Automobile Trade," paper prepared for the Japan-United States Economic Relations Group, December 1980.

67. *United States-Japan Trade Report*, 1980, p. 20.

68. See Henry Scott Stokes, "Japan and U.S. Face New Strains on Ties That Bind," *New York Times*, December 28, 1980.

69. Interview with Ambassador Sunobe Ryozo, June 14, 1979, Seoul.

70. David B. Yoffie and Robert O. Keohane, "Responding to the 'New Protectionism': Strategies for the Advanced Developing Countries in the Pacific Basin," paper presented to the 11th Pacific Trade and Development Conference, Korea Development Institute, September 1-4, 1980, Seoul, p. 24.

71. Ibid., p. 5.

72. See Destler, Fukui, and Sato, *The Textile Wrangle*.

73. See Hideo Sato, "U.S.-Japan Textile Issues in the Changing Postwar International System: A Macro-Systemic Analysis," unpublished paper, Yale University, 1979, pp. 38-39.

74. Kym Anderson and Ben Smith, "Changing Economic Relations Between the Advanced Developing Countries and Resource-Exporting Developed Countries," paper presented to the 11th Pacific Trade and Development Conference, September 1-4, 1980, Korea Development Institute, Seoul, Table 9.

75. South Korean Agency of Customs Administration, *Statistical Yearbook of Foreign Trade*. Hugh Patrick, "Economic Trends in Asian-Pacific Region: An Overview," paper for the Conference on Political, Economic, and Security Trends and Problems in East Asia, Williamsburg, Virginia, January 5-9, 1981, p. 31. There is a descrepancy between the two sources. According to the former source, the deficit is $229 million, but the latter says $202 million.

76. See *Long-Term Prospect*; and *A New Strategy toward the 1980s* (Seoul: Economic Planning Board, 1979).

77. *A New Strategy toward the 1980s.*

78. David C. Cole, "Free Enterprise vs. Government Regulation: Decisionmaking and Regulation in the Korean Economy," *Asian Affairs*, November-December 1979, p. 82.

79. Interview with Kim Jae-ik, director-general, Bureau of Economic Planning, Economic Planning Board, June 22, 1979, Seoul.

80. *Wall Street Journal*, November 7, 1979.

5

SUMMARY AND CONCLUSION

This has been a study of an influence relationship among three members of the same Western alliance system, including the bloc leader, and of the effects of the contextual shift away from the cold war, bipolar international system. The traditional, realist conception of international politics has been of limited use in illuminating this relationship. First, this study suggests that military force *per se* has clearly not been a usable and effective instrument of policy within the Western alliance; it is difficult to conceive of a situation in which the United States would threaten to use force against its own allies, as the Soviet Union has done within its own sphere of influence. More importantly, with the recent perception of decreasing military threats from the other bloc, the United States' ability to translate its military superiority into actual policy influence over its allies seems to have diminished greatly.

Second, military security alone no longer dominates the agenda of international relations in Northeast Asia. As we have seen, nonmilitary issues (including economic and human rights issues) have become "high politics" issues demanding the attention of top policy makers. Third, it has not always been useful to treat the United States, Japan, and the Republic of Korea as coherent, unitary actors, which the realist approach of world politics requires. Since neither the governments nor the domestic groups involved have united in their views on every issue, transnational channels and alliances have often proven useful to our study.

In general, it has been more productive to look at relations among the United States, Japan, and South Korea in terms of what Keohane and Nye call "complex interdependence" than from the perspective of traditional power politics.[1] This does not mean that power (defined in economic-technological and military terms) is irrelevant to an understanding of this trilateral influence relationship. Indeed, it has been necessary to examine the changing power structure – particularly economic – among the three countries for clues regarding the character and dynamics of their influence relationships. But, as Rubinstein states, "the exercise of influence is . . . not at all a mere reflection of the differential in motivations and in power base."[2] Whether country A can effectively translate its power resources into influence over country B or C depends on a number of factors, such as: the credibility of country A's leadership as perceived by country B or C; the level of domestic policy consensus in country A; the appropriateness of country A's negotiating style; the existence or absence of intergovernmental or transnational alliances; the nature of linkage politics involved; and the perception of threats from the other bloc. Let us now summarize the key points discussed in each of the three issue areas.

DIPLOMATIC RELATIONS

In the immediate postwar years, the U.S. influence over Japanese foreign policy was virtually total. As a condition for restoring Japanese independence, the United States made Japan join the U.S. cold war coalition. From the early 1950s, Japanese foreign policy evolved around the U.S. policy of containment against communist nations. Japan's China policy is a case in point. In 1952, under U.S. influence, Japan reluctantly signed a peace treaty only with Chiang Kai-shek's Formosan-based government, which claimed to represent the whole of China. Japan agreed not to recognize the PRC government on the mainland, not to move toward diplomatic normalization, and to restrict trade relations with the communist regime in accordance with the United States-sponsored COCOM and CHINCOM regulations. In dealing with the PRC, Tokyo separated politics from economics, undertaking only the gradual expansion of trade relations allowed under existing political conditions. Although at times the United States became concerned about the level of Japanese economic transactions with the PRC, Japan always deferred to the United States for initiating any major policy change on China.

In the summer of 1971, Washington's sudden reversal in its China policy – as signaled by the announcement of President Nixon's scheduled visit to the PRC, which was arranged without consulting Japan – had an immediate and dramatic policy effect on Japan. It quickly altered the power balance within the governing LDP in favor of those desiring to normalize diplomatic relations with the PRC, leading to Prime Minister Tanaka's Peking trip in September 1972. Did the United States *influence* Japan to normalize relations between Tokyo and Peking? If anything, U.S. influence in this direction was indirect and unintended. In part, Nixon's sudden shift in China policy, undertaken without consulting

Japan, was prompted by his frustration and resentment over Japan's "uncooperative" attitude on bilateral economic issues, particularly the issue of textile imports. His intention was to punish the government of Prime Minister Sato. The president's action did succeed in chastising Sato, who was forced out of office. But it had another important, unintended effect besides Japan's quick normalization of diplomatic relations with the PRC. The insensitive, unilateral way in which the United States in 1971 initiated a major policy shift regarding China and also international trade and monetary issues (in the form of Nixon's New Economic Policy) *substantially damaged the credibility of U.S. leadership* in the minds of Japan and other U.S. allies.

Thereafter, Japan's China policy more or less followed its own logic and momentum. Japan's inability to conclude the peace and friendship treaty with the PRC (called for at the time of diplomatic normalization) before August 1978 had less to do with U.S. influence as such than with the dynamics of triangular relations among Japan, China, and the Soviet Union over the "antihegemony" clause. The United States did influence the timing of the Sino-Japanese peace and friendship treaty only in the sense that Japan, believing that the United States would normalize diplomatic relations with the PRC sooner or later, wanted to keep one step ahead of the United States in developing relations with China. In fact, the Japanese peace and friendship treaty with China paved the way for the Sino-United States diplomatic normalization in that the timing of Peking's decision to proceed with normalization was probably linked to the signing of the Soviet-Vietnamese friendship treaty of November 1978, which was itself partly a response to the Sino-Japanese treaty.

Although the United States is now reemphasizing the global Soviet threat, Washington's allies probably will not accord the same degree of deference to U.S. leadership as they formerly did at the height of the cold war. This is a likely consequence of a series of U.S. actions, which ignored the interests of these U.S. allies not only with regard to China but in other matters.[3] This interpretation also recognizes that the allies increasingly have been forced to follow the imperatives of internal politics and economics as domestic groups in industrial democracies become more self-assertive vis-à-vis the state.

While the U.S. shift in China policy induced Japan to pursue a relatively more independent path in foreign policy, the same policy shift reduced South Korea's maneuverability and threatened to reduce whatever leverage Seoul had on U.S. policy toward the Korean peninsula. Insofar as South Korea's ability to influence the level of U.S. military and economic assistance to Seoul was conditioned by the level of tension existing among the United States, the Soviet Union, and China, as well as that between the two Koreas, *a reduction in levels of tension portended a loss of influence*. The U.S. criticism of President Park's repressive policies and human rights violations was another factor that negatively affected Seoul's ability to influence U.S. policy. We learned that Seoul resorted to the influence-buying practices in the United States because South Korea's own professional diplomats appeared less and less effective. But, in view of the two factors mentioned above, such decline in the effectiveness of South Korean diplomats was more or less inevitable. Park's attempt to bribe U.S. legislators in order to preclude the feared reduction in military and economic assistance to Seoul eventually backfired under the Carter Administration, which was particularly critical of Park's human rights violations and weary of continued U.S. military commitment in Asia.

As symbolized by the June 1978 U.S. House vote eliminating PL 480 aid to South Korea, the Koreagate scandal temporarily undermined Seoul's ability to secure further U.S. military and economic aid. However, what is surprising is not that the bribery scandal detrimentally affected U.S.-South Korea relations, but that *it did not produce any major long-term shift* in U.S. Korean policy. One major reason for this is that notwithstanding the rapprochement and detente among the major powers a still-divided Korea remains the potential source of a major East-West confrontation. In other words, the United States remains a hostage of the strategic balance on the Korean peninsula. Partly for the same reason, Seoul's influence-buying practices were long overlooked in the United States. South Korea also succeeded in limiting the scope of Congressional Koreagate investigations. Park Tong-son was exempt from criminal prosecutions in exchange for his testimony, which did not directly implicate the South Korean government, and Seoul managed to prevent the extradition and testimony of Kim Dong-jo, South Korea's former ambassador to Washington. The Park government cleverly invoked the universal principle of diplomatic immunity, which the U.S. State Department could not oppose. Washington may have decided not to press the issue any further, since it was doubtlessly aware that Kim Dong-jo's testimony exposing the involvement of the South Korean government would have forced the United States to take severe punitive measures against that government.

The Reagan Administration has reaffirmed the United States' strong military and economic support for South Korean President Chon Du-hwan, regardless of the latter's human rights record. This indicates, *ceteris paribus*, that a small country like South Korea, which was created as a product of the cold war conflicts, would enjoy relatively more leverage in Washington under an administration emphasizing the traditional power-politics model of international relations. Conversely, such a country would have less influence in the United States under an administration espousing the logic of "complex interdependence."

MILITARY AFFAIRS

The decrease in the U.S. willingness to commit its military resources for the defense of its allies was the central theme of the chapter on military affairs. The Carter Administration wanted to reduce the U.S. military presence in South Korea and also wanted Japan to assume a greater military burden. In both cases, the U.S. government failed to realize its desired outcomes — the withdrawal of ground troops from South Korea and the substantial increase in Japan's defense budget. In other words, Japan and South Korea were able to resist U.S. pressure and attempted to influence U.S. policy in their preferred direction.

It seems certain that the South Korean opposition alone would not have changed the mind of the Carter Administration. Washington expected and probably discounted resistance from the Park government, which was determined to maintain maximum strength vis-à-vis North Korea. In this context, Japanese opposition was crucial insofar as Japan was the United States' most important Asian ally and antiwithdrawal arguments that referred to Japanese security could be dismissed less easily by Washington. Thus, the consensus among South Korean and Japanese officials that the two countries had a shared security interest significantly strengthened the case against the withdrawal. Even then, they were successful largely because they were able to "ally" themselves with those U.S. domestic groups – the military establishment, Congress, and part of the government bureaucracy – who also opposed Carter's withdrawal plan. In short, President Carter lost on this issue due to the powerful forces of alliance politics and domestic politics.

Unlike the troop withdrawal issue, there existed in the United States a substantial domestic consensus regarding the need for a greater defense contribution by Japan. Nevertheless, Washington was unable to get Japan to do what the United States wanted, or at least as much as it wanted. This was in marked contrast to the pattern of early postwar years when the United States could virtually dictate Japan's defense policy. After demilitarizing Japan at the end of World War II and playing a key role in drafting the "peace constitution" that denied Japan's rights to bear arms, the United States pressured Japan to rearm itself at the beginning of the cold war. In response, Prime Minister Yoshida created the National Police Reserve, which was subsequently developed into the Japan Self-Defense Forces. As a condition for restoring Japanese independence, the United States was also able to get Japan to conclude an "unequal" mutual security treaty with Washington. But the Japanese government eventually grew more assertive and, in 1960, when many Japanese were calling for total abrogation of the treaty, secured revisions from Washington making the mutual security pact substantially more equal. Partially to assure the automatic extension of the security treaty with Japan, the U.S. government agreed in 1968 to give up its control of Okinawa on Japanese terms.

As we have seen, Japanese defense consciousness has been increasing slowly, but, from the U.S. point of view, remains at an inadequate level. In light of the traditional balance-of-power conception, the U.S. demand seems reasonable. In recent years, with a "diminished" U.S. presence in the Asian-Pacific region, the Soviet Union has rapidly enlarged its military capabilities. Consequently, Japan, now a major economic power, should drastically increase its defense capabilities to lighten the burden of the economically troubled bloc leader. But, Prime Minister Suzuki's "comprehensive security policy" implies that the Japanese concept of security is much broader, putting as much or more emphasis on economic (and diplomatic) efforts. Moreover, the Japanese government must worry about highly politicized domestic groups and hypersensitive Asian neighbors. As indicated above, highly visible U.S. attempts to pressure Japan into undertaking greater rearmament that disregard that country's delicate domestic and regional political environment may backfire and produce a more nationalistic Japanese defense policy, which is possibly divorced from the United States-Japan security system. This would be even more likely should the United States put similar pressures on Japan in the economic arena as well.

ECONOMIC RELATIONS

Of the three issue areas, the decline of U.S. influence is most visible in the economic relations. With the emergence of Japan and Western Europe as economic competitors in the late 1960s, the economic power of the United States has undergone a relative decline. The U.S. economic leadership position in the free world has also eroded because, as the cold war climate gave way to detente, the United States began to pay more attention to narrower domestic interests, particularly the difficulties of the domestic economy, for example, the declining productivity of U.S. industries. As the Japanese economy has grown larger and as Japan has demonstrated the ability to beat the United States in most manufacturing industries, the U.S. economy has become increasingly sensitive to economic changes in Japan. In short, the United States and Japan have become more economically interdependent.

During the 1950s and early 1960s, the Japanese government and industry basically supported the U.S. foreign economic policy of "free trade for the free world" because such a policy was generally beneficial to the Japanese. The United States provided a relatively open market for Japanese products but at the same time allowed Japan to deviate from the free-trade principle to a large extent. Therefore, when the United States asked the Japanese to restrain certain exports, such as textiles, Tokyo rather willingly agreed to voluntary export control. However, the situation changed gradually. As U.S. economic problems increased, Washington became *more demanding*, and the Japanese, increasingly confident and proud of their economic accomplishments, became more self-assertive and adamant in the face of U.S. pressures. The bitter textile wrangle of 1969-71 was a product of this development. Only by threatening to invoke the "Trading with the Enemy" Act was the United States able to win concessions from Japan.

Since then, no bilateral economic issues have proven so intractable or divisive; yet the same, basic conditions remain. Japan continues its relatively higher economic growth than the United States and is challenging U.S. higher-technology industries. However, Japan is basically more vulnerable than the United States, insofar as the former depends heavily on U.S. markets and U.S. agricultural and raw materials, while the United States could produce practically all the products currently imported from Japan, even if the results might be less efficient. Thus, the United States is always tempted to use this asymmetry to exert pressure on Japan regarding economic issues. Even if the Japanese government is ready to cooperate with the United States (and indeed, it has lately demonstrated a greater awareness of the need to coordinate economic policies with the United States and Western Europe because of its perception of economic interdependence), it has become increasingly less able to persuade domestic groups to make necessary concessions, notwithstanding the image of "Japan, Inc."

South Korea remains highly dependent on the U.S. economy but has been able to make an impact on U.S. markets through such competitive exports as textiles, footwear, color television sets, and steel. This is also true of South Korea's economic relations with Japan, except that South Korea's economic dependence on Japan is increasing because Japan is replacing the United States as the principal trader and capital investor in that country. The South Korean economy is extremely vulnerable because Seoul is not only heavily dependent on the U.S. and Japanese markets but also on U.S. and Japanese capital and technology to sustain its growth.

However, since South Korean economic stability is assumed to be closely linked to the political stability of the Korean peninsula and also to the security of Japan, the Seoul government can exploit the economic vulnerability as an important leverage to secure economic cooperation from both the United States and Japan. For the same reason, even when the United States pressures Seoul to restrain its exports to the U.S. market, Washington feels obliged to offer some economic compensations. For example, in October 1971 Washington agreed to increase U.S. development loans and to expand the PL 480 program in exchange for the South Korean textile export restraint. However, this factor has not precluded the temporary withdrawal or reduction of economic assistance to express dissatisfaction with a particular South Korean policy, as Japan did in connection with the KCIA kidnapping of Kim Dae-jung in 1973 and his planned execution in 1980 and as the United States did as a punitive response to Seoul's influence-buying scandal in 1978.

Issue Linkages

It is evident from the preceding discussion that economic, military, and political issues are often explicitly or implicitly linked. Each country resorts to a particular type of issue linkage or nonlinkage to maximize its leverage of influence.

South Korea, the smallest and most vulnerable of the three, tends to link the strategic importance of the Korean peninsula to economic discussions in an attempt to maximize economic assistance from the United States and Japan or to minimize economic concessions to them. The most recent example is

South Korea's effort to obtain $10 billion in aid and loans from Japan over a five-year period starting in 1982. While Seoul contends that Japan should help South Korea's economic recovery in view of their shared security interest, Washington urges Tokyo to support South Korea economically as part of Japan's greater regional security contribution.[4] On the other hand, Seoul has tried to separate the human rights issue from discussions of other issues important to South Korea, particularly in dealing with U.S. military support.

Japan, whose strength derives from its superior economic performance, has often emphasized economic rationality in refusing trade concessions and thus avoids the linkage of economic and noneconomic arguments (for example, charges that Japanese economic concessions are used to compensate for its defense "free ride," or textile exports are restrained in exchange for Okinawa's reversion). Even when discussing security issues, Japan stresses the economic dimension of security to counter narrow military-strategic arguments often presented by the United States.

The United States — which remains a military superpower despite its declining economic leadership — predictably emphasizes, though usually implicitly, the value of U.S. military protection (or the value of the overall relationship) when discussing economic and other nonmilitary issues with its allies.

Intergovernmental Alliances

Theoretically, country A and country B will form an intergovernmental political alliance to influence country C, particularly when country C happens to be the most powerful of the three. Surprisingly, few cases of this kind of alliance have been identified in this study. Such an alliance between Japan and South Korea was formed, though not overtly orchestrated, in order to influence President Carter's plan to withdraw U.S. ground troops from the Korean peninsula. But, as noted earlier, the "transnational alliance" of the two countries with the influential U.S. domestic groups opposed to the Carter plan was equally or more important.

An intergovernmental political alliance can be formed between the two larger allies to influence the smallest, for example, in 1980 when the United States and Japan jointly pressured Seoul to prevent the execution of Kim Dae-jung. Another variation is possible, as in 1965 when the United States helped Japan and South Korea to normalize their relations and in 1973-74 when the United States played a role of mediation between Seoul and Tokyo in the aftermath of Kim Dae-jung's abduction and Mrs. Park Chung-hi's assassination. These are examples of the bloc leader providing assistance for the resolution of issues between its allies. Thus far, South Korea's efforts to receive U.S. help in resolving another Seoul-Tokyo disagreement regarding Japan's economic and cultural contact with North Korea have not been successful because Washington and Seoul do not hold the same views on this matter. Having examined relations among the United States, Japan, and South Korea in the three issue areas, we can infer that *there is not much intrabloc alliance formation* against the third member of the same Western bloc.

Alliance Management

Rubenstein observes that "in the present international system, power has less obvious utility in non-war situations than at any previous period of modern history."[5] This is particularly true in relations among the Western allies. How does a country most effectively influence a given policy of another country belonging to the same Western alliance system? The answer seems to lie not in simple pressure tactics, but in subtle alliance management based on mutual political sensitivity.

Above all, suasion — rather than coercion — should be the rule of the game, for repeated use of coercive tactics or insensitive public pressure may eventually undermine the very foundation of the Western alliance system. Our study demonstrates that the adoption of subtle and appropriate style is often more important than the merit of substantive policy argument in managing alliance politics and in influencing allies, especially if these allies are conditioned by the Confucian behavioral norms. However, the United States has frequently used pressure tactics to influence Japanese economic and defense policies, while ignoring internal politico-economic problems in that country. Sometimes Japanese officials have invited U.S. pressures in order to force concessions from reluctant domestic groups instead of persuading them on the merit of concessions per se. Repetition of this practice may encourage a nationalistic backlash in Japan, making future United States-Japanese relations more difficult to manage. As we have seen in the bilateral issue over the Japanese defense budget, pressure tactics may also prove counterproductive in the short run. Many Japanese politicians did not want to support a major increase in the defense budget precisely because the United States was pressuring them to do so. In a pluralist democracy such as Japan (and the United States), there are highly politicized, domestic groups whose positions the government cannot afford to ignore. Therefore, the government must walk a tightrope between domestic politics and alliance politics. Any ill-conceived pressure from outside would not be conducive to the maintenance of the precarious balancing act. Although South Korea is an authoritarian polity with tighter control over the media and political expression, much the same can be said about Washington-Seoul or Tokyo-Seoul relations. If necessary, the South Korean government can intentionally mobilize "public resentment" against either the United States or Japan, as it did against the United States in 1978 with regard to the Koreagate investigations and against Japan in 1974 in the wake of Mrs. Park's assassination by a Korean resident of Japan. In view of the history of Japan's colonial rule over Korea, the Korean people are especially sensitive to any sign of mistreatment by Japan. Thus, as Ambassador Sunobe suggested, Japan would do well to approach South Korea "with tender care."

In the final analysis, managing relations among "friends" is not necessarily easy. As Richard E. Neustadt remarked, "Indifference and hostility may not breed paranoia; friendship does."[6]

NOTES

1. Robert O. Keohane and Joseph S. Nye, *Power and Interdependence* (Boston: Little, Brown, 1977), p. 47.

2. Alvin Z. Rubinstein, ed., *Soviet and Chinese Influence in the Third World* (New York: Praeger, 1975), p. 8.

3. In spring 1981, for instance, the Reagan Administration lifted the U.S. grain embargo against the Soviet Union for domestic political reasons without closely consulting their allies in advance.

4. See *New York Times*, August 12, 1981.

5. Rubinstein, *Soviet and Chinese Influence*, p. 8.

6. Richard E. Neustadt, *Alliance Politics* (New York: Columbia University Press, 1970), p. 72.

SELECTED BIBLIOGRAPHY

Acheson, Dean. *Present at the Creation*. New York: W. W. Norton, 1969.

———. *The Korean War*. New York: W. W. Norton, 1971.

Allison, John M. *Ambassador from the Prairie: or Allison Wonderland*. Boston: Houghton Mifflin, 1973.

Baerwald, Hans H. *The Purge of Japanese Leaders under the Occupation*. Berkeley: University of California Press, 1959.

Baldwin, Frank, ed. *Without Parallel: The American-Korean Relationship Since 1945*. New York: Pantheon Books, 1973.

Boettcher, Robert. *Gifts of Deceit: Sun Myung Moon, Tongsun Park, and the Korean Scandal*. New York: Rinehart and Winston, 1980.

Cho, Soon Sung. *Korea in World Politics, 1940-1950: An Evaluation of American Responsibility*. Berkeley: University of California Press, 1967.

Clough, Ralph N. *Deterrence and Defense in Korea: The Role of U.S. Forces*. Washington, D.C.: Brookings Institution, 1976.

Destler, I. M., Haruhiro Fukui, and Hideo Sato. *The Textile Wrangle: Conflict in Japanese-American Relations, 1969-1971*. Ithaca, N.Y. and London: Cornell University Press, 1979.

Eisenhower, Dwight D. *The White House Years: Mandate for Change, 1953-1956*. Garden City, N.Y.: Doubleday, 1963.

Fukase Tadakazu, ed. *Senso no hoki* [Renunciation of War]. Tokyo: Sanseido, 1977.

Goodman, Grant K., ed. *The American Occupation of Japan: A Retrospective View*. Lawrence, Kans.: Center for East Asian Studies, 1968.

Hellmann, Donald C. *Japan and East Asia*. New York: Praeger, 1972.

Henderson, Gregory. *Korea: The Politics of the Vortex*. Cambridge, Mass.: Harvard University Press, 1968.

Hilsman, Roger. *To Move a Nation*. Garden City, N.Y.: Doubleday, 1967.

Hong, Wontack, and Anne O. Krueger, eds. *Trade and Development in Korea*. Seoul: Korea Development Institute, 1975.

Hsiao, Gene T., ed. *Sino-American Detente: And Its Policy Implications*. New York: Praeger, 1974.

Japan, Defense Agency. *Boei Hakusho* [Defense of Japan]. Various issues. Tokyo: Okurasho.

Japan, Ministry of Foreign Affairs. *Comparative Economic Statistics for Canada, Japan, and the United States*. April 1980.

_____. *Waga gaiko no kinkyo* [Recent State of Our Diplomacy]. Various issues. Tokyo: Gaimusho.

Katzenstein, Peter J., ed. *Between Power and Plenty*. Madison: University of Wisconsin Press, 1978.

Kennan, George F. *Memoirs 1925-1950*. Boston: Little, Brown, 1967.

Kim, Kwang Suk, and Michael Roemer. *Growth and Structural Transformation*. Cambridge, Mass.: Council on East Asian Studies, Harvard University, 1979.

Kissinger, Henry. *White House Years*. Boston: Little, Brown, 1979.

Krause, Lawrence B., and Sueo Sekiguchi, eds. *Economic Interaction in the Pacific Basin*. Washington, D.C.: Brookings Institution, 1980.

Kuznets, Paul W. *Economic Growth and Structure in the Republic of Korea*. New Haven: Yale University Press, 1977.

Lee, Chae-Jin. *Japan Faces China: Political and Economic Relations in the Postwar Era*. Baltimore: Johns Hopkins University Press, 1976.

Long-Term Prospect for Economic and Social Development 1977-91. Seoul: Korea Development Institute, 1978.

MacArthur, Douglas. *Reminiscences*. New York: McGraw-Hill, 1964.

Meade, E. Grant. *American Military Government in Korea*. New York: King's Crown Press, 1951.

Meyer, Armin H. *Assignment: Tokyo – An Ambassador's Journal*. Indianapolis: Bobbs-Merrill Co., 1974.

Murphy, Robert D. *Diplomat among Warriors*. Garden City, N.J.: Doubleday, 1964.

Nagano Nobutoshi. *Gaimusho kenkyu* [A Study of the Foreign Ministry]. Tokyo: Simul Press, 1975.

Nixon, Richard M. *RN: The Memoirs of Richard Nixon*. New York: Grosset and Dunlap, 1978.

Oksenberg, Michel, and Robert B. Oxnam, eds. *Dragon and Eagle: United States – China Relations: Past and Future*. New York: Basic Books, 1978.

Oliver, Robert T. *Syngman Rhee and American Involvement in Korea, 1942-1960: A Personal Narrative*. Seoul: Panmun Book Co., 1978.

Oshima, Keiichi, and Mason Willrich, eds. *Future U.S.-Japanese Nuclear Energy Relations*. Tokyo and New York: National Institute of Research Advancement and Rockefeller Foundation, 1979.

Packard, George R., III. *Protest in Tokyo: The Security Treaty Crisis of 1960*. Princeton, N.J.: Princeton University Press, 1966.

Packard, George R., and William Watts, *The United States and Japan: American Perceptions and Policies*. Washington, D.C.: Potomac Associates, n.d.

Pempel, T. J., ed. *Policy-making in Contemporary Japan*. Ithaca, N.Y.: Cornell University Press, 1977.

Rees, David. *Korea: The Limited War*. Baltimore: Penguin Books, 1970.

Reischauer, Edwin O. *The United States and Japan*. rev. ed. New York: Viking Press, 1957.

Republic of Korea, Agency of Customs Administration. *Statistical Yearbook of Foreign Trade*. Various issues. Seoul.

Republic of Korea, Bank of Korea. *Economic Statistical Yearbook*. Various issues.

Rubinstein, Alvin Z., ed. *Soviet and Chinese Influence in the Third World*. New York: Praeger, 1975.

Saxonhouse, Gary, ed. *Innovations and Diffusion of Technology in Japan*. Forthcoming.

Sebald, William J. *With MacArthur in Japan: A Personal History of the Occupation*. New York: W. W. Norton, 1965.

Sodei Rinjiro. *Makasa no nisennichi* [MacArthur's Two Thousand Days]. Tokyo: Chuo Koronsha, 1974.

Thompson, W. Scott, ed. *From Weakness to Strength*. San Francisco: Institute for Contemporary Studies, 1980.

Truman, Harry S. *Memoirs: Year of Trial and Hope*. Garden City, N.Y.: Doubleday, 1956.

Tsou, Tang, *America's Failure in China: 1941-50*. Chicago: University of Chicago Press, 1963.

U.S. Arms Control and Disarmament Agency. *Japan's Contribution to Military Stability in Northeast Asia*. Washington, D.C.: USGPO, 1980.

U.S. Comptroller General. *United States-Japan Trade: Issues and Problems*. Washington, D.C.: USGPO, 1979.

U.S. Congress, House Committee on Armed Services. *Review of the Policy Decision to Withdraw United States Ground Forces from Korea: Report of the Investigations Subcommittee*. Washington, D.C.: USGPO, 1978.

U.S. Congress, House Committee on Foreign Affairs. *Report of Special Study Mission to Japan, Taiwan, and Korea*. Washington, D.C.: USGPO, 1974.

_____ . *Human Rights in South Korea: Implications for U.S. Policy*. Washington, D.C.: USGPO, 1974.

_____ . *New China Policy: Its Impact on the U.S. and Asia: Hearings*. Washington, D.C.: USGPO, 1972.

_____ . *American-Korean Relations: Hearings*. Washington, D.C.: USGPO, 1971.

U.S. Congress, House Committee on International Relations. *Investigation of Korean-American Relations*. pts. 1-7, report, and app., vols. 1-2. Washington, D.C.: USGPO, 1977-78.

U.S. Congress, House Committee on Standards of Official Conduct. *Korean Influence Investigation*. pts. 1-2 and report. Washington, D.C.: USGPO, 1977-78.

U.S. Congress, House Committee on Ways and Means. *United States-Japan Trade Report*. Washington, D.C.: USGPO, January, 1980.

_____ . *Task Force Report on United States-Japan Trade*. Washington, D.C.: USGPO, 1979.

U.S. Congress, Senate Committee on Armed Services. *United States-Japan Security Relationship — The Key to East Asian Security and Stability: Report of the Pacific Study Group.* Washington, D.C.: USGPO, 1979.

U.S. Congress, Senate Committee on Foreign Relations. *Taiwan: Hearings.* Washington, D.C.: USGPO, 1979.

_____. *U.S. Troop Withdrawal from the Republic of Korea: An Update, 1979.* Washington, D.C.: USGPO, 1979.

_____. *United States Security Agreements and Commitments Abroad: Japan and Okinawa: Hearings.* Washington, D.C.: USGPO, 1970.

_____. *United States Security Agreements and Commitments Abroad: Republic of Korea: Hearings.* Washington, D.C.: USGPO, 1970.

U.S. Congress, Senate Select Committee on Ethics. *Korean Influence Inquiry.* vols. 1-2 and report. Washington, D.C.: USGPO, 1978.

U.S. Department of Defense. *Congressional Presentation: Security Assistance Programs.* Various issues.

U.S. Department of State. *Foreign Relations of the United States.* 1944-51. Various issues. Washington, D.C.: USGPO, 1965-77.

_____. *United States Relations with China.* Washington, D.C.: USGPO, 1949.

_____. *Occupation of Japan: Policy and Progress.* Washington, D.C.: USGPO, n.d.

_____. *U.S. Policy Toward China.* Washington, D.C.: Department of State Selected Documents no. 9, n.d.

United States-Japan Trade Council. *Yearbook of U.S.-Japan Economic Relations 1979.*

Van Aduard, E. J. Lewe. *Japan: From Surrender to Peace.* The Hague: Martinus Nijihoff, 1953.

Ward, Robert E., ed. *Political Development in Modern Japan.* Princeton, N.J.: Princeton University Press, 1968.

Weinstein, Martin E. *Japan's Postwar Defense Policy, 1947-1968.* New York: Columbia University Press, 1971.

Yi Hyo-jae, *Hanguk woegyo jongchekui yisang gwa hyonsil* [Ideals and Reality of Korean Diplomatic Policy]. 3rd ed. Seoul: Bommunsa, 1975.

Young, Kenneth T. *Negotiating with the Chinese Communists: The United States Experience, 1953-1967.* New York: McGraw-Hill, 1968.

INDEX

ABOUT THE AUTHORS

Chae-Jin Lee is professor of political science and codirector of the Center for East Asian Studies at the University of Kansas. He graduated from Seoul National University and received his doctoral degree from the University of California at Los Angeles. He was a foreign research scholar at Tokyo University and taught at the University of Washington. He has authored *Japan Faces China: Political and Economic Relations in the Postwar Era* (Johns Hopkins University Press, 1976) and *Communist China's Policy Toward Laos* (Kansas, 1970) and has coauthored *The United States and Japan in the Western Pacific* (Westview, 1981). He has also coedited *Political Leadership in Korea* (University of Washington Press, 1976).

Hideo Sato is associate professor of political science at Yale University. A graduate of International Christian University in Tokyo, he holds M.A. and Ph.D. degrees from the University of Chicago. He was a Brookings research associate in 1973-75. He has coauthored *Managing an Alliance: The Politics of U.S.-Japanese Relations* (Brookings Institution, 1976) and *The Textile Wrangle: Conflict in Japanese-American Relations 1969-1971* (Cornell University Press, 1979) and has coedited *Coping with United States-Japan Economic Conflicts* (Lexington, 1982).